AF560721

STUDIES IN SCHOOL EDUCATION

STUDIES IN SCHOOL EDUCATION

Edited by

JAGANNATH MOHANTY

UGC Emeritus Fellow,
Ravenshaw (Autonomous) College, Cuttack,
Professor of Education and Former Principal,
Radhanath, IASE, Cuttack

DEEP & DEEP PUBLICATIONS PVT. LTD.
F-159, Rajouri Garden, New Delhi-110027

STUDIES IN SCHOOL EDUCATION

ISBN 978-81-8450-103-2

© 2008 JAGANNATH MOHANTY

All rights reserved with the Publisher, including the right to translate or to reproduce this book or parts thereof except for brief quotations in critical articles or reviews.

Typeset by VERONICA GRAFIC ARTS,
VP-216A, Pitampura, Maurya Enclave, Delhi-110088.

Printed in India at MAYUR ENTERPRISES,
WZ Plot No. 3, Gujjar Market, Tihar Village, New Delhi-110018.

Published by DEEP & DEEP PUBLICATIONS PVT. LTD.
F-159, Rajouri Garden, New Delhi-110027.
Phones: 25435369, 25440916
E-mails: ddpbooks@yahoo.co.in

Showroom:
2/13, Ansari Road, Daryaganj, New Delhi-110002 • Telefax; 23245122

Contents

PART II

RURAL, TRIBAL AND MINORITIES DEVELOPMENT IN EDUCATION

PART III

NUTRITION, CREATIVITY AND METHODS OF TEACHING

Preface

School Education is the foundation of the entire educational infrastructure. It is imperative that its strength and stamina must determine the quality and quantity of educational panorama in the country. It is, therefore, felt essential to study various aspects of school education in order to know the *status quo*, identify the problems faced and conduct experiments for improving the existing systems and schemes in execution. In this book as many as 27 studies have found places to give an idea about the status, issues and concerns in the field of School Education. The studies are, however, only suggestive and symbolic, not exhaustive and representative.

The studies have been classified into four categories, such as

(i)	Democracy, Sociology and Economics of Education	5
(ii)	Rural, Tribal and Minorities Development in Education	6
(iii)	Nutrition, Creativity and Methods of Teaching	8
(iv)	Learning through Media	8

The first category contains five studies relating to Democracy, Sociology and Economics. Attempts have been made not only to delve deep into the issues, but also to find out the shortcomings and suggest measures for bringing about improvement in the existing conditions.

The second category consists of six studies as regards rural, tribal and minorities and their educational problems. These studies have shown some directions and solutions, which might promote quality, equality and equity in the society.

The third category contains eight studies that relate some crucial issues like nutrition, super learning, creativity and various methods of teaching in school child subjects. The studies have pointed out that nutrition has positive correlation with physical and mental development, super learning accelerates creativity, and suitable methods of teaching help learning science and social studies very effectively.

The fourth category consisting of eight studies also deal with various electronic media particularly radio and television which have identified strengths and weaknesses of these media, their role in promoting academic achievement of students and professional growth of teachers. Some studies have revealed the special roles of Radio and TV in language learning, skill development, attitude and interest development. These studies have not only pointed out the skills in production of the programmes, but also in their proper utilization.

It may be concluded that similar studies are necessary for creating adequate awareness and interest, imparting requisite psychomotor skills, developing positive attitudes and so on. Such studies would throw light on the dark corridors of our teaching-learning system and activate the idle and inert agencies and motivate the sincere workers in the field of school education. Among these studies, there are surveys, experiments, empirical and analytical studies. All these are merely indicative or suggestive. The findings and conclusions of these studies are in no way sanctitious or sanctifying. These are as pointed out earlier are merely indicative and suggestive.

Since school education is a vast area, there is no limit to the research activities that are essential for effecting desirable changes by identifying the existing problems and shortcomings. Teachers, students, researchers, planners and supervisors have to be responsive to the challenges faced and do the needful to tackle the problems, which are never-ending and eternally emerging. Any comments and suggestions from readers for improving this book are always welcome.

Bhubaneswar JAGANNATH MOHANTY

Acknowledgements

I am grateful to a host of educationists, researchers, educators and educational institutions for their valuable contributions to this book.

In expressing my gratitude in various degrees to these persons, I am constrained to categorise them, although it is not so imperative. Firstly, out of these 27 studies about 20 were developed by me alone or through joint efforts as these studies have been endowed their authors with Ph.D. or D.Litt. degrees. They are Dr. M.R. Panda, Dr. J.R. Bohidar, Dr. (Miss) A. Pattnaik, Dr. P.K. Prusty, Dr. S.C. Patra, Dr. Sadasiba Maharana, Dr. R. Mohanty and Dr. Suresh C. Behera whom I thank for their valuable cooperation.

Some of the researchers on their own have developed their studies for their Ph.D. or D.Litt. Degrees, or for presenting them in some academic or institutional programmes. They are Dr. K.C. Behera, Dr. N. Pradhan, Dr. A.P. Behera, Sri P.C. Nayak and Dr. P.C. Mohanty. I express my gratitude to them. A few of them have gone ahead and conducted studies in their academic interests. These papers presented in the National Seminars have found place in this book and I thank the concerned authors for their academic gesture. Besides, I extend my thanks to the various educational institutions who published them earlier in some way or other.

Lastly, I appreciate the timely interest and action taken in publishing this book by the publisher Mr. G.S. Bhatia, Managing Director, Deep and Deep Publications Pvt. Ltd., New Delhi.

Bhubaneswar JAGANNATH MOHANTY

List of Contributors

Amarendra Prasad Behera, Reader, Central Institute of Educational Technology, NCERT, New Delhi.

Anjali Pattanaik, PG Dept. of Home Science, Berhampur University, Berhampur, Ganjam, Orissa.

Haritha N., PG Dept. of Home Science, Berhampur University, Berhampur, Ganjam, Orissa.

Jagannath Mohanty, UGC Emeritus Fellow, Ravenshaw Autonomous College, Cuttack, Director Academic Staff College, Utkal University, Bhubaneswar and Principal, Radhanath, IASE, Cuttack and Dr. P.M. IASE, Sambalpur, Orissa.

Jyoti Ranjan Bohidar, Head of Dept., Education, Boudh College, Boudha.

Kailash Ch. Behera, Research Fellow, Kurukshetra University, Kurukshetra, Haryana.

Manoranjan Panda, Senior Lecturer, Kamaksha Nagar College, Kamaksha Nagar, Dhenkanal.

Nityananda Pradhan, Senior Lecturer, PG Dept. of Education, DAV College, Koraput, Orissa.

P.C. Mohanty, Senior Lecturer, SIET, Orissa, Bhubaneswar.

P.K. Nayak, Ex-Principal, Baragarh Training College, Baragarh.

Pramod Kumar Prusty, Lecturer, Head, Dept. of Education, Narasinghpur College, Narasinghpur, Cuttack.

Rajashree Mohanty, Teacher Educator, DIET, Keonjhar, Orissa.

Suresh C. Behera, Senior Lecturer, Government Training College, Balasore, Orissa.

Shreelekha Dei, Lecturer, Nigamanand Mahavidyalaya, Charichhaka, Puri.

Sadasiba Maharana, Head, Dept. of Education, Sailabala Women's College, Cuttack.

Subash Chandra Patra, Headmaster, Kutasingha High School, Phulbani.

Editorial Notes

I. DEMOCRACY, SOCIOLOGY AND ECONOMICS OF EDUCATION

In the study entitled "Impact of Democracy on Primary Education in India with Special Reference to Orissa" (Mohanty, 1979) is a very comprehensive one and has encompassed the historical growth of democracy, the concept and development of Democracy in various aspects in India after Independence (1947). In this context, the relevant literature of the East and West was surveyed and studies conducted were considered from the past to the present. With a view to studying the impact of democracy on various dimensions of Education, data were collected with multifarious types of tools and techniques, and the findings were gleaned out. The major findings and recommendations thereon would be helpful for democratization of Education at all levels.

The study "Socio-economic Background of the Students Studying in the High Schools of Bhubaneswar" (Mohanty, 1987-88) was sponsored by Government in the Human Resource Development (Education). It was a pioneering study and data were collected from different types of High Schools in the Bhubaneswar Municipality and cross-sections of the society. The National Policy on Education, 1986 laid emphasis on expansion and quality of Education and various attempts were made for removal of disparities. The society has not yet availed itself of educational opportunities. On account of various disparities, students' academic achievement was very adversely affected and the school interventions to make up the deficiencies were not up to expectation.

In the next paper, "The Relationship between Socio-economic Status and Achievement of Class IX Students" (Panda, 1999) has been studied taking samples from different sectors of the society. The researcher has corroborated the findings of the previous study and suggested measures for removing the Socio-economic barriers in order to promote educational performance of students at all levels.

As per the Constitutional Directive and for success of Democracy, Universalisation of Elementary Education has not been achieved over six decades after Independence. With a view to identifying the difficulties and augmenting Universalisation of Elementary Education, another study, "Early Childhood Education (ECE) for Universalisation of Elementary Education (UEE)" was conducted with financial support from the NCERT, New Delhi (1995-96).

The next one is "An Investigation into the Problems and Prospects of School-Community Cooperation for Democratization and Improvement of Education", (Mohanty, 1979). This is an attempt to find out the areas of cooperation between the school and the society and show their mutual relationships for democratizing the whole process and bringing about improvement both in quality and quantity of education at various stages and in different regions.

II. RURAL, TRIBAL AND MINORITIES DEVELOPMENT IN EDUCATION

The Navodaya Vidyalaya Scheme is an innovative project to cater to the needs of talented children largely from rural areas and provide educational opportunities to the deprived sections of the society. With a view to finding out the shortcomings and suggest ways and means for improving the existing system, the study, "An Evaluative Study of Navodaya Vidyalayas in Haryana" was conducted by the researcher for his Ph.D. Degree (Behera, 1998). The findings of this study are quite revealing.

In another Ph.D. study attempt has been made to identify the "Problems of Tribal Education in the Context of National Policy on Education, 1986" (Bohidar, 1995). In this work various incentives and facilities available to the tribal communities were assessed, reasons for their poor attendance ascertained and recommendations were made for improving the tribal education.

The paper, "Research in Education of Minorities in India: Gaps and Priorities" (Pradhan, 2004) the author has sought to review the studies already conducted and to point out the research needs as well as priorities for bringing the minorities to the national main stream. This would help the researchers to take up suitable studies according to their expertise. The same researcher has reported a case study of a tribal village entitled, "Sustainable Solutions of Environmental Problems Through Community-based Education." The educational implications of the study are quite helpful for ecological sustenance through community support.

In the next study, "Family Life Values in the Tribal Communities" (Pradhan and Shreelekha Dei, 2003) the researchers have tried to identify the values in the Paraja tribal community relating to adolescent fertility, responsible parenthood, marriage and women's status. The findings were useful for planning the Paraja families in a better way. In the next study, "Anthropometric Status of Child Labourers" the researcher (Pattnaik and Haritha) have tried to ascertain the growth status of child workers and the related health problems. The findings would help solving these problems.

III. NUTRITION, CREATIVITY AND METHODS OF TEACHING

Since nutrition plays an important part in the physical and mental development of the child, it was felt imperative on the part of a good number of researchers to conduct studies in this area from various angles. Some of such studies have been discussed as follows. In her Ph.D. study Dr. Anjali Pattanaik (1990) assessed. "The Nutritional Status and its Effect on Physical Development and Educational Achievement of Students." The findings of the study were very helpful for planning suitable projects for removing the deficiencies and improving the present conditions.

Sometimes miracles are found even among the children with physical, mental and emotional disabilities. With adequate care taken and treatment made, these individuals not only become normal, but also do wonders. Here is a study of creativity among children with different disabilities conducted by Dr. Anjali Pattanaik (1997). She has reported that although normal children are better than the deformed ones, with proper training and medication, the latter ones may be creative as well as productive.

Dr. Pramod Kumar Prusty has presented a study, "Effect of Creative Method of Teaching English (CMTE) on Development of Creativity and Achievement: An Experiment on Secondary School Students." It was an experiment on secondary school students and the utility of such method was proved beyond doubt. Dr. Prusty in his next study, "Effect of Creative Method of Teaching English on Development of Creative Thinking of Secondary School Students" has showed the importance of such method for developing creative thinking of students. Since it is an experiment, various steps and strategies were followed in teaching. His another experiment was entitled "Multi-grade Learning—An Innovation in Primary Level Education" is also quite revealing.

The "Study of the Efficacy of the Field Trip in the Teaching of Social Studies in Primary Schools" (Mohanty, 1973) is an interesting and experimental one and presents the importance of field trip for gaining knowledge, interest and motivation for learning.

Dr. Rajashree Mohanty in her Ph.D. Study, "Science Education Programme in Secondary Schools" (2003) has tried to identity strengths and weaknesses in the teaching of science in Secondary Schools and suggest a number of measures for improving the Science Education Programme.

In a D.Litt. study, "Effect of Super Learning Technique (SLT) on Development of Creative Thinking" the researcher (Prusty, 2005) has tried to find out the difference between the scores with and without super learning and also the relation between creative and intelligence as an effect of super learning technique. The findings were quite interesting and useful.

IV. LEARNING THROUGH MEDIA

The "Study of the Educational Implications of Community TV Programmes" (Patra, 2002) seeks to show the special significance of such programmes for accelerating community development and for imparting skills, interest, knowledge, etc., of the audience. The findings of the study have wide-ranging educational implications as discussed by the scholar.

The study "Effect of Radio Interventions on the Language and Cognitive Development of Pre-school Level Children" (Behera, 1997), has given interesting findings which should be utilized for planning and implementing language and cognitive development programmes for young children in early childhood education.

In the "Study of the Effectiveness of Educational TV Programmes for Primary Schools," the researcher (Maharana, 1996) has sought to show the effect of ETV Programmes on primary school children in terms of academic achievement, their positive attitude and motivation for learning. The findings were found useful for providing suitable programmes, getting feedback from the audience, "An Evaluative Study of ETV programmes under INSAT" (Mohanty and Nayak, 1984) has shown the strengths and weaknesses of ETV Programmes and suggested measures for making them appropriate and relevant to the needs and interests of students. The next two studies (Mohanty and Maharana, 1986-87) were relating ETV Programmes for the students in the age-group 9-11 years and the findings of the studies were quite interesting and useful for planning, producing and utilizing suitable ETV programmes.

Another study, "Impact of Educational Television on the Competency of Elementary School Teachers" (Behera, 1986) has shown significant contribution of ETV Programmes for improving. teachers competence thereby helping them to teach effectively.

Besides improving, students' academic achievement and teachers' performance ETV Programmes also contribute immensely to the growth of attendance and enrolment in schools. The study, "Impact of SITE on Attendance and Enrolment" (Mohanty and Mohanty) bears testimony to this evidence.

PART I

DEMOCRACY, SOCIOLOGY AND ECONOMICS OF EDUCATION

Impact of Democracy on Primary Education in India
With Special Reference to Orissa

JAGANNATH MOHANTY

The study aimed at ascertaining the impact of democracy on education in India with special reference to Orissa. With a view to providing a theoretical framework to the investigation, the historical background of democratic education in the country and the State has been presented along with a detailed discussion on the philosophical and sociological foundations.

BACKGROUND

In ancient India, democracy found its expression in various institutions called "Sabha," "Samiti," "Sangha" and "Gana" and democratic spirit was adumbrated in its ideals of universal peace, brotherhood, fellow-feeling, freedom and sympathy through the glorious cultural heritage and literature like the Vedas, the Bhagawat Gita, the Jatakas, the Ramayan and the Mahabharat. The democratic values permeated the entire educational system prevalent in the Vedic and Buddhist age.

The medieval India witnessed a dark age of democracy as evident from the continual wars and rivalry among kings and monarchs. The teaching-learning methods followed in Islamic education also did not promote democratic principles and practices.

In the British period, the East India Company accepted the responsibility for education of Indians since 1913. When most of its time and energy was spent on "Commerce, conquest, consolidation" the Missionaries accomplished pioneering achievements in the field of women's education and modern Indian Languages. The main objective of the British education in the beginning was to prepare a group of persons for manning white-collar jobs for the British Empire. However, after 1853 a number of democratic features were introduced in the educational system.

After Independence, consequent on the introduction of the Indian Constitution, a number of provisions were made for the success of democracy in general and for democratisation of education in particular. An important Constitutional Directive was the Universalisation of Elementary Education by 1960 which is still far away from being realized. Although there has been unprecedented expansion of education at all levels, it is felt that its quality is still to be improved and democratic spirit is yet to permeate the educational system fully.

THE PROBLEM

Democracy is not merely a political system or a form of Government, but a way of life and a comprehensive and integrated concept meaning liberty, equality and fraternity. Democratisation of education is essential as well as imperative for the success of democracy.

There are two aspects of democratisation, qualitative and quantitative: Expansion of physical facilities, enrolment, attendance, etc., is quantitative aspect and diffusion of democratic spirit and values like individual dignity, self-discipline, freedom, initiative, cooperation, participation and fellow-feeling, etc., is qualitative. In the context of the latter, the progress seems to be miserable. Authoritarian as well as autocratic practices are still prevalent in various aspects of Primary Education.

As primary education is the foundation of the entire educational superstructure and is the nursery for developing desired qualities and habits in the young children, democratisation for this stage is not only a necessity but also a prerequisite for success of democracy in the country.

PURPOSE OF THE STUDY

The study was primarily intended to determine the impact of democracy on all aspects of primary education curriculum, teaching methods, school organisation, administration, supervision, evaluation finance, etc. The objectives were as follows:

- to find out conceptual background of the teachers and supervisors,
- to ascertain as to what extent they are aware of their responsibilities in the context of democracy,
- to make a stock-taking of the democratic practices and programmes in vogue,
- to determine the impact of democracy on various aspects of primary education,
- to find out the consequences of democratisation,
- to identify the hurdles and handicaps standing in the way of democratising primary education,
- to pool the suggestions of all concerned for their removal,
- to evolve suitable methods and techniques of democratisation, and
- to suggest the guidelines for early democratisation.

SCOPE OF THE STUDY

All kinds of institutions and all the practices and programmes at the primary stage in the State of Orissa were brought under the scope of this study. The aspects of primary education taken under its purview were: (1) Democracy and Primary Education; (2) Curriculum and Syllabus; (3) Methods and Materials; (4) School Administration; (5) Inspection and Supervision; (6) School Organisation; (7) Finance and School Improvement; (8) Examination and Evaluation, and (9) Status and Service Conditions of Teachers.

METHODOLOGY

The study mainly came under descriptive research involving data collection, tabulation, interpretation and evaluation leading to inferences and conclusions. Two sets of identical questionnaires were prepared—one in English for supervisors and another in Oriya for head-teachers.

Observation technique was adopted to study the on-the-spot practices and programmes. A number of interviews were conducted with selected educationists, administrators and Senior Inspecting Officers for eliciting their views on some crucial points of problem and a structured schedule was used for making data guided and controlled. Besides, the experiences of the researcher in the UK, France, Switzerland, Netherland and West Germany provided additional data and greater insight.

SAMPLE

The questionnaire was administered on 580 supervisors and 3,176 head-teachers of whom 410 (71 per cent and 1 per cent) responded respectively. The total number of interviewees was 25, of whom 10 were interviewed personally and 5 had extended their comments in response to an interview schedule. Thus the total percentage of interviewees was 60.

FINDINGS

Democracy and Primary Education

1. Most of the respondents understood democracy either as a political or a social or an ethical concept and not as a comprehensive and well-integrated one in its true perspective.
2. The concept of Primary Education was not clear to a large number of supervisors and head-teachers.
3. Although majority of supervisors and head-teachers opined that India was a true democracy. Most of the interviewees observed that she was in the process of becoming a true democracy slowly, but steadily.
4. According to most of the responses the eradication of mass illiterate and mass poverty would make India a true democracy.
5. Due to educational, economic, political and social difficulties, schools did not yet belong to the society.

6. The school as a conservative agency was not in a position to assume leadership for bringing about desired social changes.
7. The students were not being trained for democracy on account of education, political, social, economic and psychological difficulties.

Syllabus and Curriculum

1. The syllabus merely enunciated but did not enforce the provisions for democracy.
2. The programmes and practices conducive to democracy were not adequately organised in the primary schools.
3. Teachers and supervisors were not properly associated with curriculum planning.
4. The preparation of the instructional materials by the teachers is not given due importance.

Methods and Materials

1. Modern methods were not followed by most of the teachers and traditional methods were adopted for case and expedience of execution.
2. Innovations and experiments in teaching were not encouraged.
3. Work experience was not given due emphasis.
4. The teachers did not make attempts to impart knowledge and skills in democracy.
5. Special methods and materials were not adopted for teaching the slow and the advanced learners.
6. Text Books and supplementary readers were not produced properly. They are also not available in time and at inexpensive prices.
7. Text Books are not accompanied with teacher's handbooks and pupils' workbooks.

School Administration

1. Careful planning was needed in setting up new schools and for efficient utilisation of the existing ones.

2. Public awareness was not properly generated and education was not made relevant to the life, needs and aspirations of the people.
3. There was no regular attendance in many schools.
4. Mass poverty and ignorance were the greatest hurdles in the Universalisation of Primary Education.
5. Democratic decentralisation was not a success due to political interference and ignorance of the personnel about their duties and obligations.

School Organisation

1. Inter-personal relationships were not satisfactory in most of the Primary Schools.
2. Villagers' inertia and teachers' indifference were the main bottlenecks in making adult education programme a success.
3. Freedom and flexibility were lacking in school organisation.
4. In most of the schools, student-government was not in existence.
5. Corporal punishment was still resorted to in many primary schools.
6. Various kinds of rewards specially non-material ones were yet to be introduced in most of the schools.
7. Community service was not provided in many schools.
8. Staff meetings were not regularly held in most of the schools.
9. School timing and holidays were not arranged according to local needs and conditions.

Inspection and Supervision

1. Class-teaching was not regularly supervised by the Inspecting Officers.
2. Mistakes were often pointed out to the concerned teachers in the classroom.
3. Demonstration lessons were not given by many supervisors.
4. Supervisors did not often hold discussion on educational matters in staff/faculty meetings.
5. Discussion by the supervisors was occasionally held with the community members.

6. Centre-meetings were not often held democratically and meaningfully.
7. Leadership qualities in teachers and pupils were not properly identified and encouraged.

Finance and School Improvement

1. Funds for physical facilities were inadequate.
2. Provision of ancillary services was poor and unsatisfactory.
3. A large number of children were not able to continue their education owing to economic, physiological and physical barriers.
4. Educational costs increased to a great extent mainly on account of reading and writing materials, donations, examination fees, dress and mid-day food.
5. Many schools were ill-equipped and unattractive.
6. School Improvement Programme was not making headway due to lack of initiative, cooperation and resourcefulness of supervisors.

Examination and Evaluation

1. Majority of supervisors and head-teachers were not aware of an important objective of examination, i.e. diagnosing and giving guidance to students.
2. Undue importance was given to cramming. Assessment of pupil growth in citizenship was not done in the examination.
3. Many of the respondents viewed the abolition of Upper Primary Public Examination and class examinations for promotion from classes I and II as the reason for deterioration of the general standard.
4. Cumulative Record was not yet introduced in most of the primary schools.

Status and Service Conditions of Teachers

1. Many head-teachers and supervisors were not satisfied with the present status of teachers.
2. Majority of the respondents were not happy with the promotional prospects and service conditions.

3. Academic freedom was not adequate for teachers' professional growth and introducing innovations.
4. Many respondents felt that teachers' organisations were not working in the right directions.
5. Teachers' Organisations were not implementing academic programmes adequately for the professional growth of teachers.

Lastly, on the basis of these findings a number of relevant suggestions were made for bringing about democratisation of Primary Education through suitable methods and techniques.

Socio-economic Background of the Students Studying in the High Schools of Bhubaneswar

JAGANNATH MOHANTY

1. INTRODUCTION

1.1 Present Scenario of Indian Education

The Constitution of India has declared the nation's firm commitment to ideals of democracy, socialism and secularism. Education has been taken as a powerful instrument for realising its ideals. But there are some social and economic barriers standing in the way of achieving the Constitutional Directive and commitment.

The Education Commission, 1964-66, has observed that education instead of bringing about an egalitarian and integrated society is itself tending to increase social segregation and class distinctions. The National Policy on Education, 1986 has, therefore, laid special emphasis on the removal of disparities and equalisation of educational opportunity.

1.2 Socio-economic Status (SES)

A number of studies conducted in India and abroad have pointed out that socio-economic status has significant role to play in the academic achievement of students. According to Kuppuswamy, the socio-economic status of a family includes education, occupation and income of the family. But the status symbols of a modern man have multiplied to include location of the residence, house type and other facilities like TV, Car, Library, etc.

1.3 Academic Achievement (AA)

Academic Achievement means knowledge attained and skills developed in the school subjects usually designed by test scores or by work assigned by teachers. It means students' performance in school subjects and behavioural changes that take place as a result of learning experience.

1.4 Relation between SES and AA

Coleman (1966), Borgan and Dunn (1976), Prakash Chandra (1975), Shah (1975), Sudame (1978), Anand (1973), Menon (1973), Dave and Dave (1971) and so on have found a high correlation between socio-economic status and academic achievement. On the contrary, Mehta (1969) has shown that students with low SES were associated with higher achievement than students with middle SES.

1.5 Educational Innovation and Intervention

With a view to making up the deficiencies of the socio-economic status of students and energizing the teaching-learning process in the schools, it is felt that educational innovations and interventions are of great significance. Some teachers committed to their work have been implementing some innovations and interventions at their level. But their actions are often found unsystematic and haphazard thereby losing significance sooner or later.

The International Commission on Education has, therefore, suggested that such innovative practices should be well-planned and broad-based. These changes can be effected in the school situations with or without structural changes on the socio-economic level. Since the teachers are the main catalytic agents of such desired changes, they should be given adequate freedom and facilities. The NPE (1986) has also suggested that the Government and the

Community should create conditions for inspiring teachers on constructive lines.

1.6 Present Study

The present study is confined to the geographical limits of Bhubaneswar Municipality. Besides, its historical importance, Bhubaneswar has developed as the Capital of Orissa since 1948 and a large number of institutions and organisations have been set-up with individual, Government and non-Government initiative and support. Bhubaneswar Municipality started functioning since 1979 and its present population is about 2.5 lakhs in an area of 65.03 sq. kms. The percentage of literacy in Bhubaneswar is 66.96 against the State's percentage 34.12. The total number of high schools under various managements is 37.

With a view to improving academic achievement of students and solving problems by the teachers and managements, the socio-economic status, school interventions and achievement were studied taking a sample of thirty high schools under various managements as follows:

Central Government sponsored	:	3
State Government Managed	:	14
State Government Aided	:	2
Municipality Managed	:	6
Voluntary organisation managed	:	5

Data were collected with the help of a questionnaire on socio-economic status and academic achievement of students. Information was collected on school interventions through interview with the Heads of the institution with the help of an interview schedule. After data collection, necessary compilation and processing of data were made taking the help of a computer.

2. MAJOR FINDINGS

The processed data on SES of students showed a skewed distribution of the sample having more concentration of students (81 per cent) with low SES. Only 18 per cent and 1 per cent of students belonged to average and high SES respectively. Thus, it is inferred that in spite of Bhubaneswar being the Capital city of Orissa a large majority (81 per cent) of students belonged to poor SES.

Unlike the SES distribution, the distribution of AA of poor, average and good students was not very much skewed. A near-normal distribution of AA was evident in central sponsored and voluntary organisations managed schools. However, in the Municipality managed, State managed, and State-aided schools a more concentration of students was found with poor AA category.

The study indicates that AA is poor in schools managed by Bhubaneswar Municipality (77 per cent), State Government (65 per cent) and State Government-aided (59 per cent). Thus, majority of students in these schools have low/poor AA. In institutions sponsored by the Government of India and voluntary organisations, the corresponding percentage is much less, i.e. 10 per cent and 17 per cent respectively. As regards to high AA, the percentage of students in Central sponsored institutions is 28 which is the highest of all the schools. In case of institutions managed under Bhubaneswar Municipality, State Government or State-aided and voluntary organisations, the percentage of students with high AA is very negligible.

As regards to the school interventions, it was found that 74 per cent of the institutions sponsored by Central Government agencies and 16 per cent of State managed schools provide good interventions, whereas no school in other categories (Municipality-managed, State-aided and voluntary managed) could provide good interventions. However, under average category of school interventions there were 26 per cent of Central-managed, 68 per cent of Municipality managed, 63 per cent of State-managed and 100 per cent of State-aided as well as voluntary-managed schools.

The study indicates that in institutions sponsored by Central Government agencies, the status of school intervention was best of all types due to availability of adequate physical facilities, periodic assessment of students and effective supervision. In state-aided and voluntary-managed schools the Status of school interventions was to some extent better. In the institutions managed by the State Government and Municipality the status of interventions was not satisfactory.

As regards the extent of influence of the SES and SIs on AA of students, the multiple correlation coefficient was found to be 0.19

which is not significant. This means the joint effect of SES and SIs on AA of students is not perceptible.

The correlation between SES and AA is significant having 'r' value of 0.31, significant at 0.01 level. Similarly, the relationship between SES and SIs, was also found to be significant having 'r' value of 0.26, significant at 0.01 level.

To conclude it may be said that the relationship of AA with SES was significant, whereas no significant relationship existed between AA and SIs. It shows school interventions were not adequate or non-existent.

In case of management categories it is found that there was significant correlation between AA and SES in Municipality-managed and State-managed schools. In other three categories the correlation coefficients between SES and AA were not found to be significant. It is however, found that excepting schools managed by voluntary organisations, in case of all others the correlation was quite nearer to be significant but for the small size of the sample. That is, SES has played a significant role in higher AA of students in all schools excepting the voluntary ones.

3. RECOMMENDATIONS

On the basis of the findings of the study the following recommendations may be made for improvement of the academic achievement of the students:

1. Since majority (81 per cent) of students belong to poor SES, better school interventions like remedial teaching, improvement of school community relations, School Broadcast programme and co-curricular activities should be effectively organised by the schools for improving students' achievement. The Headmaster and Teachers are to be entrusted with this task with provision of adequate facilities.
2. As a high percentage of students reading in Municipality-managed, State-managed and State-aided schools are of poor academic achievement specific programmes should be taken up by the Municipality and State Government for improving pupils' academic growth. The state educational authorities in consultation with respective head-teachers should plan out such programmes.

3. Since in the State-managed and Municipality-managed schools the status of school interventions is not satisfactory, adequate physical facilities should be provided, periodic assessment of students be made and the existing facilities are to be utilised to the optimum and effective supervision be ensured to a great extent.
4. As the relationship between academic achievement with socio-economic status was significant, necessary steps need be taken for improving home situations, parents' awareness, physical facilities, etc., so that improved socio-economic status would lead to better achievement of students.
5. Since remedial teaching is felt essential for improving achievement of weaker students which are in large number in almost all schools, Government, voluntary agencies and Municipality should take necessary action for provision of remedial teaching in all schools and the teachers, head-teachers of the schools are to be encouraged to undertake different programmes.
6. In view of the specific importance of parent-teacher associations in improving school conditions as well as pupils' growth the head-teachers should take interest and initiative for organising parent-teacher organisations in their school. This will go a long way in solving many of the problems in the school including the AA of the students.
7. With a view to solving the day-to-day problems of the schools as well as students, improving the physical facilities of schools and performance of students, parents/ guardians meeting should be convened by head-teachers from time to time so that the parents could be kept updated with the academic progress of their ward. Besides, they will be motivated in evincing interest in the school programmes and school developmental programmes.
8. As the annual day celebration is a means of encouraging students in various subjects, of motivating parents in the school programmes, of associating the community with the school and of informing the higher officers about the school achievement and its problems, the annual day should be celebrated invariably, and effectively in all schools.

9. Since school Broadcasting programme aims at enriching and supplementing teachers' teaching work it should be properly organised by the head-teachers as well as concerned teachers.
10. With a view to enabling students to participate in the school programmes with renewed energy and interest, efforts should be made by the Government and voluntary agencies to provide mid-day meals/tiffin during recreation period in all schools.
11. In order to improve physical facility and curricular programmes of schools, adequate steps should be taken by the head-teachers for effective community participation in school programme. The head-teacher with community leaders/parents has to identify the areas and programmes and plan accordingly.
12. With a view to improving school community relations and students' behaviour in-and-outside the school, frequent personal contacts should be made with the parents and students by the head-teachers and the assistant teachers.
13. Since all teachers of a school need be involved in decision-making and in jointly solving day-to-day problems in respect to curricular and co-curricular programmes, staff council meetings should be held as frequently as possible.
14. With a view to developing different interests, abilities of students different types of co-curricular activities like games and sports, debate competitions, essay writing competitions, field trips, etc. should be effectively organised in all schools.
15. Since the head-teachers are the key persons in implementing various programmes in the schools they should be given adequate freedom, facilities and incentives in organising various curricular and co-curricular programmes in their schools.
16. The head-teachers should involve their colleagues in decision-making and assign suitable responsibility to teachers for ensuring success of all programmes in schools.
17. Since supervision is an important element in improving AA of students, supervisors should extend necessary cooperation, encouragement and guidance to schools for organising various useful programmes.

18. Government, voluntary organisations, and local self-government, should provide necessary funds and facilities for successful implementation of various programmes in schools.
19. The public in general and parents/guardians in particular should realise the importance of different programmes for improving the academic achievement of the pupils and support the schools in organising such programmes.
20. With a view to making the school interventions effective, various innovative programmes should be given formal shape with organisational and infrastructural support. The teachers and head-teachers are to be encouraged to undertake innovative practices for improving academic achievement of pupils.

References

Abraham, M., *Some Factors Relating to Under-achievement in English of Secondary School Pupils*, Ph.D. Education, Kerala University, 1974.

Anand, C.L., *A Study of the Effect of Socio-economic Environment and Medium of Instruction on the Mental Abilities and the Academic Achievement of Children*, Ph.D. Education, Mysore University, 1973.

Basavayya, D., *Effect of Bilingualism on Language Achievement*, Central Institute of Indian Languages, Mysore, 1974.

Bhubaneswar Municipality, *Paur Samachar* (Oriya), 1986-87.

Borgan, John *et al.*, *Psychology and Education . . . A Science for Instruction*, John Wiley and Sons Inc., 1974.

Dave, P.N. and Dave, J.P., *Socio-economic Environment as Related to the Non-Verbal Intelligence of Rank and Failed Students*, Regional College of Education, Mysore, 1971.

Dewal, O.S., *A Study of Difficulties in Teaching English and Effectiveness of Programmed Teaching*, Ph.D. Education, M.S. University, 1974.

Ebel, R.L., *Measuring Educational Achievement*, Englewood Cliffs, N.J.: Prentice-Hall, Inc., 1965.

Government of India, *National Policy on Education—1986*, MHRD (Deptt. of Education), New Delhi, 1986.

Government of India, *The Report of the Education Commission*, 1964-66, Ministry of Education, New Delhi, 1966.

International Commission on Education, *Learning to Be*, UNESCO, Paris (1972).

Kuppuswamy, B., *Socio-economic Status (Urban) Manual*, Manasayana, Delhi, 1962.

Mehta, Prayag, *The Achievement Motive in High School Boys*, Research Monograph—NCERT, New Delhi, 1969.

Menon, S.K., *A Comparative Study of the Personality Characteristics of Over-achievers and Under-Achievers of High Ability*. Ph.D. Psychology, Kerala University, 1973.

Mohanty, J., *Indian Education in the Emerging Society*, Sterling Publishers, New Delhi, 1983.

NCERT, *National Curriculum for Primary and Secondary Education*, New Delhi, 1986.

Ottaway, A.K.C., *Education and Society*, Routledge and Kegan Paul, London, 1962.

Prakash, Chandra, *A Study of the Problems of High School Students in the Varanasi Education Region of U.P. and their Relative Effect on Achievement*, Ph.D. Education, Gor University, 1975.

Reddy, E.L.N., *A Study of Certain Factors Associated with Academic Achievement in the First Year Degree Examination*, Ph.D. Education, M.S. University, Baroda, 1973.

Rogers, Everett M. (1964): *Diffusion of Innovations*, Macmillan, New York.

Shah, B., *Construction and Standardisation of the Omnibus Test of Intelligence in Gujarati for Age Group 13+ to 16+*, Ph.D. Education, Bombay University, 1975.

Sudame, G.R., *A Study of the Effect of Library Use on Academic Achievement of Post-Graduate Students*, Ph.D. Education, M.S. University, Baroda, 1973.

3

The Relationship between Socio-economic Status and Achievement of Class IX Students

MANORANJAN PANDA

1. STATEMENT OF THE PROBLEM

The Constitution of India in its preamble has clearly indicated the vision and commitment of the nation to the ideals of democracy, socialism and secularism securing to all citizens Justice, Liberty, Equality and fraternity Article 46, therefore, declares "The state shall promote with special care the educational and economic interest of the weaker sections of people and in particular, of the scheduled caste and scheduled tribes and shall protect them from social injustice and all forms of exploitation. The framers of the constitution were quite conscious that Indian society has suffered from age-old superstitions and discriminations which have resulted in various social and economic barriers and disparities.

Since education has been regarded as a potential instruments of social transformation, the Constitution of India in Article 45, under the Directive Principles of State Policy stated, "The state shall endeavour to provide within a period of ten years, from the commencement of this constitution for free and compulsory education for all children until they complete the age of 14 years. It has been a bitter experience that universalisation of elementary education has not been achieved even after fifty years of the attainment of Independence.

Although a good number of steps have been taken by the Government of India and State Government as well for achieving to this objective, it is eluding the grasp on account of varied reasons, mainly social and economic in nature. These seasons are also equally applicable to secondary education which suffers from heavy drop out and stagnation, poor attendance, high percentage of failures and so on.

It has been the responsibility of the educational system to ensure education both in quantity as well as in quality with a view to bringing the different social classes and groups together, and this promoting the emergency of an egalitarian and integrated society.

It is evident from the above statement that social and economic factors have been influencing education to a great extent and stand on the way of realising the constitutional objectives as well as scholastic and vocational goals. For this the investigator felt that an in-depth study should be conducted to know the relationship between socio-economic status and academic achievement pertaining to secondary schools. Thus, the investigator chose to take up the present problem entitled, "A study of the relationship between socio-economic status and achievement of class IX students."

2. OBJECTIVES OF THE STUDY

The following objectives were formulated for the study:

(i) To identify various factors determining the social and economic background of students.
(ii) To make a survey of the school interventions that have a bearing on the achievement of students.
(iii) To assess inter-relationship between socio-economic status academic achievement and school intervention in different categories of schools.
(iv) To find out the effect of socio-economic status, school intervention on academic achievement in different categories of schools.
(v) To predict academic achievement with the help of socio-economic status and school intervention in different categories of schools.

3. HYPOTHESES

The following hypothesis were formulated for the study:

(i) There is no significant difference in socio-economic status of students studying in different categories of schools.
(ii) There is no significant difference in academic achievement of students studying in different categories of schools.
(iii) There is no significant difference in school intervention score in different categories of schools.
(iv) There is no significant relationship between socio-economic status and academic achievement of students studying in different categories of schools.
(v) There is no significant relationship between academic achievement of students and school intervention scores in different categories of schools.
(vi) There is no significant relationship between socio-economic status and school intervention score in different categories of schools.
(vii) Socio-economic status and school intervention together do not contribute significantly to the academic achievement of class IX students studying in different categories of schools.

4. SAMPLING

With a view to improving academic achievement of students and solving problems by the teachers and management the socio-economic status academic achievement and school intervention were studied taking samples of 55 high schools under various managements as follows:

Welfare Schools	:	4
Government Schools	:	14
Non-Government Schools	:	37

5. COLLECTION OF DATA

Data were collected with the help of scale on socio-economic status of students. To assess the academic achievement, the marks of the last annual examination of the same students were collected from the office record as provided by the Headmasters. Information was collected on school interventions through interview with the Heads of the institution with the help of an interview schedule. After data collection, necessary compilation and processing of data were made taking the help of a computer.

6. ANALYSIS OF DATA

The data were analysed through the following headings keeping the objectives of the study in view:

(i) Conversion of raw scores into standard scores and comparison of frequency distributions.
(ii) Significance of difference between means.
(iii) Inter-relationship between variables under study.
(iv) Multiple correlation and predication of dependant variable on the basis of independent variables. For analysing the data the following statistical techniques were used:
  (i) Conversion of raw score to standard score.
  (ii) Test of significance.
  (iii) Co-efficient of correlation among socio-economic status, academic achievement and school intervention.
  (iv) Regression technique.
(v) Partial and multiple correlation.
(vi) Standard error of multiple R.

7. MAJOR FINDINGS

1. There is significant difference in socio-economic status of students studying in different categories of schools.
2. There is significant difference in academic achievement of students studying in different categories of schools.
3. There is no significant difference in school intervention score between government and non-government schools.
4. There is significant difference in school intervention score between welfare and government schools.
5. There is also significant difference in school intervention score between welfare and non-government schools.

6. There is no significant relationship between socio-economic status and academic achievement of students studying in difference categories of schools.
7. There is no significant relationship between academic achievement and school intervention in government and non-government schools.
8. There is marked relationship between academic achievement and school intervention in welfare schools.
9. There is no significant relationship between socio-economic status and school intervention in different categories of schools.
10. As regards the extent of influence of the socio-economic status and school intervention on academic achievement of students the multiple correlation co-efficient is found to be 0.077 which is not significant. This means the combined effect of socio-economic status and school intervention on academic achievement of students is not perceptible.

8. RECOMMENDATIONS

On the basis of the findings of the study the following recommendations may be made for improvement of the academic achievement of students:

1. Since remedial teaching is felt essential for improving achievement of weaker students who are in large number in almost all schools, Government may take necessary action for provision of remedial teaching in all schools and the teachers as well as head-teachers of all the schools are to be encouraged to undertake different programmes for the purpose.
2. With a view to solving day-to-day problems of the schools as well as students, improving the physical facilities of the schools and performance of students, parents/guardians meetings should be convened by head-teachers from time to time so that the parents can be well informed about their wards. Besides, they will be motivated to participate in the school developmental programmes.
3. With a view to developing different interests, abilities of students, different types of co-curricular activities like

games and sports, debate competitions, essay writing, field trips, etc., should be effectively organised in all schools.

4. As the annual day celebration is means of encouraging students in various subjects of motivating parents in the school programmes and informing the higher officers about the school achievement and its problems, the annual day should be celebrated invariably and effectively in all schools.
5. In service teacher training should be compulsory for all teachers. One teacher must attain an orientation course once in every five years to refresh his/her knowledge in content as well as techniques of teaching.
6. Teachers are to be encouraged to conduct action research on the burning problems of the schools and its students.
7. Selection of appropriate persons to the post Headmasters need be based not only an experience but also on qualification and efficiency. A teacher to become a headmaster should have not only fifteen years of teaching experience but also higher qualifications, i.e. a post-graduate besides, CCR may be taken into account for considering efficiency.
8. Headmasters are to be trained time and again to enrich their content knowledge to acquaint themselves with modern methodology of teaching and evaluation techniques and to develop administrative and supervisory practices.
9. A laboratory-*cum*-science room is the basic requirement of the school. Steps in this direction should be taken. In science room chart, diagrams, graphs are to be displayed and laboratory equipment and chemicals are to be stored as per requirement.
10. Attention must be given to upgrade library conditions keeping in view of the needs of students and teachers. There should be reference books. Magazines, journals and for updating teachers knowledge.
11. Now it is recommended that the audio-visual aids like TV, cassette, recorder, projector, cinematography, VCR and Radio sets should be provided to each school and be incorporated in teaching method in all the secondary schools. Through these, the demonstrations to the students are made more attractive, acceptable, lively and under-

standable. The students not only easily memorise the content but also can assimilate it better for longer duration. The creative potentiality of the child is also augmented because of it.

12. Every school should organise science fairs at least once a year. The programmes should include exhibits prepared by the students. Talks by experts, film show on scientific topics, music shows, scientific plays, quiz, etc., can also be organised. Both the teacher and pupils should co-operate and contribute towards the success of such fairs.
13. Learning in the classroom cannot be sufficient for a student of modern time. So excursion and visits to different place of scientific importance should be organised annually to give an opportunity to the participants to get direct and practical learning experiences in an interesting manner. Science teacher must arrange tours to radio station, telephone exchange, gardens, factories, planetarium which will supplement class room instructions.
14. Inspection and supervision in the school is very essential. The inspecting personnel should inspect the following items:
    - Time table.
    - Teachers diary.
    - The scheme of work.
    - Notebooks of students.
    - Laboratory, library and stock registers.
15. Objective system of testing the achievement of students and personality assessment should be introduced.
16. As socially disadvantaged children have internalised their parents low motivation and aspiration, it becomes necessary to involve the parents in the process of education and orient them regarding the value of education through non-formal educational programmes.
17. In small families the children receive individual attention and personal care. It is, therefore, advisable to keep the family small. The state should take positive measures in this direction and involve the teachers also in such programmes.
18. Local community is to be involved in the school improvement programmes since community possesses abundant resource—Men, Money and Material. On the other hand, school should also be made a centre of community work.

19. Attempts should be made to remove social and economic disparity. The Government should try to improve the conditions of people living below the poverty line.
20. Since all teachers of a school need be involved in decision-making and in solving day-to-day problems in respect to curricular and co-curricular programmes, staff council meetings should be held as frequently as possible.

4

Early Childhood Education (ECE) for Universalisation of Elementary Education (UEE)

JAGANNATH MOHANTY

1. NEED AND IMPORTANCE OF THE STUDY

Early childhood extending from two to six years of age is a period of great importance, when the child seeks to acquire control over the environment. He gets himself ready to explore his environment, know its components, to know how it works and how it feels. This period is, therefore, ideal for learning. He acquires new knowledge and skills through curiosity, adventure and activities.

The child develops egocentrism and animism. Still, he learns the basics of social behaviour and as a member of the gang he gets interested in the company of others. Many leadership qualities develop at this stage and shows his interest in toys, plays, drawings, dance, music, etc.

Educationally, this period is, therefore, very significant and paves the way for effective learning. It enables the child to profit from early childhood education in all respects. There are mainly two reasons for giving importance to ECE, firstly, for bringing about development—physical, social, emotional and intellectual and secondly, for reducing the high wastage and drop-outs in primary schools. The Kothari Commission emphasized ECE for the first generation learners and as a support for working mothers. Some studies also revealed that children passed through pre-school education show regular attendance and better progress at the primary stage. The National Policy on Education (NPE—1986) and the revised one, 1992 have pointed out the importance of SCE for child development as a whole, through nutrition, health, social, mental, physical, moral and emotional development. That is why, these documents have termed ECE as Early Childhood Care and Education (ECCE).

ECCE has received high priority from the government due to its contribution towards universalization of elementary education. At present, besides Anganwadis and Balwadis, a number of ECE centres have been established through private initiatives and most of them are English Medium Schools. Since UEE is a matter of great national concern, ECE has been emphasized by various Committees and Commissions as supportive and contributory to the success of Elementary Education.

A comprehensive review of related studies gave no conclusive findings about the contribution of ECE towards enrolment, attendance and achievement of children. Especially, no adequate studies have been undertaken relating to the role of ECE in UEE in India in general and in Orissa in particular. It was, therefore, felt necessary to conduct a in-depth study of the ECE centres for ascertaining their effectiveness and relevance to UEE.

2. OBJECTIVES OF THE STUDY

The objectives of the study were as follows:

(a) To make a survey of ECE centres in all aspects and managements.
(b) To find out the strengths and weaknesses of their programmes.
(c) To know their contribution towards the achievement of UEE.
(d) To make a comparative study exposed and non-exposed groups of children in ECE centres with Oriya and English Medium as regards their achievement and dropout.

(e) To suggest measures for improving ECE centres so that UEE can be promoted and be a success.

3. SCOPE AND LIMITATIONS

The entire state of Orissa was taken as the universe and all kinds of ECE centres were brought under its purview. ECE centres both in English and Oriya were selected through the method of random sampling from all the three Revenue Divisions taken as clusters. The study was also delimited to the curricular and co-curricular programmes, management and other aspects of ECE centres with special reference to their efficiency for realization of UEE.

4. SAMPLES

One sample of 100 Anganwadi Centres (AWCs) with Oriya medium and another sample of 56 ECE centres in English Medium Schools viz., Convents, DAV, Sri Aurobindo Integral School, Saraswati Sishu Mandir, Maharshi Vidya Mandir, Satya Sai Schools and other such schools were taken from three Revenue Divisions, Central, Northern and Southern. The districts of Balasore, Puri and Cuttack in the Central Division, Sambalpur and Dhenkanal in Northern Divisions and Ganjam, Phulbani and Koraput in Southern Division were selected for collection of data. One sample of 25 managements and another sample of 25 educationists, administrators and supervisors were taken for eliciting their views through interview.

5. TOOLS AND TECHNIQUES

For making a survey of ECE Centres, a detailed questionnaire for heads of ECE centres was developed and tried out for collecting data relating to general information about the teachers, and ECE centres, academic programmes, structure, media, materials, management, supervision, finance and other relevant aspects. Prior to this, two conferences of the ECE centres and experts were held at Bhubaneswar and Sambalpur to identify the problems and issues relating to ECE and feedback of the conferences was taken into account for developing the questionnaire.

One interview schedule was developed for enlisting the views of managements of ECE centres regarding various their issues and problems. An opinionnaire was drafted and finalized for pooling the opinions of the educationists, senior administrators and supervisors on different aspects of ECE centres and their contribution towards UEE. Besides, two information sheets were developed, one for children of exposed group and another for non-exposed group under both English and Oriya Medium, for collecting data regarding their attendance, dropout and achievement. Data regarding achievement and dropout were collected from the school documents like Examination and Admission Registers in respect of the students from Class I to Class V during the period 1990-91 to 1994-95. However, daily attendance registers were not available in most of the primary schools and as such data regarding attendance could not be collected.

All these tools were administered and data were collected personally by the Principal Investigator and Junior Project Fellow (JPF) through on the spot visit of the ECE centres. During such visits it was possible to observe the programmes, discuss with teachers and managements and interact with students and other persons concerned. Therefore, both quantitative and qualitative data were collected for better analysis and interpretation.

6. ANALYSIS AND INTERPRETATION

Data were compiled and analysed with the help of percentages in most of the cases. As regards the achievements of children belonging to exposed and not exposed groups both in Oriya and English, Standard Error of Difference Between Means (SED) was employed and calculation of 't' value was made for better comparison.

Analysis of data regarding ECE centres (both English and Oriya) revealed a number of interesting findings about teachers, students, accommodation, qualification, pay, methods, etc.

Table 4.1 indicates that all Anganwadi workers belong to female sex whereas 71 per cent and 29 per cent were male and female teachers respectively in ECE (E) centres. The ECE (O) and (E) centres were established during the period from 1974 to 1993. Most of the AWCs were located in villages and slum areas whereas 100 per cent of ECE (E) centres were located in urban and semi-urban areas. Most of the ECE (E) centres (76 per cent) were housed in rented buildings whereas only 42 per cent of ECE (O) centres were running in rented houses. Only 24 per cent and 8 per cent belonging to these former and latter groups had their own buildings.

TABLE 4.1

Information of Workers/Teachers Regarding Sex

(In percentage)

	Central Divn.		*Northern Divn.*		*Southern Divn.*		*Total*	
	Male	*Female*	*Male*	*Female*	*Male*	*Female*	*Male*	*Female*
ECE (O)	Nil	100	Nil	100	Nil	100	Nil	100
ECE (E)	50	50	83	17	80	20	71	29

In majority of the ECE (O) centres workers were matriculate (33 per cent) having in service training whereas, a great majority of teachers (85 per cent) in ECE (E) centres were graduates with in-service training (40 per cent). Table 4.2 shows the qualification of teaching staff.

TABLE 4.2

Information about Qualification of the Teaching Staff

(In percentage)

	General Qualification					*Professional Qualification*	
	Matric	*Under Matric*	*Post Matric*	*Graduate*	*Post Graduate*	*In-Service*	*Pre-Service*
ECE (O)	53	31	16	–	–	100	–
ECE (E)	–	–	–	85	15	40	7

The workers of ECE (O) centres were paid according to their qualification and experience, but there is no rationality in the pay of the teachers working in ECE (E) centres.

Table 4.3 gives an idea about the distribution of students according to their sex in ECE centres (both O and E).

TABLE 4.3

Distribution of Students according to Sex

(In percentage)

	Central Divn.		*Northern Divn.*		*Southern Divn.*		*Total*	
	Boys	*Girls*	*Boys*	*Girls*	*Boys*	*Girls*	*Boys*	*Girls*
ECE (O)	51	49	36	64	63	37	50	50
ECE (E)	71	29	78	22	80	20	76	24

It is interesting to note that the distributions of boys and girls in ECE (O) Centres were equal whereas, in ECE (E) centres the percentage of girls (24 per cent) was less than that of boys (76 per cent).

In ECE (O) centres children were in the age group 3 to 5 whereas in ECE (E) centres they were in the age group 2 to 5 years. In the former education was quite non-formal and in ECE centres it was formalized to a great extent. Table 4.4 gives the information about the age level, and structure of ECE centres.

It is evident from Table 4.4 that 100 per cent children attended Anganwadi centres of two years whereas, in 85 per cent of ECE centres students attended K.G. classes and 15 per cent attended nursery classes.

TABLE 4.4

Information about the Age Level and Structure of ECE Centres

Age Level			*Structure*	*Per cent of centres*
ECE (O)	(a)	3+ to 4+	Anganwadi classes	100
	(b)	4+ to 5+		
ECE (E)	(a)	2+ to 3+	Nursery	15
	(b)	3+ to 4+	K.G.I/L.K.G., etc.	85
	(c)	4+ to 5+	K.G.II/U.K.G., etc.	

In ECE (O) centres, a set of guidelines has been provided by the government to carry on various activities and in ECE centres syllabi have been developed by their concerned agencies. In the former, activities were organised due to heterogeneity of the syllabi. The nature of such activities was recreational and developmental in the former category. It was mostly academic in the latter. In the AWCs the activities were stereotyped and in ECE (E) centres they were mostly unintelligible and traditional. However, in the former the children had the pleasure and joy of participation, which was lacking in ECE (E) centres. Due to lack of space, sports and games were occasionally organised in both kinds of ECE centres.

In ECE (O) centres, books, story chart, alphabets chart, dolls, maps and pictures, etc., were provided by government long back and most of them were found broken and damaged. In ECE (E) centres mechanical toys and quizzes were purchased but rarely used. The primers, nursery rhymes, stories, etc., printed in English were supplied to students on payment. Students in these centres were actually hard pressed due to the demands of parents and joyful learning was found absent. Workbooks were found unnecessary in ECE (O) centres whereas, in ECE(E) centres workbooks were used in most of the subjects. There were no guide books either in ECE (O) or in ECE (E) centre. But the guidelines provided by the concerned authorities were taken as guide books.

In ECE (E) centres Oriya was the medium of instruction with some difficulties for children of the minority communities and tribes. In ECE (E) centres English was the medium of instruction with difficulties of understanding and enjoyment. English was preferred by 84 per cent of parents for its social and economic values. In ECE ('O' and 'E') centres story telling and recitation of poems were followed generally. Activity and playing methods were followed in most of the centres. In ECE (O) centres there were no formal examinations whereas, in ECE (E) centres both written and oral and different types of formal examinations were held without adequate understanding and appreciation.

All the ECE (O) centres were managed by the government, whereas, the ECE (E) centres were managed by Missionaries and other non-government agencies. Although most of ECE (E) centres said to have been set-up to spread education but actually profit motive was found to be an important cause. In case of ECE (O) and ECE(E) centres no accounts were made available and there were some elements of commercialisation due to lack of transparency in the financial management of ECE (E) centres. The former was supervised by Supervisors. CDECs and DWOs and the latter by Secretaries, Presidents, heads and other important members of the Advisory Committees. In spite of free education and provisions of supplementary food the percentage of attendance widely ranged from 36 to 94 in the ECE (O) centres but due to payment of fees and parents' awareness, the range of such attendance was found to be very narrow, i.e. from 90 to 100 in ECE (E) centres.

As revealed from the responses of heads in case of ECE (O) centres the academic problems were lack of training (39 per cent), dearth of teaching aids (29 per cent), heavy workload (22 per cent) and the administrative problems were inadequate accommodation (53 per cent), low salary (36 per cent), irregular inspection (28 per cent) and irregular salary (26 per cent). In case of ECE (E) centres, the heads have pointed out academic problems like heavy course of study (73 per cent), lack of in-service training (47 per cent), lack of pre-service training (41 per cent) and the administrative problems viz., absence of play ground (57 per cent), low salary (55 per cent) and inadequate accommodation (54 per cent).

According to 77 per cent and 72 per cent of interviewees of ECE (O) centres the academic problems were low educational qualification and inadequate learning materials respectively and under administrative problems low and irregular payment (97 per cent), inadequate contingency (89 per cent), poor quality materials (85 per cent) and poor accommodation (85 per cent). In case of ECE (E) centres the highest percentage (91 per cent) pointed out inadequate accommodations, lack of government assistance, low salary, etc. under administrative problems and as high as 91 per cent have felt workload on students too heavy as the most important academic problem.

Table 4.5 shows the significance of academic achievement of students exposed and not-exposed to ECE (O). And the result has shown that there exist no such significant difference (t = 1.95) between these two groups of students in their achievement.

TABLE 4.5

SED of Exposed and Not-exposed to ECE (O) Groups on Overall Achievement

Group	*N*	*M*	*SD*	*t*	*s/ns*
Exposed	49	218.50	50.63	1.95	ns both at .01 and .05
Not-exposed	54	214.23	64.27		

Table 4.6 shows the significant difference between exposed and not-exposed ECE (E) students in their achievement scores (t = 4.53). But the matter of great surprise that the students not-exposed to ECE (E) are at higher degree in their mean score (M = 421.50) than their counterparts (M = 361.90). It may be due to the coaching of educated parents and their personal attention.

The findings on inter-class achievement indicated that children exposed to ECE in the regional language have shown gradual improvement in their course whereas, those exposed to ECE in

TABLE 4.6

SED of Exposed and Not-exposed to ECE(E) Groups on Overall Achievement

Group	N	M	SD	t	s/ns
Exposed	78	361.90	55.80	–	–
				4.53	s
Not-exposed	42	421.50	74.70	–	–

English have not shown such gradual improvement in their achievement.

It is evident from the Table 4.7 that the continuance of children exposed to ECE (O) in primary classes was not found to be better and rather the children not exposed to ECE(O) have recorded less dropout. On the other hand, the continuance of children exposed to ECE (E) was found to be better than their counterparts, since the percentage of their dropout was less in primary classes than the children not exposed to ECE (E).

TABLE 4.7

Percentage of Dropout of Students Exposed and Not-exposed to ECE (O) and ECE (E)

Groups	Exposed		Not-exposed	
	No.	Per cent	No.	Per cent
ECE (O)	53	51.90	47	46.7
ECE (E)	22	23.97	55	69.88

7. MAJOR FINDINGS AND RECOMMENDATIONS

(a) Major Findings

On the basis of analysis and interpretation, the following were major findings:

(i) Although in Anganwadis all workers were female. In English Medium ECE Centres, percentage of female teachers (29 per cent) was less than male teachers (71 per cent).

(ii) Almost all ECE (E) Centres were located in urban and semi-urban areas, whereas most of the ECE (O) were located in villages and slum areas of towns.

(iii) As high as 76 per cent of ECE (E) centres were housed in rented buildings, whereas 42 per cent of ECE (O) centres were running in rented houses. In the former case 24 per cent and in latter case 8 per cent have their own buildings.

(iv) Most of the AWs were found to be less qualified, but trained whereas most of the teachers in ECE Centres were highly qualified and some of them trained.

(v) The teachers' emoluments both in ECE (O) and ECE (E) were not found adequate in comparison to their qualification and workload.

(vi) In the ECE (O) centres the percentage of boys and girls were the same, whereas, in ECE (E) centres the percentages of boys (76 per cent) was higher than that of girls (24 per cent).

(vii) The structure of ECE (O) was uniform and ungraded, whereas in ECE (E) centres the structure was diversified and multi-graded.

(viii) In ECE (O) centres curriculum was mostly uniform and informal, whereas in ECE centres the curriculum were very much divergent and too much formal.

(ix) The nature of activities in the ECE (O) centres was mostly recreational and developmental, whereas in ECE (E) centres it was mostly instructional and academic.

(x) In ECE (O) centres the teaching-learning materials were quite inadequate and occasionally provided, whereas in ECE (E) centres there were too many of them either brought out by their own agencies or by private firms.

(xi) In the ECE (O) no workbook was used, whereas in ECE (E) there were workbooks used in some subjects.

(xii) As high as 100 per cent of ECE (O) centres and 81 per cent of ECE (E) centres reported to have used guide books, but actually they have misunderstood guidelines given by their concerned authorities as guide books.

(xiii) Oriya was invariably used as the medium of instruction in ECE (O) centres with difficulties to tribal and minority communities and English in all ECE (E) centres with difficulty in understanding and enjoyment.

(xiv) Both in ECE (O) and (E) centres, story telling and action songs were emphasized and activities and play ways were occasionally used as methods of teaching.

(xv) In ECE (O) centres there were no formal examinations, whereas in all ECE (E) centres there were formal examinations—written, oral or both.

(xvi) ECE (O) centres were managed by the Government of Orissa and ECE (E) centres were managed by various private agencies like Missionary, New Life Education Trust, Siksha Vikas Samiti, Sai Baba Trust, etc.

(xvii) Although 85 per cent of ECE (O) and 81 per cent of ECE (E) centres reported that they have been set-up to satisfy local needs, actually ECE (E) centres came into existence to earn money.

(xviii) No accounts were made available in the ECE (E) centres and their financial management seems to have some elements of commercialisation.

(xix) The ECE (O) centres were supervised by supervisors, CDPOs and DWOs and ECE (E) centres by the Secretaries and other members of the Advisory Committees.

(xx) In ECE (O) centres the percentage of daily attendance ranged from 36 to 94 and in ECE (E) centres from 90 to 100.

(xxi) As reported by the head of ECE (O), the academic problems were—lack of training, difficulty in using teaching aids and heavy workload with less importance on educational activity and administrative problems were inadequate accommodation, low payment of salary and irregular inspection.

(xxii) In ECE (E) centres the academic problems were—heavy course of study, lack of in-service and pre-service training and the administrative problems were inadequate accommodation, low salary, etc.

(xxiii) The difference between exposed and not-exposed groups of ECE (O) was not found significant in achievement, whereas the difference in achievement between such groups of ECE (E) was found significant in favour of not-exposed ECE (E) group.

(xxiv) As regards ECE (O) in case of exposed group there were more dropouts than not exposed group in primary classes, whereas, this result was reverse in case of ECE (E).

(xxv) In primary classes continuance of children exposed to ECE (O) was not found better than that of ECE (E).

(b) Recommendations

In the light of the findings mentioned above, the following recommendations are made for improving the system in order to achieve the desired objectives of ECE.

(i) Since ICDS is likely to cover the entire country. ECE centres should be set-up both in villages and towns in order to provide facilities for school readiness so that UEE will be a success.

(ii) Irrespective of management whether government or non-government, the ECE centres have not been provided adequate and suitable accommodation which has resulted in adversely affecting the progress of students and smooth functioning of centres. It is, therefore, suggested that, early steps need be taken for provision of suitable accommodation in all ECE centres in a planned manner.

(iii) In ECE centres well-qualified and well-paid teachers should be appointed irrespective of medium of instruction and nature of management.

(iv) Teachers working in ECE centres should be provided both pre-service and in-service training with due emphasis on practical activities and methods of teaching oriented to the needs and conditions of young children.

(v) Since different structures of ECE were in vogue, there is scope for more heterogeneity, duplication and commercialisation. It is, therefore, suggested that ECE should be provided for two sessions for the children in the age group 3 to 5 years.

(vi) The curriculum for ECE should be flexible, activity-based and need-oriented, according to the psycho-social and cultural ethos.

(vii) In all ECE centres activities should be organised mostly for giving them different learning experiences through joyful and playway methods.

(viii) In ECE centres, no workbook should be used and more comprehensive guidebooks with detailed instructions for organising various activities should be provided free of cost.

(ix) Psychologically it is unsound to impose English on young children who are not able to enjoy and understand the instructions and activities. Hence in all the ECE centres mothertongue should be used as the medium of instruction particularly during the first year.

(x) There should not be any formal examination and students' progress can be evaluated through teachers' personal observation of their participation and interest in various activities and behaviour.

(xi) Excepting Anganwadis, all the ECE centres were managed by private agencies with various interests and motives, leading to unhealthy environment, over-loaded curriculum and commercialisation. In view of the great importance of ECE it is suggested that a well-organised institution or Board should be set-up under Government for fixation of standards and norms of establishing and maintaining ECE centres in the State.

(xii) Due to lack of transparency in the school accounts and high rates of collection from the students, it is suggested that action deemed suitable should be taken up to check such commercialisation.

(xiii) There should be an Advisory Committee in each ECE centre for extending their advice both for academic and administrative issues. These committees should be representative, active and sensitive to the problems of the children.

(xiv) The ECE centre should be supervised regularly by competent authorities, not haphazardly, but in a planned manner for giving practical guidance and suggestions for improving their activities and functioning.

(xv) The ECE centres should be made attractive, motivating and congenial for promoting daily attendance of students.

(xvi) Like the students of ECE (E) centres, almost all children of ECE (O) centres should go to primary classes for making UEE a great success.

(xvii) The ECE (O) centres should be supplied good quality materials and sufficient contingencies.

(xviii) In all ECE centres rich learning experiences should be provided by teachers through provision of better working conditions and infrastructural facilities so that better achievement of children could be evident.

(xix) Since teachers are expected to play a significant role, particularly in ECE centres, they should be appointed with due consideration of their genuine interest and attitude for working with young children with love and commitment.

REFERENCES

Bakshi, A., *Performance of Primary School Children with and without ICDS Exposure*, Department of Human Development and Family Studies, Baroda, M.S. University, 1986.

Buch, M.B. (ed.), *Fourth Survey of Research in Education*, Vol. II, NCERT, New Delhi, 1991.

Government of India, *National Policy on Education*, MHRD, Department of Education, New Delhi, 1986.

Government of India, *National Policy on Education*, MHRD, Department of Education, New Delhi, 1992.

Government of India, *Programme of Action*, MHRD, Department of Education, New Delhi, 1992.

Government of Orissa, *A Report—20 Years of ICDS in Orissa*, Department of Women and Child Development, 1995.

Kaul, V. and Bhatnagar, R., *Early Childhood Education*, NCERT, Department of Pre-School and Elementary Education, Sri Aurobindo Marg, New Delhi, 1992.

Kaul, V., *Early Childhood Education Programme*, NCERT, New Delhi, 1991.

Mohanty, J. and Mohanty, B., *Early Childhood Care and Education*, Deep and Deep Publications, New Delhi, 1994.

Mohanty, J. and Mohanty, B., *Pre-School Education* (*Early Childhood Education*), Cuttack Publishing House, Cuttack, 1984.

Mohanty, J., *Education for All*, Deep and Deep Publications, New Delhi, 1994.

Mohanty, J., *Indian Education in the Emerging Society*, Sterling Publishers, New Delhi, 1981.

Mohanty J., Mohanty, C., Tripathy, S., *Research Abstracts*, Dr. PM IASE, Sambalpur, 1994.

Paul, J. and Srinivas, R., *The Future School Strategies in the Classroom*, Educational Planning Group, 4, Rajnivas Marg, New Delhi, 1995.

Verma, A., and Mohite, B., "Research in Early Childhood Education—A Trend Report" (pp. 1217-48), *4th Survey of Research Education*, Vol. II, NCERT, New Delhi, 1991.

5

An Investigation into the Problems and Prospects of School Community Cooperation for Democratisation and Improvement of Education

JAGANNATH MOHANTY

1. NEED FOR THE STUDY

In a democratic set-up, close cooperation between the school and the community is not only essential but also imperative. But unfortunately such cooperation seems to be absent and a gap is being maintained between the two. The school works in isolation without concern for the community which in turn does not care to look after the needs of the school. The school is said to be working in an "Ivory Tower" and the community in a house with the doors closed. But for democratisation of education there must be two-way traffic between them and the gap as existing must be bridged through inter-communication and interaction.

The community, even at the stage of its under development, possesses abundant resources like farms and forts, old and new buildings, temples and monuments, places of social, economic, historical, cultural, technological, artistic and aesthetic importance.

Besides, there are fairs and festivals, rich heritage and customs as well as abundant human resources like artists and artisans, craftsman and clergymen, doctors, teachers and so on.

On the other hand, schools have buildings, equipment, furniture, libraries and laboratories, etc. They are not merely meant for children. The whole community must benefit from these resources. The Community Schools in the Philippines, the Folk Schools of Denmark, the Tushegee Institute for Negroes and the Gary Schools in the USA, are the notable instances of the school-community interaction. Thus the resources of the school must be thrown open for public use after the regular school hours are over and community resources should be utilised for school purposes.

The Education Commission, 1964-66 have aptly observed that since it is very costly to provide and maintain the physical plant of educational institutions, it becomes necessary to utilise it as fully as possible, for the longest time on each day and for all the days in the year by making suitable administrative arrangements. The libraries, laboratories, workshops, craft-sheds, etc., should be utilised for community service, adult education and so on.

But it is found that such cooperation and mutual sharing between the school and community are not encouraged under various pretexts. Hence a study is felt desirable to find out the real facts in the field.

2. OBJECTIVES

The following are the objectives of the study:

(i) to find out the extent of utilization of the school plant by the society;

(ii) to ascertain the advantages and disadvantages in such utilization;

(iii) to find out the extent of the use of community resources for the school;

(iv) to make a stocktaking of both pros and cons in using community facilities for the school; and

(v) to make suggestions for the betterment of school community cooperation.

3. SCOPE

All categories of institutions at the Primary stage were brought under the scope of the study. The utilization of both the physical and human resources belonging to schools for the community and *vice-versa* was taken under its purview. Both advantages and disadvantages in such utilization were studied for the purposes.

4. METHODOLOGY

Although data were collected mainly by means of two sets of identical questionnaire, one for the inspecting officers and another for Primary School teachers, observation techniques was adopted to study the problem directly and interview was conducted with some selected educationists and senior inspecting officers for eliciting their views on the problem. Besides, the experiences of the researcher in the United Kingdom in this context provided adequate data and insight.

5. SAMPLE

The questionnaire was administered on 580 supervisors out of whom 419 responded. The overall percentage of responses to the sample was 71.1. Another questionnaire was administered on 3,716 head-teachers out of whom 1170 responded and the overall percentage of responses to the total sample was 37.2.

6. ANALYSIS AND INTERPRETATION OF DATA

6.1 Utilization of School Resources for the Community

In order to know whether the physical facilities of the school were utilized by the society, a relevant question was asked to both the groups of the respondents. 40.8 per cent of the supervisors and 48.6 per cent of the head-teachers admitted that physical resources of the school were utilized by the community, whereas 33.6 per cent of the supervisors and 28.0 per cent of the head-teachers replied negatively. Further 25.6 per cent of the Supervisors and 23.4 per cent of the head-teachers remained silent. This shows that the physical facilities of the school were not always utilised by the community.

With a view to ascertaining the kinds of advantages that were gained due to utilization of the school plant for the community, an open-ended question was asked. The responses of the supervisors and the head-teachers may be classified into four main categories and their frequency distribution may be seen from the Table 5.1.

TABLE 5.1

Distribution of Advantages of Utilization of School Resources by the Community

Sl. No.	*Advantages*	*Supervisors*		*Head-teachers*	
		N = 293	*Per cent*	*N = 598*	*Per cent*
1.	Better school-community relations can be established	135	32.9	583	49.8
2.	School resources can be utilised to the maximum	85	20.7	153	13.0
3.	Needs of the Schools can be fulfilled by the community	123	30.0	254	21.7
4.	Reciprocal involvement in each other's life activities	50	12.2	–	–

It is evident from Table 5.1 that the head-teachers (49.8 per cent) are more conscious of the better school community relations consequent on the utilization of the school resources than the supervisors (32.9 per cent). On the other hand, supervisors (30.0 per cent) are more aware of the advantage of this in community cooperation for improving the physical resources of the school than the head-teachers (21.7 per cent). But neither of the two groups of respondents found to be adequately conscious of the maximum utilization of the school resources by the community will promote reciprocal involvement and interest in each other's activity. But this point has been marked only by 12.2 per cent of the supervisors and by nobody from among the head-teachers. Besides, silence on the part of the 29.2 per cent supervisors and 34.0 per cent head-teachers indicate their indifference or their lack of interest in the programme. However, 88 per cent of the interviewees observed that school community relations could be improved due to use of the school resources by the community.

It is also complained that a large number of difficulties is experienced by teachers in such utilization of the school resources by the community. In response to the question "What are the disadvantages in the utilization of the school resources for the community purpose?," the supervisors as well as the head-teachers gave a number of difficulties which have been categorised as follows with the frequencies mentioned against each.

TABLE 5.2

Disadvantages in the Utilization of School Resources for the Community

Sl. No.	*Advantages*	*Supervisors*		*Head-teachers*	
		N = 318	*Per cent*	*N = 658*	*Per cent*
1.	Mishandling of the school resources like furniture, library, etc.	138	33.6	283	24.1
2.	Undue interference and trespassing by the villagers in school matters	91	22.2	–	–
3.	Petty village politics and bickerings adversely affecting school organisation and administration	89	21.8	375	32.0

It transpires from the above table that comparatively a large percentage of the respondents of both the groups (supervisors) 33.6 per cent and head-teachers (24.1 per cent) were concerned with mishandling of the school resources like furniture, equipment, libraries, etc. Further 22.2 per cent supervisors pointed out that undue interference and trespassing by the villagers in the school matters was another disadvantage; whereas all the head-teachers were silent on this point. Closely related to this was another difficulty felt by 21.8 per cent of the Supervisors and 32.0 per cent of the head-teachers. That as the petty village politics and bickerings adversely affecting school organisation and administration. As high as 43.9 per cent of the head-teachers and 22.4 per cent of the Supervisors gave no responses.

It may be concluded that the advantages undoubtedly outnumber the disadvantages in the utilization of the physical resources of the school by the community. While the use of the physical plant of the school would contribute to better school community relations, maximization of the resources, improvement of public support, greater involvement, etc. It is also apprehended that mishandling of the school resources, undue interference of the villagers in the school affairs and petty village politics and quarrels might adversely affect the school organisation. But a large number/majority of senior supervisors and educationists advised for the extensive use of school resources by the community.

6.2 Utilization of Community Resources for the School

With a view to knowing whether the primary schools used the physical resources like buildings, furniture, playground, etc., belonging to the community for organising various activities, a question was asked. 47.0 per cent of the supervisors and 45.3 per cent of the head-teachers responded affirmatively, whereas respectively 14.4 per cent and 22.7 per cent gave negative responses. Besides, 38.6 per cent of the supervisors and 32.0 per cent of the head-teachers kept silent.

In order to ascertain whether the school gets the benefit of human resources such as the village craftsmen, specialists, unemployed young men and others, a question was asked to both the groups of respondents. It is equally encouraging to note that 42.6 per cent of the supervisors and 49.3 per cent of the head-teachers reported affirmatively and 16.6 per cent and 21.8 per cent negatively.

As regards advantages accruing from such utilization of the community resources by the school, both the groups of respondents pointed out a number of benefits. These responses have been classified mainly into three categories and the respective frequencies are given below.

TABLE 5.3

Advantages in the Utilization of Community Resources by the School

Sl. No.	*Advantages*	*Supervisors*		*Head-teachers*	
		N = 272	*Per cent*	*N = 747*	*Per cent*
1.	Making up Inadequacy of Facilities	90	21.9	495	43.3
2.	Improving School Community Relations	205	50.0	518	44.2
3.	Bringing Awareness in the Community of the School's Needs	85	20.7	468	40.0

It is evident from the above data that more head-teachers (42.3 per cent) than supervisors (21.9 per cent) were conscious of the advantage of making up inadequacy or deficiency of the school facilities through utilising community resources. But according to the highest percentages of the supervisors (50.0 per cent) and of the head-teachers (44.2 per cent) school community relations were improved by this. As many as 40.0 per cent of the head-teachers were concerned with bringing about awareness of the school's needs.

Similarly, responses about the disadvantages in utilizing community resources for the school purposes may be classified into three categories with the frequency given against each.

TABLE 5.4

Disadvantages in Utilization of the Community Resources for the School

Sl. No.	*Disadvantages*	*Supervisors*		*Head-teachers*	
		N = 310	*Per cent*	*N = 905*	*Per cent*
1.	More Public Interference in School Affairs	120	29.3	486	41.5
2.	Discipline to be Adversely Affected	68	16.5	378	32.2
3.	Academic Activities Likely to be Hampered	132	32.3	61	3.7

It may be seen that as high as 41.5 per cent of the head-teachers were conscious of more public interference in school affairs, whereas only 29.3 per cent of the supervisors were of the same opinion. 16.5 per cent of the supervisors and 32.2 per cent of the head-teachers apprehended that discipline would be adversely affected on account of the school's utilization of the community resources. It is surprising to see that when 32.3 per cent of the supervisors were concerned about academic activities likely to be hampered, only 3.7 per cent of the head-teachers expressed their apprehensions about this. It is also interesting to note that 75 per cent of interviewees were of the opinion that local resources, both human and physical should be utilised for organising various school programmes, which would promote social awakening and better relations.

It may be concluded that in the case of utilization of community resources by the school also there are advantages like making up deficiency of facilities, improving school community relations, bringing about awareness in the community above the school needs. There are also apprehensions that there would be more public interference in school affairs, that the discipline would be adversely affected and that academic activities are likely to be hampered on account of this.

It is, however, felt that with experience and training in citizenship not only these difficulties would be reduced to the minimum, but also the school would be made self-dependent and community centres. Only in those cases where the school could properly maintain its discipline and status, it would utilise the resources of the community both, human and material and the school resources would also be allowed to be used by the community. This would facilitate better school community relations and improve the school programmes and practices.

The Third Educational Survey (1979, pp. 144-45) has recorded some relevant data which reveal that the total number of Primary Schools where the school participates in community activities is 3,946 constituting 12.4 per cent and the total number of Primary Schools where the community participates in school activities is 8,364 constituting 26.2 per cent of all the Primary Schools in Orissa. Although it transpires from the above data that the community participation in the school activities is greater than the school participation in the community activities, the position in fact as evident through on-the-spot study, is not encouraging and is left with much to be desired. It may be emphasized that for democratization and improvement of education, such cooperation and collaboration should be promoted between the school and the community.

It is also found by the researcher himself and mentioned in the pamphlet of the British Information Service (1974, p. 46) that as per the recommendation of the Plowden Report on "Children and their Primary Schools," community schools were set-up as "open beyond the ordinary school hours for the use of children, their parents, and exceptionally for other members of the community," community schools have been established mostly in educational priority areas where they would try to improve the educational experience of disadvantaged children and adults. As a result of Education Priority Area Project, several schools have developed a community approach. These community schools not only have given ample scope for mutual cooperation and involvement of the schools and community, but also have improved their relations and quality of education in general.

7. MAJOR FINDINGS

7.1 48.6 per cent of head-teachers and 40.8 per cent of supervisors were of the opinion that school resources were being utilised by the community.

7.2 More head-teachers than supervisors were conscious of better school community relations and aware of the fact needs of the schools as fulfilled through the utilization of school resources for the community.

7.3 Although more supervisors than head-teachers were of the opinion that school resources could be utilized to the maximum they were mishandling of the school resources in utilization by the community.

7.4 Although Supervisors were particularly scared by the undue interference of the villagers in school matters, more head-teachers than supervisors were afraid of petty village politics adversely affecting school organisations.

7.5 47 per cent of the supervisors and 45.3 per cent of the head-teachers were of the opinion that physical resources of the community were being utilised by the school.

7.6 According to 42.6 per cent of the supervisors and 49.3 per cent of head-teachers human resources of the community were being utilised by the school.

7.7 50 per cent of supervisors and 44.2 per cent of head-teachers have opined that school-community relations would be improved due to the utilization of community resources in schools.

7.8 More head-teachers (42.3 per cent) than supervisors (21 per cent) were conscious of making up the deficiency in school facility through utilising community resources but were concerned about the public interference in day-to-day affairs in and academic activities of schools.

8. SUGGESTIONS

8.1 With a view to promoting better school-community relations school resources could be intensively used by the community.

8.2 In order to make an efficient as well as economic utilization of resources in the developing society, the physical facilities of the schools should be allowed to be used by the people to the maximum.

8.3 Mishandling or misuse of resources, undue interference or local politics, infringement of school discipline, etc., can be minimised by giving civic training and generating adequate civic awareness among the people.

8.4 Community resources, both material and human should be utilised by the school for making up the deficiency as well as for enriching the learning experiences;

8.5 Primary schools should be developed into community centres for making education more democratic and relevant to the life, needs and aspirations of the people.

REFERENCES

A.K.C., Ottaway, *Education and Society*, Routledge and Kegan Paul, London, 1952.

British Information Service, *Education in Britain*, London, 1974.

Burgess, Tyrrel, *A Guide to English Schools*, Penguin Books, 1970.

Central Advisory Council for Education: The Plowden Report, *Children and Their Primary Schools*, HMSO, 1962.

Directorate of Public Instruction, Orissa, Bhubaneswar, *Report of the Third Educational Survey*, Orissa, 1978.

PART II

RURAL, TRIBAL AND MINORITIES DEVELOPMENT IN EDUCATION

6

An Evaluative Study of Navodaya Vidyalayas in Haryana

KAILASH CH. BEHERA

1. INTRODUCTION

In a democratic country citizens have the right not only to maintain themselves by way of their physical up keep, but also of their proper education and training so that they are not only allowed to grow, as much as possible, their best self but also as useful citizens standing on their own legs and not remaining as a parasite on society. Teachers, educationists, administrators, social workers and the general public should be concerned with the education or training of not only the normal but also of the deviants whom we may call exceptions.

In democracy, progress comes through the efforts of all but it follows the plans or ideas of some. While supporting this view Grisworld (1954) has quoted that, "If the spark from the heaven falls, who will pick it up? The crowd? Never. The individual? Always. It is he and she (Gifted or Talented) as an artist, inventor, educationist, explorer, scholar, scientist, spiritual leader or statesman, who stands nearest to the source of life and transmits its essence to his fellow men."

According to Witty (1955) Fliegler and Bish (1959), Kirk (1962) and Renzulli (1975) gifted or talented are those children whose performance in a worthwhile human endeavour is consistently remarkable and those who are academically superior and possesses a high intellectual ability and creativity. Since the word gifted or talented is used for both the creative and intelligent so it is not surprising that sometimes people think that intelligence and creativity are similar and synonymous. But indeed they are not same as convergent thinking is the basis of intelligence and divergent thinking forms the basis of creativity. In convergent thinking only one correct response is required, whereas divergent thinking allows as many responses as possible.

Intelligence and creativity of masses affect scientific progress and the commercial life of nations. Many of our present means of transport, communication and production can be traced back to intelligent and creative thinking.

It is expected that nations which become conscious of identifying, developing and encouraging intelligent and creative potential in their people may find themselves in a very advantageous position. Thus a more complete knowledge of man can stem a balanced world. But it may not be possible for the nations to depend upon sheer quantity of manpower as the complex society of tomorrow would need high quality personnel, specifically intelligent and creative persons to deal with the vital problems. Conant (1959) supports this view and says that, "ten second-rate men are not substitute for one first-rate man." His comment is justified as all great inventions and discoveries, are fruits of intelligent and creative thinking, made by intelligent and creative persons.

Furthermore, the need to understand intelligence and creativity in greater details seems to be substantiated in the form of the importance emphasized by various authors in one form or the others. Bruner (1962) argues that man's intelligent and creative faculties restore his dignity in this computer-dominated age. Toynbee (1962) stated that, "To give a fair chance to potential creativity is a matter of life and death for any society."

Taylor (1964) has accepted intelligence as any human quality in changing history and in reshaping the world.

Intelligence and creativity have their implications for education as well. The goal of education in terms of increased capabilities, personal expression, greater inventiveness and blossoming of gifted leaders cannot be fully realized in the absence of adequate and accurate knowledge or intelligence and creativity.

Terman (1954) defines, "Intelligence as the capacity to carry on abstract thinking." Wechsler (1949) defines "Intelligence as the aggregate or global capacity of the individual to act purposefully, think rationally and deal effectively with his environment."

Stoddard (1943) defines that "Mental ability or intelligence is the ability to undertake activities that are characterised by difficulty, complexity, abstraction, economy, adaptiveness to a goal, social value and the emergence of originals and to maintain such activities under conditions that demand a concentration of energy and a resistance to emotional forces."

At the same time creativity which results in evolution of new methods, new concepts, new understanding and new inventions has also been defined by various persons. According to Drevdahl (1956), "Creativity can be defined as the capacity of a person to produce compositions, products or ideas of any sort which are essentially new, novel and previously unknown to the producer." Torrance (1969) thinks of "creative thinking as the process of sensing gaps or distributing mission elements, forming ideas or hypotheses concerning them and testing the hypotheses."

History of gifted education very clearly depicts that in ancient Greece over 2000 years ago, education for the gifted and talented was started, when Plato advocated that children with superior intellect be selected at an early age and offered a specialized form of instruction. In sixteenth century, Suleman, the magnificent king of Turkey, made special efforts to identify the gifted Christian youth throughout the Turkish empire and provided with education in Muslim faith and in war, art, science and philosophy. During the 19th and 20th centuries a few organized efforts were made in Europe to select gifted children to offer them special education. But in the year 1950, for the first time identification of the gifted was started in the USA with the help of psychological tests and also special instructions were offered to them.

The cultivation of intelligent and creative potentiality, in spite of its crucial importance, so far, however, been neglected (Flescher, 1963).

In India, until 1986 there were no such special provisions for intellectually superior and creative children. Although there are central and public schools throughout the country, yet their sole aim is not to nurture the highly intelligent and creative children. The main drawback of these schools is that they only cater to the needs of a few people and these schools are mainly situated in urban areas. Hence, the rural masses, which constitute a large number of the population, are deprived of such type of facilities provided by the government of India.

But in order to identify the gifted/talented, i.e. diamond from the coal, largely from rural areas and to nurture them for the all round development of the country, our government adopted National Policy on Education (NPE) 1986, popularly known as the New Education Policy 1986, which was declared by the then Prime Minister Mr. Rajiv Gandhi in his first broadcast to the nation on January 5, 1985. There were various important features in NPE. The Navodaya Vidyalaya Scheme is one of them and the present work is an attempt to evaluate the effectiveness of this scheme.

2. SCHEME OF NAVODAYA VIDYALAYA

In pursuance of the National Policy on Education (1986) the Government of India has launched a scheme called "Navodaya Vidyalaya Scheme." With the aim to provide good quality modern education including strong component of culture, inculcation of values, awareness of the environment, adventure activities and physical education to the talented children, predominantly from the rural areas without regard to their family's socio-economic condition. In the policy, it was decided to set-up such residential and co-educational schools, on an average of one in each district during the Seventh Five Year Plan. The main purpose of these Vidyalayas is to nurture talented students coming largely from rural areas (75 per cent from rural areas and 25 per cent from urban areas). The scheme also envisages that at least one-third of the students in each Navodaya Vidyalaya should be girls.

The Programme of Action (POA, 1986) further emphasised for establishing a Navodaya Vidyalaya in each district before the end of the Seventh Five Year Plan, but this objective could not be achieved for want of sufficient resources. Moreover, the three state governments of Assam, Tamil Nadu and West Bengal did not accept the schemes. But soon after the installation of Congress Party in Assam, the government has accepted the scheme subsequently. Nevertheless, the Navodaya Vidyalaya Scheme has achieved a significant degree of success and popularity, which is reflected in the demand for more Navodaya Vidyalayas.

The programme of Action envisaged that the Navodaya Vidyalayas would make available good quality education irrespective of the parents' capacity to pay and their socio-economic background. The Navodaya Vidyalaya scheme has achieved a certain level of measure of success in regard to this objective. According to a survey made in 1989, 40.7 per cent of students belonged to families below the poverty line, 16 per cent of the students were first generation learners. Students are selected on the basis of an all India level test of objective type questions. Further, it is intended to be a culture-free and designed to judge potential rather than academic achievement. The academic results of the scheme have generally been better than those of other group of schools affiliated to CBSE, including private schools.

The Navodaya Vidyalayas are largely intended to cater to rural talented children (for whom 75 per cent seats are reserved) with reservation for SCs and STs and girls. This social objective has been achieved to a great extent. An important feature of the scheme is the migration of a proportion of the students from one region to another (generally from Hindi speaking regions to non-Hindi speaking regions) and *vice-versa* for promoting national integration by providing opportunities to talented children from different parts of the country to live and learn together.

3. OBJECTIVES OF NAVODAYA VIDYALAYAS

(a) Major Objectives

(i) To promote national integration through a specific programme of education.

(ii) To nurture talent particularly in the rural areas/especially among the weaker section of the society.

(iii) To make equality education accessible to the talented children without constraints.

(iv) To establish institutions of high quality at district level to serve as pace-setters and models to stimulate pursuit of excellence in the surrounding institutions.

(v) To emphasize all round development and inculcation of moral values through education by establishing institutions that strive in an effective manner, for these components in child development.

(b) Specific Objectives

(i) To provide good quality modern education including a strong component of culture, inculcation of values, awareness of the environment, adventure activities and physical education to the talented children predominantly from rural areas, without regard to their family's socio-economic condition.

(ii) To ensure that all students of Navodaya Vidyalayas attain a reasonable level of competence in three languages as envisaged in the three language formula.

(iii) To serve, in each district, as focal point for improvement in the quality of school education in general through sharing of experiences and facilities.

Navodaya Vidyalayas are residential and co-educational institutions, primarily for children from rural areas. Hence, admission of children from urban areas is restricted to a maximum of one-fourth. Efforts are made to ensure that at least one-third of the students in each Navodaya Vidyalaya are girls.

Education in Navodaya Vidyalayas including boarding and lodging as well as expenses on uniform, textbooks, stationery, rail/bus fare from and to the home is free for all students. The Navodaya Vidyalayas are affiliated to the Central Board of Secondary Education (CBSE).

The role of Navodaya Vidyalayas as pace-setting institutions *vis-a-vis* other schools is attempted to be realised through their participation in the training of staff, in jointly organised activities, in the extension of new methods of teaching and in dissemination of information and in evaluation. They establish rapport with schools in their vicinity and provide guidance to primary schools for improvement of standards, sharing of facilities such as audio-visual equipments, micro-computers, etc.

Navodaya Vidyalayas aim to provide adequate modern infrastructural facilities in terms of school building, laboratories, hostels, boarding houses and staff quarters for these Vidyalayas. In addition to appropriate accommodation facilities, sufficient facilities for development of games and sports are also provided. The Navodaya Vidyalaya building complex on completion, aim to provide appearance of a modern school and also provide adequate scope for children to develop various facets of their personality. Till such time the permanent buildings are completed, existing school buildings, project buildings which are not in use and other similar government and voluntary organisations premises with adequate land and water supply are utilised for starting new Vidyalayas.

Navodaya Vidyalayas are run by the 'Navodaya Vidyalaya Samiti', an autonomous organisation under the Ministry of Human Resource Development, Dept. of Education, Government of India. The objective has been to cover all districts in states accepting the scheme before the completion of the Eighth Plan period and preferably within three years. This meant opening about 50 Navodaya Vidyalayas every year.

4. JUSTIFICATION OF THE STUDY

Before this scheme of Navodaya Vidyalayas, there had been no special provisions for intellectually superior and creative rural children in India. Although there were central and public schools throughout the country which were basically catering to the needs of urban students and rural students were not at all taken care of. For nurturing the creative ability of rural students, Navodaya Vidyalayas have been established. And there is always a felt need to evaluate and review from time to time, such educational schemes or provisions especially those which are in their infancy as a huge amount of money is being spent on this ambitious scheme.

In order to find out whether these institutions have been achieving their objectives, and also from the point of view of further improvement in the functioning/working of these institutions, the task in hand is justified.

Further, there has always been a controversy amongst educationists with regard to existence of these Vidyalayas and the very basis of this controversy are also due to uncertainty and doubts about the workability and performance of these Vidyalayas. Therefore, this study is also justified on this ground.

Lastly, while reviewing the related literature, the investigator had not come across any such study on Navodaya Vidyalayas as there has been hardly conducted any evaluative study for these Vidyalayas. Hence the present study is the need of the day.

5. STATEMENT OF THE PROBLEM

"AN EVALUATIVE STUDY OF NAVODAYA VIDYALAYAS IN HARYANA."

6. OPERATIONAL DEFINITIONS OF KEY WORDS

Navodaya Vidyalaya

In the present study, the Navodaya Vidyalaya implies those vidyalayas which have been set-up by Government of India to nurture talented students coming largely from rural areas. These vidyalayas are residential and co-educational institutions. In the policy, it was decided to set-up residential and co-educational schools, on an average of one in each districts during the Seventh Five Year Plan. The main aim of these Vidyalayas is to nurture talented students coming largely from rural areas (75 per cent from rural areas and 25 per cent from urban areas). Efforts are made to ensure that at least one-third of the students in each Vidyalayas are girls.

Evaluation

Evaluate means to work out the 'value' of (a quantitative expression); to find a numerical expression for (any quantitative fact or relation). To "reckon up," ascertain the amount of; to express in terms of something already known.

Evaluation is the systematic assessment of the worth or merit of some object. Cronbach (1963) describes evaluation as the "collection and use of information to make decisions about an educational programme." C.E. Beeby (1977) who described evaluation as "the systematic collection and interpretation of evidence, leading, as part of the process, to a judgement of value with a view to action." In the present study evaluation implies up to what extent the envisaged objectives of the Navodaya Vidyalaya Scheme have been achieved by the Navodaya Vidyalayas.

7. OBJECTIVES OF THE STUDY

The present study was conducted with the following objectives:

1. To find out actual admission pattern of students in the Navodaya Vidyalayas in terms of residence, sex and other reservations.
2. To study the infrastructural facilities existing in Navodaya Vidyalayas.
3. To study the migration pattern of students from Hindi-speaking areas to Non-Hindi-speaking areas and *vice-versa.*
4. To study the aspect of staff sanctioned and in position.
5. To study the opinion of neighbouring school teachers as well as community members towards Navodaya Vidyalayas.
6. To study the family background of Navodaya Vidyalaya students and views of their parents regarding the Navodaya Vidyalaya Scheme.
7. To study the placement of pass out students in professional institutions.
8. To study the problems and difficulties faced by Navodaya Vidyalayas in achieving the envisaged objectives and to suggest measures for their improvement.

8. DELIMITATION OF THE STUDY

The present study was delimited to four Navodaya Vidyalayas (JNV Titram of District Kaithal, JNV Kaloi of District Jhajjar, JNV Khunga Kothi of District Jind and JNV Butana of District Sonepat) of the Haryana State.

9. RESEARCH METHOD

Keeping in view the nature, main purpose of the study and its objectives, survey method was considered to be most appropriate for undertaking this investigation.

9.1 Sample

The present study was carried out to evaluate the Navodaya Vidyalaya Scheme in Haryana. Therefore, all the Navodaya Vidyalayas of Haryana State constituted the population of the present study. For drawing the sample of the present study, at the first stage, four Navodaya Vidyalayas were selected by employing simple random sampling technique (by Lottery Method).

The Navodaya Vidyalayas thus selected were Jawahar Navodaya Vidyalaya, Kaloi (District Jhajjar), Jawahar Navodaya Vidyalaya, Titram (District Kaithal), Jawahar Navodaya Vidyalaya, Khunga Kothi (District Jind) and Jawahar Navodaya Vidyalaya, Butana (District Sonepat). At the second stage all four principals and 40 teachers of these Navodaya Vidyalayas (10 teachers from each Navodaya Vidyalaya) were selected on purposive basis. At the third stage all those students of Class X of the Vidyalayas were selected (on purposive basis) who had been migrated from these four Navodaya Vidyalayas to Navodaya Vidyalayas of non-Hindi-speaking regions (Andhra Pradesh and Maharashtra) during their IX class. At the fourth stage, 20 community members and 20 teachers of neighbouring schools of Navodaya Vidyalayas (5 community members and 5 teachers from surrounding of each Navodaya Vidyalaya were selected on purposive basis). At the fifth stage, 80 parents of the students of X class of Navodaya Vidyalayas (20 parents of each Navodaya Vidyalayas' X class students) were selected on purposive basis.

9.2 Procedure

The plan of the study has been described in the preceding part of this chapter. It is followed by the actual procedure adopted in conducting the study. The same is given in the following pages.

9.3 Tools Used

In order to collect data, the researcher used self-developed information and interview schedules. These schedules are given in the appendices. Keeping in view the nature of the study, the investigator consider these tools as most appropriate for collection of data. The following tools were developed and used by the investigator for the collection of data.

1. Schedule I : Information Schedule Regarding Infrastructural Facilities.

2. Schedule II : Information Schedule for Teachers.
3. Schedule III : Information Schedule for Parents.
4. Schedule IV : Interview Schedule for Community Members and the Neighbouring School Teachers.
5. Schedule V : Information Schedule for Principals.
6. Schedule VI : Information Schedule Regarding Staff Sanctioned and in Position.
7. Schedule VII : Information Schedule for Students' Enrolment.
8. Schedule VIII : Information Schedule for the Students Migrated to other Navodaya Vidyalayas.

9.4 Collection of Data

After the development of the tools it was the responsibility of the researcher to administer the tools in an organised manner. The researcher collected data in three phases. In the first phase, data was collected from the Vidyalaya itself. The principal, the teachers, non-teaching staff and the students studying in Navodaya Vidyalayas were contacted for collection of the data. First of all, respondents were explained about the research work. Then they were requested to provide the required information on the schedules used for the collection of data. The first phase took two to three days for data collection of each Vidyalayas.

In the second phase, the data was collected from the community and the teachers of the neighbouring schools of Navodaya Vidyalayas. In this phase the researcher visited the village community and neighbouring schools to collect information from them. They were asked to give their free and frank views about the Jawahar Navodaya Vidyalaya Scheme. The second phase took two days for data collection of each Vidyalaya.

In the third phase, the data was collected from parents of children studying in Jawahar Navodaya Vidyalayas through mail service by sending a self-addressed stamped envelope so as to enable the parents to return back the schedule at the earliest. For this purpose, students were also asked to intimate their parents for filling up the required information in the schedule and earliest return of the same. The information schedule was sent to 160 parents of class X students (40 parents of each Navodaya Vidyalaya's students).

9.5 Statistical Techniques Used

The responses of the respondents collected through interview schedules/information schedules in "Yes" or "No" and "Agree," "Disagree" and "Undecided" were counted for their frequencies and percentages were calculated for the same. There were also some open ended items requiring descriptions were scored accordingly.

10. MAIN FINDINGS

For the sake of convenience and clarity, the findings of the present study have been presented under seven sections. Section I deals with the findings regarding the admission pattern of the Navodaya Vidyalayas. Section II covers the findings related to the infra-structural facilities in Navodaya Vidyalayas. In Section III, the findings regarding the migration policy of Navodaya Vidyalayas have been presented. Under Section IV, findings related to the staff sanctioned and in position have been given. Section V covers the findings based on the opinion of the neighbouring school teachers and community members. Section VI deals with the findings pertaining to the family background of students and opinion of these parents about Navodaya Vidyalayas. In Section VII, the findings related to Placement of Passouts in Professional Institutions have been provided. Section VIII covers the findings based on the suggestions of the principals, teachers, community members, parents and migrated students for improving the functioning of the Navodaya Vidyalayas.

SECTION I

10.1 Findings Regarding the Admission Pattern of the Navodaya Vidyalayas

1. The admission pattern followed by all the four sample Navodaya Vidyalayas reveals that the admission was done as per the norms of the Navodaya Vidyalaya Samiti (NVS). It further reveals that the representation of the students from the rural and urban background, different category (SC/ST/General) and sex (boys/girls) were as per the norms.
2. It is clear from the results that the specified number of seats (80) in VI class of Navodaya Vidyalayas was not totally

filled and the seats remained vacant in almost all the four Vidyalayas during all the sessions.

3. It is clear from the results that there was a high rate of drop-out in Navodaya Vidyalayas.

SECTION II

10.2 Infrastructural Facilities in Navodaya Vidyalayas

1. All the four Jawahar Navodaya Vidyalayas were located in interior areas and their distance ranged from 10 to 48 Kilometres from their respective District Headquarters.
2. The land areas of these Vidyalayas' premises varied from 21 acres to 50 acres.
3. There were inadequate number of office buildings, hostels and staff quarters (teaching/non-teaching) in all the four Navodaya Vidyalayas (though the buildings were under construction).
4. There was inadequate number of urinals for the staff as well as students.
5. In the Vidyalayas water supply was done either through tube-well or from the well with pump sets.
6. There were proper arrangements for sewerage disposal.
7. All the Jawahar Navodaya Vidyalayas were provided with a vehicle and a dispensary.
8. Two Vidyalayas were having post-office on their campus itself and the remaining two (JNV Kaloi and JNV Titram) were having a post office located at the distance of 10 kms. and 5 kms. respectively.

SECTION III

10.3 Migration Policy for the Students of Navodaya Vidyalayas (from the Hindi Speaking Areas to Non-Hindi Speaking Areas and *vice-versa*)

1. As per the norms of Navodaya Vidyalayas Samiti 30 per cent students at the level of IX standard, were migrated from the four sample Navodaya Vidyalayas of Haryana to the Navodaya Vidyalayas of Non-Hindi speaking areas. From

Haryana, the students of Jawahar Navodaya Vidyalaya Khunga Kothi (District Jind) and Titram (District Kaithal) were migrated to Jawahar Navodaya Vidyalaya Sarubujjili (District Shrikakulam) of Andhra Pradesh and those of Butana and Kaloi to Navodaya Vidyalaya, Selukate (District Wardha) and Navodaya Vidyalaya Navsari (District Amaravati) of Maharashtra respectively.

2. The students migrated to the Vidyalayas of Non-Hindi-speaking regions did not face any difficulty to adjust with their peer groups and teachers in those Vidyalayas where they were migrated.

SECTION IV

10.4 Staff Sanctioned and in Position

1. There was inadequate academic and administrative strength of staff in all the four sample Vidyalayas.
2. Most of the teachers (63 per cent), including PGTs and TGTs had attended in service training programmes.
3. For effective teaching, majority of the teachers adopted programmed learning approach.

SECTION V

10.5 Opinion of Neighbouring School Teachers and Community Members

1. Both the community members and neighbouring school teachers opined that Navodaya Vidyalayas were of great help to the pupils belonging to weaker sections/backward community and pupils of rural areas.
2. Some of the community members and teachers of neighbouring schools indicated that these Vidyalayas created two classes of citizens.
3. 85 per cent of the neighbouring school teachers and community members viewed these Vidyalayas as institutions of wasteful expenditure.
4. 60-70 per cent community members and neighbouring school teachers reported that these Vidyalayas should be

started/opened in non-represented districts of the country and they regarded these Vidyalayas useful in achieving national integration and communal harmony.

5. The community members and teachers of neighbouring schools suggested full utilisation of community resources. They also indicated that there must be full time lady wardens for girl students, they should be invited in all the functions of JNVs and sometimes also for observing classes.

SECTION VI

10.6 The Placement of Students in Professional/Vocational Courses

1. The study reveals a disheartening picture about the placement of students in professional/vocational courses as a very limited number of students qualified in the entrance tests (PMT, CEET, NDA, JBT, etc.) for admission in the professional courses.

SECTION VII

10.7 Family Background of Students and Opinion of Parents Towards Navodaya Vidyalayas

1. The study revealed that among the parents of Navodaya Vidyalayas' students, 19 per cent were labourers, 32 per cent were farmers, 18 per cent were businessmen and 31 per cent were government servants.
2. The study indicated that the annual income of the parents of 28 per cent students was below Rs. 20,000, those of 20 per cent ranged from Rs. 21,000 to 40,000. Annual income of the parents of 18 per cent students ranged from Rs. 61,000-80,000 and those of 12 per cent it was Rs. 81,000 and above.
3. The study revealed that parents of 21 per cent students were landless, those of 26 per cent were having landed property of 1-5 acres. Land holding ranged from 6-10 acres, and above 10 acres in case of parents of 23 per cent and 30 per cent students respectively.

4. With regard to the educational background of the parents of students, the study revealed that 16 per cent were illiterate, 19 per cent were matriculate, 30 per cent were intermediate, 20 per cent were graduate and 15 per cent of the parents were post-graduate.
5. Majority of the parents (42 per cent) were having Radio as the recreational media.
6. Parents of about 50 per cent students were using drinking water from the public sources.
7. About 38 per cent of the parents had no electricity connection.
8. Most of the parents were taking interest in the studies of their wards and discussed their problems with the Vidyalayas' authorities/teachers.
9. Majority of parents were satisfied with the arrangements related to hostel accommodation, boarding, sports and recreational facilities, type of education imparted, organisation of extra-curricular activities and examination system.

SECTION VIII

10.8 Suggestions for Improving the Functioning of the Navodaya Vidyalayas

(a) *Suggestions given by the community members and teachers of the neighbouring schools to improve the Navodaya Vidyalaya Scheme are given as under:*

(i) Intelligent, creative and experienced teachers should be selected and appointed on the basis of written and personality test.

(ii) Non-detention policy up to class IX level should be abolished and replaced with public examination at middle school level.

(iii) These Vidyalayas should also start vocational and professional courses. Community members and teachers of neighbouring schools be invited in all the functions of JNVs.

(iv) Appointment of teachers on part time basis should be stopped and permanent teachers should be appointed.

(v) A qualified and experienced doctor should be appointed in these Vidyalayas to take care of the health of students.
(vi) Free coaching centres should be started at Navodaya Vidyalayas to help the poor students in their preparation for seeking admission in Navodaya Vidyalayas.
(vii) The authorities of Navodaya Vidyalayas should regularly monitor the activities of these Vidyalayas.
(viii) The quality of food and accommodation facilities in the hostels should be improved and there must be full time lady wardens for girl students. Community resources should be fully utilised by JNVs.
(ix) The condition of electricity and water supply should be improved.
(x) Transportation facilities should be improved to connect the Navodaya Vidyalaya with nearest towns.

Some respondents also reported that the standard of these schools was going down day-by-day and therefore, NVs authorities should take a serious note of it.

(b) *Suggestions of Principals for Improvement of the Navodaya Vidyalaya Scheme:*

When the Principals were asked to give their suggestions for improvement for Navodaya Vidyalaya Scheme, it was found that almost all the principals agreed to the following:

(i) The Navodaya Vidyalaya should be restricted to less number of students at the entry level, so that it may not cause management problems.
(ii) Admission to the Navodaya Vidyalaya should given to only those children whose parents income is low and for admission of students in the Navodaya Vidyalaya, the age range should be 11 to 13 years instead of 9 to 13 years.
(iii) Education in Navodaya Vidyalayas should be free of cost to the needy and academically extra-ordinary students only.
(iv) The Vidyalaya could be made partly day schools and partly residential by which accommodation problem can be solved.
(v) There should be migration policy for all the students of IX class instead of 30 per cent of the students of this class.

(vi) Mini migration at the level of XI and XII class (in the absence of non-availability of the particular course in any NVs) may be immediately stopped.

(c) *Suggestions of Teachers for Academic Improvement of Navodaya Vidyalayas*

- Recruitment of teachers (on permanent basis) of better quality and experience.
- Compulsory promotion up to class IX should be discouraged/ withdrawal of non-detention policy.
- Extra coaching should be given to students.
- Stress should be on practice than theory.
- The entrance test pattern should be changed.
- Teacher should be kept free from other duties like purchasing, wardenship, etc.
- There should be conducted weekly oral tests for the students.
- Audio-Visual aids should be available and used for making the teaching effective.
- There should be co-operation among teachers of JNVs.
- There should be also started nursery and primary school classes in Navodaya Vidyalayas for the wards of the staff of NVs.
- Enough attention should be given to the students of lower classes.
- Enough drill and repetition should be given to the average students.
- There should be full time wardens for girl students of NVs.
- Medium of instruction should be English right from the VIth class.
- Provisions and opportunities should be there for the professional growth of teachers.

(d) *Suggestions of Teachers for Administrative Improvement in the Navodaya Vidyalayas*

(i) Staff position:

- Appointment of teachers should be made on regular basis.
- Vacant post of teaching staff must be filled immediately.

- Post of hostel warden must be created and teacher must be kept free from Wardenship. In case of girl students, full time lady wardens should be appointed at the earliest.

(ii) There should be improvement in the boarding and lodging arrangements in the hostels.

- Sufficient and separate hostel facilities should be provided for boys and girls.
- A maximum of ten students should be accommodated in one dormitory.
- Students should be involved in the purchasing for Mess with a view to give them chance of exposure in the day-to-day life.

(iii) Improvement in residential facilities of staff

- Sufficient number of staff quarters should be constructed to accommodate all the staff members (teaching and clerical) of the Vidyalayas.
- Water and electricity problems must be solved.

(iv) For the professional growth of the members of the teaching staff:

- In-service training in computer education should be given to all the staff members.
- Allowance for purchase of recent books and should be given to the teaching staff.
- The In-service training programme arranged twice in a year by Navodaya Vidyalaya Samiti should be supported by innovations and experienced resource persons.

(v) For improving recreational facilities:

- Students should be taken to places of historical importance as a part of the educational tours/trips.
- Proper playground facility and TV, VCR, Radio should be provided and should be in working order.
- Patriotic films should be shown to children.
- Separate TV set must be arranged for both boys and girls.
- Games and cultural activities should be organised regularly.

(vi) For improving public relations:

- Students and teachers of neighbouring schools should be invited on various occasions/functions of Vidyalayas.
- Local people should be invited in functions of Vidyalayas.
- Parents of the children studying in Navodaya should be invited in school to discuss the problems of their children. They should be also invited on different functions.

(vii) For improving the administrative aspects.

- All the vacant posts should be filled immediately.
- Strict disciplinary action should be taken against students for violation of Vidyalayas norms/rules.

(viii) For improving teacher-pupil relationship.

- Teacher should be friendly with students and share their problems.
- Regular parent-teacher meetings should be organised to discuss problems of students.

(ix) For the welfare of staff.

- Provision for pre-school and primary class/school should be made in the JNV campus itself for the education of children of the staff.
- There should be a hospital facility for the JNV campus staff and students.
- There should be staff welfare club to look after staff problems.

(x) For promoting national integration.

- Migration period should be for larger duration.
- Frequent educational trips should be organised to different regions.
- Inter-Region transfer of teachers should be encouraged.

(xi) For promoting communal harmony.

- Festivals of different religious groups should be celebrated in each JNV.
- Students should be taken to surrounding villages for creating awareness related to social problems.

(xii) Any other suggestion.

- The Vidyalaya should be located in such a place so that the basic facilities like Post Office, Bank, Health

Centre/Hospitals and Market Complex should be there for the convenience of the students as well as staff

- JNVs should be converted into day schools.
- Some extra allowances should be given to the teacher as the JNVs are residential and located in remote rural areas.

(e) *Suggestions of the Parents of the Children Studying in Navodaya Vidyalayas*

- Staff (on permanent basis) should be appointed.
- Vacant posts, if any should be filled immediately.
- Construction work (of hostels) should be completed on priority basis.
- There must be full time lady wardens for girl students.
- Provision of negative marking should be made in the entrance test.
- Classrooms should be airy and laboratories should be separate for different practicals and should be maintained properly.
- For admission in the JNVST continuity condition of passing class III to V in the preceding three continuous academic sessions should be abolished for rural students.
- Adequate facilities for games and sports, music and dance should be provided to the students.
- Age and class relaxation should be given to the students of rural background.
- The Vidyalaya surroundings should be kept clean.
- Proper attention should be given for the maintenance of boys and girl hostels.
- Special attention should be given to the new entrants, i.e. VI class students, so as to enable them get accustomed with new environment.

11. EDUCATIONAL IMPLICATIONS

The present study has greater significance as the Navodaya Vidyalaya Scheme is an innovative idea and cater to the needs of the talented children largely from rural areas.

The study has its implications for Navodaya Vidyalaya Samiti, policy-makers, administrators, curriculum framers, and teachers, of Navodaya Vidyalayas as the findings of the present study can help the authorities to implement the Navodaya Vidyalaya Scheme in an effective manner. The study has indicated that all the specified seats (80 seats in each school per year) for VI grade were not totally filled up in NVs and there remained many seats vacant.

This state of affairs raises question mark on the popularity, propaganda and effectiveness of this scheme and the very purpose of nurturing rural talent through Navodaya Vidyalaya Scheme will be in doldrums if this issue of cent per cent non-filling up of seats in Navodaya Vidyalayas is not taken up seriously by Navodaya Vidyalayas Samiti/authorities. Besides, the study has also highlighted many other issues of serious nature such as problem of accommodation, inadequate or dilapidated buildings, no provision for full time wardens especially lady wardens for girls, high rate of dropouts, lack of interest on the part of district administration for Navodaya Vidyalayas, poor performance of Navodaya Vidyalaya students in entrance tests (PMT, CEET and NDA) of professional streams like medical, engineering and defence services. All these problems of Navodaya Vidyalayas need immediate attention.

12. SUGGESTIONS FOR FURTHER STUDIES

1. The present study was delimited to a limited number of Navodaya Vidyalayas of Haryana. In this study, the admission pattern, infrastructural facilities, staffing pattern, migration policy for students to other Navodaya Vidyalayas and opinion of Navodaya Vidyalayas principals, teachers, community members, neighbouring school teachers and parents were studied. Similar study can be undertaken for drawing wider generalisations covering large number of schools and larger geographical areas and different socio-cultural backgrounds.
2. An investigation into causal factors of dropouts in Navodaya Vidyalayas can be a good study.
3. In the present study the researcher had also tried to study the problems of Navodaya Vidyalayas as viewed by principals, teachers, community members, parents and neighbouring school teachers, and sought suggestions thereof for improv-

ing the functioning of Navodaya Vidyalayas. A similar independent study can be conducted in this direction for other Navodaya Vidyalayas.

4. There can also be conducted a study on the training needs of Navodaya Vidyalayas' staff.
5. One of the objectives of Navodaya Vidyalayas is to promote national integration among the students through a policy of migration of students from Hindi-speaking areas to non-Hindi-speaking areas and *vice-versa*. Similar systematic attempts can be made for other Navodaya Vidyalayas to study the migration policy with a view to determine its success in promoting national integration.
6. A detailed study can be conducted to follow up the Navodaya Vidyalayas' students who have successfully passed class XII so as to know the placement of these students in different professional/vocational institutions.

Problems of Tribal Education in the Context of National Policy of Education, 1986

JYOTI RANJAN BOHIDAR

1. INTRODUCTION

The tribal population of Orissa characterised by sheer backwardness and staggering poverty provides excellent sample to study their socio-economic educational backwardness. Lack of proper education among tribal people is recognised as the main stumbling block which deters their progress and prosperity.

In spite of Constitutional safeguards like Directive Principles for State Policy, various reservation policies and other special provisions for enhancement of tribal education, it is noticed that the tribal people are still lagging behind. Although four decades have elapsed since the promulgation of Indian constitution, policies after policies are formulated and recommended for the upliftment of tribals, no conspicuous results are achieved regarding tribal, educational development. So it has remained a headache on the part of every Government to change tribal ways of life and revolutionize a tradition-based society into modern one. Education plays a pivotal role in bringing about desirable changes in any society, but implementation of educational policies have proved ineffective so far.

However, the N.P.E. 1968 and N.P.E. 1986 and recommendation of Rammurti Committee are laudable efforts by the Indian Government to open up new vistas for educational development of the tribals.

A comparative study of demographic status of tribals at the national level of Orissa has been undertaken. The tribal population of Orissa comprise 22.21 per cent of the total population. The percentage of tribal literacy in Orissa is as low as 18.10 per cent of the total tribal population.

The effect of poverty on tribal education, ecology of school and home, uncongenial home environment, language problems in imparting education, wastage and stagnation in tribal area, methods of teaching, curricular and syllabi and lack of suitable teachers are dealt with at length.

2. OBJECTIVES, SAMPLES AND TOOLS

Objectives

The present study has the following five major objectives:

(i) To delineate the institutional and behavioural characteristics of tribal children.

(ii) To study various incentives and facilities available to tribal communities in order to increase their effectiveness.

(iii) To ascertain the causes of low enrolment and attendance.

(iv) To suggest remedial measures for improving the existing situation.

(v) To recommend a series of measures that can be taken up and implemented to bring improvement in tribal education.

3. SAMPLES

Samples of this study have been chosen broadly from three categories of tribal region—(i) Hilly region of Phulbani and Kalahandi thickly populated by tribals, (ii) Tribal district like Sambalpur, Sundargarh, Bolangir wherein tribal population is almost evenly distributed both in plain and hilly areas, (iii) Coastal district like Puri and Ganjam which represent the tribal people scattered over the areas.

Tools

Questionnaire and interview schedule were used as tools to gather data. Questionnaire for the Heads of the Institutions was administered to collect data about tribal schools and the educational problems. Interview schedule was administered on educational administrators like Circle Inspector of Schools (both for Tribal and General) and District Welfare Officers.

4. MAJOR FINDINGS

1. Slow Progress in the Spread of Secondary Education

Till 1960, there was no tribal secondary schools in the sample area. Expansion of secondary education and the progress in the establishment of secondary schools in the sample districts has been very slow. Only 55 schools for a tribal population of 31,07,826 indicates the tardy growth of educational awakening among the tribals.

2. Distance as a Stumbling Block

In some areas students have to walk two to five kilometres to reach the school. It was the load of poverty and not the burden of the school bag that they used to carry. Natural barriers like rivers, forests, infested with ferocious wild animals are a potent cause for adversely affecting spread of education. Road communication was in a deplorable condition.

3. Lack of Amenities

Amenities provided to teachers and students were far from satisfactory. Condition of quarters supplied to the teachers was very poor. Poor play ground and ill furnished library were clear signs of poor education.

4. Health and Sanitary

Proper drinking water facilities were not at all provided to schools. Health care was totally non-existent. Residents were experiencing thirst for water in the scorching heat as tubewells in the area were lying defunct. Food materials supplied to students were of poor quality. Hardly any Doctor used to visit the school for students health inspection.

5. Irrelevant Curriculum

All Harijan and Tribal schools provided a stereotyped curriculum devoid of any relevance, to practical life. The tribal students did not evince any interest for the curricula which were alien to their environment.

6. SUPW and Co-curricular Activities

Introduction of socially useful productive works into curricula has failed to achieve anything substantial. Implementation of SUPW programme in a perfunctory manner, without the required equipment needed for the purpose, did not bring about the desired result, i.e. economic self-reliance for students. Co-curricular activities in most schools meant only a few outdoor games and occasional performance of drama, music, drawing, painting and literary magazines were seldom utilised to explore and enhance creative talent of students.

7. Media and Materials

In all Harijan and Tribal schools, the medium of instruction was Oriya. Most of the tribal students used to speak their own tribal languages at home. Hence the influence of mother tongue could not be ignored for imparting education effectively. Although some educationists were trying to introduce tribal script in presenting educational materials like text books, most tribal communities did not have any script of their own.

However, mass media like TV and Radios could be effectively utilised for teaching the tribal children in their mother tongue. Electronic teaching aids like tape-recorders, VCP can be fruitfully manipulated to impart education in science and language subjects. Though some of the tribal schools were in possession of TV sets and radio-sets, lack of good and useful instructional programmes in their telecast/broadcasts caused despair.

8. Provision for Mid-day Meal and School Uniforms

Tribal school students got regular supply of uniform even if they were of not good quality and not adequate. Mid-day meals were not at all supplied to them. Free uniform and mid-day meal would certainly be an allurement to the students and would prove a great assistance to the poverty stricken guardians.

9. Stipend and Scholarship

Stipend amount was meagre to make their both ends meet. Food materials supplied to them were of poor quality. Tribal students seldom obtained the scholarship like NRTS (National Rural Talent Scholarship) or any other scholarship for academic brilliance.

Even if they fared well in the field of games and athletics, their talent for games and athletics were not properly harnessed.

10. Administration and Supervision

Lack of transport and communication facilities and inconducive climate of hilly regions were the reasons which hinder administration and supervision of tribal schools. Inspecting Officers were too over-burdened with official works to properly supervise the work of the schools and to check up whether their instruction/guidelines were carried out in actual action.

11. School Hostel

School hostels were poorly improvised. Supervision work in the hostels were rarely conducted.

5. RECOMMENDATIONS

In the light of the above findings and the weightage given by the respondents the following recommendations may be made:

1. Unlike other resources, human resources should be treated with careful consideration where human sentiment and emotions are involved. The tradition bound Adivasis

should be rescued from social and cultural isolation and alienation.

2. A good band of teachers with missionary zeal and genuine love for the tribal people can transform the tribal society and may be able to bring about wonderful changes.
3. Government should be liberal in providing adequate financial assistance for enhancing educational standard of secondary school.
4. Curriculum should be so designed as to meet the practical needs of tribal life. Curriculum should be enriched with cultural heritage of the tribals, elements of self-reliance and self-employment. Secondary education should be job-oriented.
5. Sufficient teaching aids, science equipment may be supplied to schools.
6. Special coaching classes may be conducted in order to bring them on par with general students. Teachers taking classes may be given incentive.
7. Laboratories and library facilities are inadequate and poorly furnished. These may be furnished and enriched for good academic performance. Up-to-date educational technology (both software and hardware) may be introduced to make teaching-learning process effective and lively.
8. Adequate number of technical instructors may be appointed for proper organisation of SUPW. Sufficient funds may be made available by Government for different type of co-curricular activities.
9. Mid-day meal and free uniform should be generally provided. Quality of good materials catered to the boarders may be improved.
10. Proper medical facility may be given to the students.
11. Care should be taken for providing potable water. Bath rooms should be made in the girls' hostel.
12. A separate and permanent hostel superintendent may be appointed to look after the boarders.
13. Heads of the institutions may be empowered to utilise contingency money to meet the immediate expenditure.
14. Administrators may be vested with more power to effectively deal with the problems. A separate inspection wings

may be established to look after academic work of the school. Supervision work should be done regularly.

15. Electronic aids like TV and Tape-recorders may be supplied to the school.
16. Annual work of the teachers may be reviewed in the context of students' performance and achievement.

8

Research in Education of Minorities in India: Gaps and Priorities

NITYANANDA PRADHAN

1. INTRODUCTION

India is the world's most complex and comprehensive pluralistic society harbouring a vast variety of races, tribes, castes, communities, religions, languages, customs and living styles. The groups of people who are perceptibly differentiated from others by race, nationality, religion or language are defined 'minorities' by the contemporary sociologists (Shukla, 1997; Reported in NCERT, 1997, p. 564). The constitution of India defines 'minorities' as communities constituted on the bases of religion or language, even when the language does not have a separate script. According to 1991 census, the religious minorities constitute 17.59 per cent of the population of which Muslims are 11.67 per cent, Christians, 2.32 per cent Sikhs 1.99 per cent, Buddhists 0.77 per cent, Jains 0.41 per cent and others 0.43 per cent. Historically, Hindus contribute to more than three-fourths of the country's population (82.41 per cent according to 1991 census) (Reported in IGNOU, 2003, p. 7). The Government of India have notified five communities, viz. Muslims, Sikhs, Christians, Buddhists and Zoroastrians as minorities at the national level. The High Power Panel on Minorities, SC/ST and other Weaker Sections appointed by Ministry of Home Affairs under the chairmanship of Dr. Gopal Singh has identified Muslims and Neo-Buddhists as educationally backward at the national level.

The population of India is divided on the basis of language and the reorganization of state according to language gives each Indian State an official language. People in these states who speak another language as their mother tongue are considered as language or linguistic minority, for example, the Bengalis or Biharis living in the States of Assam and Tripura. The minorities, whether religious, linguistic or other groups, generally lack power and hence are subject to certain exclusions, discrimination and other differentiated treatment. It, thus, becomes imperative to protect their interests *vis-a-vis* the majority groups, and, therefore, attempts should be made to bring them at par with the majority groups even in a secular system.

2. CONSTITUTIONAL PROVISION FOR MINORITIES

The Constitution of India has made provisions to safeguard the rights of religious and language minorities, particularly to conserve the language, script and culture and to establish and administer educational institutions of their choice, whether based on religion or language. The constitutions, under Article 29, states that the "minorities with a district language, script or culture have the right to conserve the same" and that they "shall not be denied admission into any educational institution maintained by the State or receiving aid out of state funds on grounds only of religion, race, caste, language or any of them." Article 30 states that all minorities, whether based on religion or language, shall have the right to establish and administer educational institutions of their choice. The state shall not, in granting aid to educational institutions, discriminate against any educational institution on the ground that it is under the management of minority, whether based on religion or language. Article 350-A of the Constitution regarding facilities for instruction in the mother-tongue at the primary stage of education states that "It shall be the endeavour of every local authority within the state to provide adequate facilities for instructions in the mother tongue at the primary stage of education to children belonging to linguistic minority groups." Article 350-B states that there shall be a special officer for linguistic minorities to be appointed by the President of India. It shall be the duty of the special officer to investigate all matters relating to the safe-guards provided for linguistic minorities under this Constitution and report to the President upon those matters at such intervals as the President may direct, and President shall cause all such reports to be laid before each house of Parliament, and sent to the Governments of the states concerned (Reported in IGNOU, 2003, p. 7; Government of India MHRD, 1992, p. 9).

3. THE STATE OF EDUCATION OF THE MINORITIES

Education of minorities acquires a special significance in a democratic country which has substantial minority population, be it a linguistic minority or a religious minority. The statistical data required to assess the nature of representation of minorities in educational sphere or to estimate the magnitude of their deprivation is not available in a consolidated form. However, the educational backwardness of minorities is revealed by the data from the National Sample Survey, 43rd Round (1987-88), the NSS data and the studies done in the field (e.g. Rao, 1995; Ahmad, 1994; Reported in IGNOU, 2003, p. 10). According to Rao (1995) in rural India 51 per cent of Hindu males were illiterate. But the figure for Muslim males was 58 per cent. The difference was more striking from urban India. The percentage of illiteracy in urban India was 25.30 per cent for Hindu males and 42 per cent for Muslim males. Moreover, the rate of illiteracy in urban India was 42 per cent for Hindu females and 60 per cent for Muslim females. Another study by Ahmad (1994) also shows that Muslims are backward than Hindu regarding literacy. According to his study, the literacy rate was 32.20 per cent and 53.65 per cent among Muslims and Hindu respectively in Diwana town of Rajasthan and 31.46 per cent and 55.17 per cent among Muslim and Hindu respectively in Kishanganj town of Bihar. The study reflects that females lagged far behind males.

The data presented in Tables 8.1 and 8.2 as follows reveals the state of education of the two minority communities, viz. Muslim and Christian, as compared to their Majority Hindu counterparts in rural and urban India, respectively during 1987-88 (cited in Kazi, 1999, p. 25):

Table 8.1 shows that figures for female literacy are almost identical for both Hindu (75 per cent) and Muslim (76.1 per cent) women in rural India. There is a marginal difference between figures for Hindu and Muslim women's primary education for rural India, which subsequently widens across middle, secondary and graduate levels. There is, however, wide difference between figures for Hindu and Christian women's education at all levels. A similar trend is observed for figures for women's education in Urban India (Table 8.2). Furthermore, 59.5 per cent of Muslim women are illiterate in urban India, as compared to 42.2 per cent of Hindu women and 22.7 per cent of Christian women who come under this category. There is some parity between urban Hindu (17.2 per cent) and Muslim (18.5 per cent) women with reference to primary education which widens considerably for corresponding figures for middle school—25.3 per cent for urban Hindu women and 16.8 per cent for Muslim women—the difference being much greater when compared to Christian women (33.4 per cent). Only 4.3 per cent of Urban Muslim women have secondary education, compared to 10.7 per cent of Hindu women and 20.8 per cent Christian women. The number of urban Muslim female is negligible (0.8 per cent against 4.2 per cent of Hindu women and 5.5 per cent of Christian women).

The relative gap between the figures for educational enrolment for Muslim women in comparison to Hindu and Christian women is highlighted in Tables 8.3 and 8.4.

Unlike the percentage difference between Muslim, Hindu and Christian women in primary education, Muslim women in both rural and urban India lag behind their counterparts in school enrolment from the very beginning. This initial disadvantage is further exacerbated across subsequent educational enrolment categories. The figure of 32.8 per cent for rural Muslim females attending school in the 5-9 age group (compared to 40.6 per cent Hindu women) or 1.4 per cent for Muslim rural female enrolment for the 20+ age group (7.4 per cent for Hindu women) is still more favourable than the corresponding figures for urban India. The enrolment figure of 52.1 per cent for urban Muslim females compares poorly to the corresponding figure of 70.7 per cent for Hindu females, which further widens across subsequent age categories. Clearly, Muslim women in urban India are much worse-off than their rural counterparts not only in terms of their overall educational status as

TABLE 8.1

Education in Rural India—1987-88 by Percentage

Educational Level	*Hindu Female*	*Hindu Male*	*Muslim Female*	*Muslim Male*	*Christian Female*	*Christian Male*	*Other Female*	*Other Male*
Illiterate	75.0	51.3	76.1	58.2	43.1	33.7	61.4	45.3
Primary	11.8	19.0	13.1	18.6	17.8	20.5	15.7	17.9
Primary to middle	11.2	22.7	9.9	19.1	29.2	35.4	19.4	25.5
Secondary	1.7	5.7	0.8	3.4	8.1	9.3	3.1	9.0
Graduate+	0.2	1.2	–	0.6	1.5	1.8	0.3	2.3

Source: The National Sample Survey, 43rd Round, 1987-88, Table 31.4.

TABLE 8.2

Education in Urban India—1987-88, by Percentage

Educational Level	*Hindu Female*	*Hindu Male*	*Muslim Female*	*Muslim Male*	*Christian Female*	*Christian Male*	*Other Female*	*Other Male*
Illiterate	42.2	25.3	59.5	42.4	22.7	18.8	31.2	18.0
Primary	17.2	18.8	18.5	20.9	17.5	16.0	14.7	15.6
Primary to Middle	25.3	30.5	16.8	26.3	33.4	36.7	8.5	30.0
Secondary	10.7	17.2	4.3	8.0	20.8	20.1	17.5	23.6
Graduate+	4.2	7.9	0.8	2.3	5.5	8.1	7.9	11.7

Source: The National Sample Survey, 43rd Round, 1987-88, Table 31.4.

TABLE 8.3

Educational Enrolment in Urban India—1987-88, by Percentage

Age	*Hindu Female*	*Hindu Male*	*Muslim Female*	*Muslim Male*	*Christian Female*	*Christian Male*	*Other Female*	*Other Male*
5-9	70.7	76.3	52.1	56.0	86.1	89.2	85.6	88.0
10-14	74.6	83.2	53.6	63.6	90.0	93.3	82.7	89.9
15-19	42.4	56.1	19.3	34.8	57.1	60.0	60.2	63.7
20+	10.2	21.8	4.7	12.1	17.0	18.2	17.2	35.8
N.R.	29.4	31.3	–	6.4	13.6	67.4	40.7	3.0

Source: The National Sample Survey, 43rd Round, 1987-88, Table 37.

TABLE 8.4

Educational Enrolment in Rural India—1987-88, by Percentage

Age	*Hindu Female*	*Hindu Male*	*Muslim Female*	*Muslim Male*	*Christian Female*	*Christian Male*	*Other Female*	*Other Male*
5-9	40.6	53.3	32.8	42.1	66.9	67.4	50.6	60.1
10-14	41.3	66.9	37.0	56.6	70.1	75.6	65.4	62.6
15-19	12.6	37.7	8.8	26.9	43.3	47.7	13.7	31.3
20+	1.8	8.8	1.4	7.4	10.4	14	1.7	9.3
N.R.	1.2	3.2	15.9	15	–	50.9	16.7	8.7

Source: The National Sample Survey, 43rd Round, 1987-88, Table 37.

citizens of India, but also in terms of their relatively poor educational status when compared to Hindu or Christian women

4. GOVERNMENT STRATEGIES AND PROGRAMMES

Some steps have been taken by the Government, especially in the last decade, to tackle the problem of educational backwardness of the minorities, especially Muslims. The details of these measures adopted by the Government are found in the Programme of Action (POA) of NPE, 1986, POA of the NPE, 1992 (the modified version of NPE, 1986) and the Annual Report of the Department of Education of Ministry of Human Resource Development (MHRD). The National Policy on Education, 1986 states the following regarding education of minorities, vide para 4.8 of the document: *"Some minority groups are educationally deprived or backward. Greater attention will be paid to the education of these groups in the interest of equality and social justice. This will naturally include the constitutional guarantees given to them to establish their own educational institutions, and protection to their languages and culture. Simultaneously objectivity will be reflected in the preparation of textbooks and in all school activities, and all possible measures will be taken to promote an integration based on appreciation of common national goals and ideals, in conformity with the core curriculum."* It may be noted that the POAs of 1986 and 1992 emphasize the need of special efforts to be made "to bring the educationally backward minorities (which includes Muslims) on par with the rest of the society and to make them participate fully in the national developmental activities." (Government of India, MHRD, 1992, p. 9). For achieving these goals the POA of 1992 mentions short-term, medium-term and long-term programmes with respect to the minorities.

5. SOME OF THE SHORT-TERM MEASURES INCLUDE

- Imparting technical skills through the Community Polytechnics setup in the areas of pre-dominant minority concentration.
- Coaching classes for students belonging to educationally backward minorities.
- Evaluation of textbooks from the stand point of national integration.

- Orientation programmes for Principles/Managers, and training programmes for teachers of minority educational institutions.
- A crash programme of School Improvement consisting of Elementary Education, Non-formal Education and Adult Education in Minority concentration areas.
- Extension of resource centres for providing training and guidance to minority educational institutions situated near these centres.
- Appointment of regional language teachers in Urdu Medium schools.
- Setting up women's Community Polytechnics.
- Implementation of Guidelines of recognition of minority managed educational institutions.
- Locating schools in the minority concentration areas.
- Appointment of Urdu teachers in Navodaya Vidyalayas and Kendriya Vidyalayas located in minority concentration areas.

6. SOME OF THE MEDIUM-TERM MEASURES INCLUDE

- Area Intensive Programme for Educationally Backward Minorities.
- Modernization of Madrasa.
- Establishment of Madrasa Boards to look after the education of the minorities.
- Appointment of Urdu teachers in the states where Urdu is spoken by a substantial number of people.
- Appointment of language teachers.
- Preparation of time-bound schedule for publication and timely availability of Urdu textbooks along with those of Hindi and English.
- Wide publicity of all programmes of minorities education through Radio, TV and Newspapers in regional and minority languages.
- Opening of Urdu medium sections in the existing secondary schools.
- Release of grants to minority institutions.
- Incentive schemes to states achieving the targets in respect of minorities.

7. SOME LONG-TERM PROGRAMMES INCLUDE

- Opening of Early Childhood Care and Education (ECCE) centres.
- Survey on availability of teacher training facilities for teachers, and availability of textbooks in minority languages.
- In-service training for minority institution teachers in Science, Mathematics, Social Sciences, English and Carrier Guidance.
- Strengthening educational trusts, foundations, and NGO, in higher education sector.
- Provision of Vocational and Technical education in higher secondary schools.
- Setting up of libraries and reading rooms in minority areas.

(Government of India, MHRD, 1992, pp. 12-16.)

8. RESEARCH IN EDUCATION OF MINORITIES

This part of the paper presents a brief sketch of researches done on education of minorities during different periods of review, followed by analysis of gaps with reference to quantum of research, methodology followed, and quality of research, etc. Based on the trends of research and research gaps in the field, certain areas of research that need attention on priority basis, are identified and listed at the end.

9. OVERVIEW OF RESEARCHES

The overview of researches on minority education presented here have been taken from the reports of survey of research in education published from time to time at the national level. The reports of survey of research in education referred here include: Third Survey of Research in Education covering a period of five years, i.e. 1978-83 (Buch, 1986); Fourth Survey of Research in Education covering a period of five years, i.e. from 1983-88 (Buch, 1991); and Fifth Survey of Educational Research (Vol. I) covering a period of four years, i.e. from 1988 to 1992 (NCERT, 1997).

Review of research on education of minorities groups conducted during the period from 1978 to 1983 (Buch, 1986) revealed that only four studies have been conducted in this area during the period (Indukumari, 1976; Rajwade, 1980; Gupta, 1980; Quadri, 1981) and all the four studies have dealt with the utilization of educational facilities by the Muslims in a district of Uttar Pradesh. He found that the Muslim enrolment at primary stage was quite in proportion to their population, but that of the Muslim teachers at the higher stage of education very low. The important elements in the society which hindered the utilization of educational opportunities were: illiteracy and low socio-economic status of parents, non-availability of Urdu as a medium of instruction, lack of confidence in the Muslim students, and hesitation of parents to send their daughters to co-educational institutions, etc. The study conducted by Gupta (1980) on 111 schools from four districts of Uttar Pradesh revealed that the difference in enrolment ratio between Hindu and Muslim population in each district was statistically significant in favour of Hindus. The major reasons as evident were: non-availability of Urdu as medium of instruction; and culture bias in drama, prayers, wall writings, paintings, etc., favouring Hindus. The other two studies (Indukumari, 1976; Rajwade, 1980) conducted on the Muslim women in Kerala and Madhya Pradesh respectively revealed that the educational and social status of the Muslim women was low due to practice of seclusion and early marriage, the absence of socially defined occupation roles, the lack of conformity between traditional and modern feminine roles, and the low level of aspiration, etc. (Indukumari, 1976). In spite of *Purdah* and seclusion, the majority of women went out marketing and also to see movies (Rajwade, 1980). In the field of marriage, their consent was taken for granted. The incidence of divorce was not very high, but the women seemed to be under the fear of divorce (Rajwade, 1980). In all the four studies reviewed here descriptive research design has been employed and thus the findings are based on the data collected from a cross-section of informants.

Review of studies on education of minorities conducted during the period from 1983 to 1988 (Sachidananda, 1991; Reported in Buch, 1991) is very disappointing as only two studies had been conducted during the review period (Basu, 1981; Ahmed, 1985). The study conducted by Basu (1981) dealt with the personality characteristics of Tibetan and East Pakistani refugee children. The study revealed a marked difference between the intelligence scores of the children of the two groups. Further, inadequate ego-formation and other personality traits like rationalization and need for autonomy was characteristics of backward children from both the groups. The study conducted by Ahmed (1985) tried to assess the extent to which the educational rights of minorities have been protected. It further tried to assess their views on secular democracy and national integration in the context of the traditional educational institutions of the Muslims as well as of other minority institutions. The study revealed that the right to cultural and educational self-determination created hurdles in the way of national integration. Education is a potent instrument to achieve national integration in a plural society like India.

It is further disappointing to note that only four studies (Joseph, 1989; Jain, 1992; Kareem, 1991; Mondal, 1992) had been conducted during 1988-92 on education of minorities (Shukla, 1997; Reported in NCERT, 1997). The study conducted at M.Phil. level by Joseph (1989) on "Education at and Politics Among Depressed Class Christians of Central Kerala" revealed that depressed class Christians, who had embraced Christianity to release themselves from the bondage of caste, could not observe the ideals of equality fully. The sub-caste feeling was so strong that they could not appreciate movements like Tennindia Savishesha Sangham, the Pratyaksha Raksha Daiva Sabha, and the separate Administration Movement. Both the Syrian and the depressed classes Christians, who were studied, continued to accept casteism and only highly publicised and highly liberation conscious individuals could delink themselves form this. These findings are mainly based on the data collected from secondary sources and through an interview schedule. The study conducted by Jain (1992) on the topic—"Minority Rights in Education in Bombay—An Exploration" revealed that the minority educational institutions may instigate communal feelings as they are vulnerable to communal pressures. Such institutions were found to be contributing towards attainment of the national goal of universal literacy through mobilization of community resources. The study of "Developmental Implications with special Reference to Indian Muslims" (Kareem, 1991) on a sample of 200 Muslims drawn from five districts, showed that their educational backwardness is caused by the general economic. A positive relationship was found to exist between education and the socio-economic advancement of the area. Mondal (1992) studied the state of education among the Muslims of West Bengal with the major objectives in study the attitudes of Muslims in West Bengal towards education; to identify the factors responsible for it; and to suggest remedies. The average literacy rate of Muslims in the sample villages was only 32.27 per cent; and the female literacy rate (22.89 per cent) was much lower than that of their male counterparts (40.87 per cent). Nearly 64 per cent of guardians expressed their desire to educate their children up to the secondary standards, while only 1 per cent showed their willingness to let their children study up to the university level. Illiteracy and dropout among children was very high and the enrolment very low. The main reasons for the backwardness of the Muslims were found to be social (e.g. *Purdah* system), cultural, economic, traditional value system, and the style of living.

Based on the objectives, methodology and findings of the researches conducted on education of minorities during the period of review, the following observations can be made:

- The number of studies conducted are few.
- Most of the studies (80 per cent) are dealt with the Muslims only.
- Most of the studies (60 per cent) are quantitative in nature, although qualitative tools of interviews have reported to been used in most of the studies.
- Most of the studies (80 per cent) are cross-sectional. Attempts have mostly been made by the researchers to generalise the findings of their studies to the population.
- In most of the studies attempts have been made to study the status, particularly socio-economic and educational, of Muslim women.
- Only one study (Joseph, 1989) has been conducted, at the M.Phil. level, on Christians.

10. RESEARCH GAP

Review researches on education of minorities, during the period from 1987-92 showed that it is a neglected are of research on account of both quantity and quality. Although the Minority Commission of India has identified Muslims, Christians, Sikhs, Buddhists and Parsis in the category of religious minorities, not a single study on education of Sikhs, Buddhists or Parsis, has been conducted during the period of review. Most of the studies (80 per cent) are dealt with the Muslims only. All the studies belong to academic category—either for the doctoral or for M.Phil. degree, and hence are of relatively less useful in solving the practical problems in the education of the minority children. It can be seen that most of the studies on minority education (80 per cent) are cross-sectional in nature and reported to have used quantitative techniques of data analysis (60 per cent), e.g. Percentage, Chi-square, Correlation, t-test, although qualitative tools of interviews have frequently been used in most of the studies. The researchers, in most of the cases, seems to have tried to generalize the findings to the population (Quadri, 1981; Gupta, 1980; Indukamari; Rajwade, 1980; Kareem, 1991; Mondal, 1992) without considering the adequacy of the sample and sampling designs. The size of sample in most of such cases seems to be inadequate. The review did not reveal a single in-depth study depicting grass-root realities associated with minority education. The exploratory study conducted by Joseph (1989), however, is a good attempt in this context, which, to some extent, throw light on the issues of Christians pertaining to education and politics. This study, on the other hand, suffers from the weakness of using secondary source data. It can clearly be observed from the studies conducted by Rajwade (1980), Quadri (1981), Indukumari (1976) and Gupta (1980) that most of the issues associated with education of Muslims, particularly Muslim women, are socio-cultural in nature. It is, therefore, considered appropriate to conduct ethnographic studies in this area in order to explore the micro-level realities in education of different minority groups. The multiple methods of data collection, i.e. combining dissimilar methods to study the same unit/phenomenon, may extensively be used in these types of studies. The present review revealed that only one or two data gathering tool(s), mostly interview, has been used by the researchers. Ethnography case studies on the functioning of minority educational institutions or non-enrolled and dropout children of different minority groups, may be of immense help in designing instruction, curriculum, teacher education programme; and preparing text-books, etc. The nature of some problems associated with education of Muslims, as reported by the researchers (Rajwade, 1980; Indukumari, 1976; Gupta, 1980), implies that action research will be of immense help in exploration and solution of problems faced by the teachers with reference to pedagogy, dropout, and organization of various co-curricular activities in schools of minority concentration areas. The practising, teachers as well as school supervisors need to be encouraged to undertake action research on the issue(s) they encounter during the course of their duty.

11. RESEARCH PRIORITIES

A brief review of the studies on education of minorities reveals many gaps in our knowledge. It is an important area of research, especially in a country like India, where a large number of linguistic and religious minorities have to be taken care of. The studies reviewed here are not only few in number, but also cover only few minority groups and few aspects of their education. Thus, the studies under review here are in no way representative of the researches required in this area. Based on the gaps with reference to aspects, quality, trends, and methodology of researches on minority education, following suggestions are made to be taken care of on priority basis:

- Research may be conducted on education of religious minority groups, so far not covered at all. These include Sikhs, Buddhists and Parsis.
- Studies may be conducted on aspects of minority education not covered so far, e.g. functioning of minority educational institutions, the relevance of curriculum and instructional materials, behavioural issues and adjustment problems of children belonging to different minority groups in the schools dominated by the children of majority groups, language problems, school climate, teacher-pupil relationship.
- Action research on the problems faced by the minority children, e.g. adjustment, language, may be conducted by the teachers who really face them.
- In-depth studies, e.g. case study, may be conducted with a view to explore the micro-level realities pertaining to the causes of dropout and non-enrolment; factors determining achievement motivation and level of aspiration; and adjustment problems, etc., in respect of the children of minority groups.
- Ethnographic studies may be conducted to understand the socio-cultural contexts of different issues associated with minority education, e.g. poor learning achievement, low rate of enrolment, low level of aspiration, functioning of minority

educational institutions. These studies may make use of triangulation (interviews, observation, documentary analysis) in the collection of data from multiple sources.

- Comparative studies may be conducted in the following areas: status of educational institutions run by minorities and by government; factors of dropout among the children of different religious groups; status of educational institutions run by different religious and linguistic minority groups, etc.
- Analysis of textbooks in different subjects and grade levels may be made to study the religious bias, if any.
- Intervention (experimental) studies may be conducted with teachers of varying religious groups/co-curricular activities/textbooks of different languages, as independent variables.

References

Buch, M.B. (Ed.), (1998): *Fourth Survey of Research in Education (1983-88)*, Vol. II, NCERT, New Delhi.

Buch, M.B. (Ed.), (1998): *Third Survey of Research in Education (1978-83)*, NCERT, New Delhi.

Government of India, MHRD (1992): *Programme of Action—1992* (National Policy on Education, 1986), New Delhi.

IGNOU (2003): *Higher Education: Its context and Linkages*, MES—101-3, New Delhi.

Kazi, S. (1999): *Muslim Women in India*, Minority Right Group International, London, UK.

NCERT (Eds.), (1997): *Fifth Survey of Educational Research (1988-92)*, Vol. I, New Delhi.

9

Sustainable Solutions of Environmental Problems Through Community-based Education: Case Study of a Tribal Village

NITYANANDA PRADHAN

1. THE RATIONALE

Sustainable development has become the catchword of our decade, used and misused in many contexts. In a dynamic system like human society, sustainability is fundamentally a question of balance maintained over time. It may be more easily defined, in practice, as the lack of forces tending to upset equilibrium over time. Our society functions in a natural environment. Therefore, seeking the sustainability of human society depends on, and intimately interrelates with, natural systems. In the present context, any other approach to development, equity, planning or environment could be considered indefensible and unethical.

Sustainable development implies central focus on people. Man lives in environment. He lives on environment. He is a part of the natural system and depends utterly, on them. Thus, natural system should be respected at all times. To respect natural system means to approach nature with humility, care and compassion; to be efficient in resource use; to be guided by the best available knowledge—both traditional and scientific; and to help shape and support the public policies that promote sustainability. People should preserve the complexity of ecosystems to ensure the survival of all species and the safeguard of their habitat. Everyone should take responsibilities for his/her impact on natural systems. They should not interfere unduly with ecological processes, diminishing bio-diversity, or over exploit renewable resources and the ecosystems that support them. People should treat all creatures decently and protect them from cruelty and avoidable sufferings. But today we find out rivers polluted, air unbreathable, soil degraded and forest denuded. The reason is that we have used and exploited environment, but have never cared for it. The present experience is that people tend to act like the proverbial farmer who killed the goose that laid the golden egg by destroying the capital of the natural resources at an alarming rate (Singh, 1998; Reported in Jerath, 1998, p. 13).

However, the situation is now changing and people are realizing the significant role of community participation in sustainable development programme. With the growth of this concern, many things have happened, particularly in terms of institutional development, enactment of legislations and regulations, and establishment of agencies for environment protection. The basic principles behind all these initiatives is to ensure people's participation in the process of environmental management and conservation, e.g. the National Forest Policy, 1988 envisages people's involvement in the development and protection of forest; the Government of India in 1990 has issued guidelines for involving village communities in the regeneration of degraded forests and envisaging the formulation of Joint Forest Planning and Management (JFPM) scheme charged with responsibility of preparing plans for development, protection and managing the same as per approved plans (Singh, 1998; Reported in Jerath, pp. 22-23). Community-based sustainable development programme works on the basic premise that people have the innate capacity to improve their quality of life and the problems confronting them can be overcome through their own efforts with some assistance from government and non-government agencies (Balagot, 1990; Reported in Sharma and Tan, 1990, p. 147). Concerns for the environment logically starts with one's community. Furthermore, involvement of community residence is considered a revolutionary aspect in environmental management (Andaya, 1989; Reported in Talisayon, 1990,

p. 211). The best advocates of an ecosystem are said to be community members whose livelihood depends on the ecosystem. The community-based environmental education, as an approach, utilizes community resources and addresses community needs and problems. The approach has been proved effective in Africa (Swift, 1983; Reported in Talisayon, 1990, p. 211) and the United States (Penick, 1984; Penick *et al.*, 1984: Reported in Talisayon, 1990, p. 211).

Review of researches on environmental education in general and community-based environmental education in particular, carried out in India and abroad, revealed that considerable number of environmental projects have been implemented in the countries like Australia, Canada, Greece, Hong Kong, Latvia, Romania, South Africa, Slovenia, Taiwan, Uganda, and USA. Most of the projects seems to have planned and implemented involving school students and young adults, and hence can be categorized as school-based/community-based environmental education projects. From the point of view of research designs, including sampling designs, statistical designs and operational designs, most of the environmental education projects seems to be weak. This is due to the fact that such projects have so far not attracted the attention of the professional researchers working at the university level to a desirable extent. It can be seen that the number of in-depth studies in this area are inadequate both in India and abroad. The case studies conducted by Rammurthy and Kausik (2001), Khan (2002), Reddy *et al.* (2002), Goyal (2002), are too narrow in scope, i.e. in terms of independent variables and sample size, to be generalized. In view of the importance of in-depth case studies in environmental education and research, a good number of such studies need to be undertaken, the findings of which would serve as basis for the formulation of major environmental education projects. The present study is one such attempt. It is grounded on the concept of sustainability, use of community resources, community involvement, wide applicability, social acceptability and application of scientific research methods.

2. OBJECTIVES OF THE STUDY

The objectives of the study are:

(i) To study the key environmental problems of the tribal village under study;

(ii) To study the resources, concerning environment of the tribal village under study, and utilization of those resources.

(iii) To study the environmental awareness, interest, and attitude of the inhabitants of the village under study;

(iv) To design an environmental education programme adapted to the needs and resources of the community, i.e. village under study; and

(v) To assess the impact of community-based environmental education programme in terms of sustainability, i.e. community participation and effective use of community resources—human and financial.

3. DESIGN OF THE STUDY

Case study research design (Merriam, 1988; Jessop, 1998) was employed in carrying out the study. A tribal village/habitation, namely, '*Padeiguda*' was considered as the case/unit for the purpose of this case study. The case was selected on the basis of convenience and experience of the investigator. The detailed data pertaining to environmental problems of the village, needs and resource; and environmental awareness, interest and attitude of the villagers were collected from a cross-section of inhabitants with the help of the tools like interviews, observation, and focus group discussion. However, the basic information in respect of all the 94 households of the habitation was collected with the help of household information schedule. The data collected through these tools were put to qualitative analysis, i.e. describe the opinion, attitude, and behaviour of the informants. The study was conducted in three phases: (i) Identifying key environmental problems of the study village and ascertaining awareness, interest and attitude of the villagers; (ii) Designing and implementing community-based environmental education programme; and (iii) Assessing the impact of the programme.

4. CASE PROFILE

A uni-tribe village, namely *Padeiguda* constitutes the 'case' for the study. The village is situated at a distance of about 10 kilometres to the west of Koraput town (a district headquarter of Orissa State). After seven kilometres on the way from Koraput to Jeypore in the National Highway No. 43, there is an approach road of about three kilometres distance to the right of the road (NH-43) that leads to the village. Out of 94 households in the habitation, 93 belong to the Paraja tribal community. The total population of the village, as revealed from household survey, is 465 out of which 223 are male and 242 are female. In one side of the village there is a small patch of teak forest down the hill. The other sides have vast patches of unutilized land wanting of trees and plants to maintain ecological balance. There is a natural stream close to the village which is utilized mostly for the purpose of bathing, cleaning utensils, washing clothes and fetching water for household use. The stream water is rarely used to grow vegetables and paddy, etc. There is also one tube-well at one end of the village. Despite bounty of natural resources, including water and land, very little attention is given to utilize or maximize them. The villagers rather prefer to work as daily wage labourers in the nearby town with lower wages than that fixed by the government.

5. RESULTS

The results pertaining to the three phases of the study, viz. (i) Identifying key environmental problems and resources of the study village; (ii) Designing and implementing community-based environmental education programme; and (iii) Assessing the impact of the programme, are presented as follows:

Key Environmental Problems of the Study Area

In the first phase of the study, the environmental problems and the related factors pertaining to five key aspects of the environment, viz. land, forest, air, water, health and hygiene, were identified. These are as follows:

Land

- Massive soil erosion as a result of cleaning of forest for the purpose of growing crops like *ragi,* oilseeds and different types of grams.
- Increasing use of chemical fertilizers, particularly for the purpose of growing vegetables, decreases the fertility of land.

- Limited practice of bounding, terracing and plantation cause soil erosion.

Forest

Felling trees by the inhabitants for the preparation of charcoal, etc. leads to growing shortage of minor forest produces like, fuel, edible leaves and roots, fodder, leaves, timber, and bamboo, etc.

Air

- Lack of windows in most of the houses for ventilation. People do not keep windows in their houses conventionally.
- Use of closed rooms (i.e. rooms without windows) for the purpose of cooking. The same room is used for all purposes, e.g. storing foodgrains, sleeping.

Water

- The tube-wells sunk by the government in the village are fully or partly defunct.
- The villagers use stream water for drinking and cooking purposes, despite availability of tube-wells. Some people are reluctant to use tube-well water due to emission of iron smell and/or iron particles seen in the water.
- People are habituated with cleaning utensils, putting tooth sticks, washing clothes, bathing domestic animals, around the tube-wells.

Health and Hygiene

- The health workers do not pay regular visit to the village, particularly due to the problem of communication. The village remains almost cut-off during rainy season.
- The inhabitants suffer from the diseases like malaria fever, dysentery and skin diseases throughout the year.
- The people consult *Disari* (the village medicine man) instead of doctor at the time of health hazards. This is due to the fact that the *Disari* is readily available, whereas the doctor is not.

- Lack of drainage system for the disposal of waste water or rain water. The village road remains unclean due to stagnation of water.
- People do not use mosquito-net, despite their awareness of the fact that malaria fever is caused by mosquito-bite.

5. INVENTORY OF RESOURCES AND RESOURCE UTILIZATION

The major resources concerning environment, e.g. land resources, forest resources, water resources, human resources, in respect of the tribal village under study can be listed as follows:

(i) The village is surrounded by vast hilly terrain lands which can be used for plantation of cashew nuts, coffee, and cardamom, etc. But plantation activities are hardly seen.

(ii) There is a natural stream with perennial flow of water very close to the village. The stream water is used for household purposes only and never used for agricultural or plantation purposes.

(iii) The village is surrounded by bounty of forest resources. The economy of the inhabitants is, therefore, forest-based. Forest provides them their prime necessities, e.g. fuel, fodder, roots, vegetables, oil seeds, leafy vegetables, timber.

(iv) The inhabitants of the study village are very docile, disciplined and receptive. Such people can easily be motivated and, therefore, their services can be utilized for attaining common goals.

6. ENVIRONMENTAL AWARENESS, INTEREST AND ATTITUDE OF THE INHABITANTS

The environmental awareness, interest and attitude of the tribal inhabitants of the study village with reference to different aspects of the environment, e.g. land, forest, air, water, were assessed with the help of interviews, observation and focus group discussions. The results are summarized as follows:

Awareness

Majority of the tribal inhabitants of the village under study:

- Are aware of the fact that upper layer of land is more fertile as compared to that of the lower layer.
- Are aware of the benefits of mixed cropping pattern.
- Are aware that use of chemical fertilizers loses fertility of land in the long-run.
- Are aware of the fact that shifting cultivation results in degradation of forest.
- Are aware of the consequences of forest degradation.
- Prefer to use stream water for all purposes, e.g. drinking, bathing, washing clothes, cooking, cleaning utensils.
- Are aware about the consequences of drinking unclean water, e.g. dysentery.
- Prefer to consult doctor at the time of health hazards but intact consult *Disari* (the village medicine man) for all types of health hazards.

Interest

Majority of the tribal inhabitants of the village under study possess low interest in environmental activities pertaining to land, forest, air, water, and health and hygiene.

Attitude

Majority of the tribal inhabitants of the village under study possess unfavourable attitude towards different aspects of environment, including land, air, water, and health and hygiene, etc.

7. COMMUNITY-BASED ENVIRONMENTAL EDUCATION PROGRAMME

An analysis of various environmental problems faced by the villagers revealed that wanting of trees and plants due to human intervention is the root cause of most of the environmental problems. Realizing this fact, a community-based environmental programme, viz. *Green Your Village*, was designed with the following objectives:

(i) To form a village green committee;
(ii) To mobilize resources—human and financial, for the project;
(iii) To establish coordination between village green committee and resource agencies, including government and NGOs;
(iv) To generate awareness among the villagers about plantation, gardening, and utilization of natural resources, including water and wasteland;
(v) To establish a nursery for the village;
(vi) To plant trees in and around the village; and
(vii) To enhance desirable attitudes and habits among the villagers to maintain trees/plants regularly.

Action Plan

Table 9.1 depicts the detailed action plan of the programme as follows on next page.

8. THE IMPACT OF COMMUNITY-BASED PROGRAMME

The impact of community-based environmental programme was assessed employing the qualitative techniques of participant observation, focus group discussions, informal discussions and the use of checklist. Regular monitoring and review of the programme for a period of one year, i.e. between launching and final assessment of the programme, was made employing standard project review protocol. The final assessment of the programme was done with reference to the following indicators:

(i) Involvement of the community;
(ii) Establishment of nursery;
(iii) Plantation of trees in the wasteland around the village;
(iv) Kitchen garden attached to each family/household;
(v) Maintained greens; and
(vi) Change in environmental interest, attitudes and habits of the community.

Table 9.2 presents the impact of community-based environmental programme with reference to the programme objectives:

TABLE 9.1

Action Plan for Community-based Environmental Programme: *Green Your Village*

Task Description	*Resources*	*Expected Result*	*Plan for Evaluation*
(1)	*(2)*	*(3)*	*(4)*
Form of Village Green Committee.	Influential and interested people of the village.	Formation of a Village Green Committee consisting of influential and interested persons to remain in charge of making the village green.	Review of minutes of meetings with reference to attendance of members and resolutions adopted.
Mobilize resources for the project.	Contribution of the villagers in terms of money and labour.	Contributions of the villagers in terms of money and labour plus existing village fund.	Review of relevant records.
Establish coordination between villagers and resource agencies/ persons.	• Experts from forest department and NGOs. • Experts from community. • Village green committee.	Active involvement of the experts from forest department and NGOs in the project activity.	• Focus group discussions. • Participant observation.
Environment building to ensure community awareness and participation.	• Community members. • Experts from forest department and NGOs.	Participation of the villagers in the project activities.	• Focus group discussions. • Participant observation.
Establish a nursery for the village.	• Local community experts. • Experts from forest department. • Money for the purpose.	Establishment of nursery in the primary school campus of the village.	• Making a list of different types of plants with numbers. • Making a list of community members involved in the process.

(Contd.)

TABLE 9.1 (*Contd.*)

Task Description	*Resources*	*Expected Result*	*Plan for Evaluation*
(1)	*(2)*	*(3)*	*(4)*
Tree Planting.	• Villagers. • Community's cultural resources such as values and beliefs.	• Plantation in and around the village. • Active participation of the village green committee and the villagers.	Making a list of seedlings planted and number of seedlings survived.
Follow-up and monitoring activities.	• Village green committee. • Villagers.	Beautiful, healthy, green and productive environment.	• Monthly follow-up by the village green committee. • Checking up various responsibilities. • Project review from time to time. • Re-planting if needed modifying some strategies.

9. DISCUSSION OF RESULTS

It can be seen from a review of the resources—land resources, forest resources, water resources and human resources, available in the village under study that it is surrounded by large patches of wastelands which can be used for plantation. The natural stream with perennial flow of water close to the village is used for the household purposes only, e.g. bathing, washing clothes, cleaning utensils, but never used for agricultural or plantation purposes. It was learnt through interviews, observation and focus group discussions that majority of the inhabitants are aware about the environmental problems their village/locality is facing and likely to face in the future. They are also aware about the major factors behind such problems, particularly those concerning land, water and forest. But they do not possess adequate interest in activities that would promote or protect their immediate environment. This is due to lack of education; systematic knowledge about the implications of environmental degradation for the family, community, nation or globe; and absence of a mechanism to organize or mobilize the inhabitants. However, the major strengths of the villagers are that they seem to be disciplined and receptive. These strengths could be optimally utilized in designing action plan for community-based environmental education programme presented in Table 9.1; and implementing the same (see Table 9.2) in an effective manner. It was found during the process that people are interested to contribute resources in terms of money and labour for the protection/ promotion of their environment. They have shown adequate interest to listen to functionaries who came forward to assist them for their development. Review of some community-based environmental education projects conducted abroad, e.g. by Atrash (1994) in Palestine; Timisina (1995) in Nepal; Pottapova (1995) in Russia; Ombe (1995) in Mozambique; Serre (1995) in France; Clover (1995) in Canada; Buchan (1996) in New Zealand; Siron (1997) in Canada; Adepoju (2001) in Nigeria; Neamt (2002) in Romania, have proved to be successful in mobilizing community to protect environment without awaiting for any external intervention. Further, the studies conducted by Dovie (1995) in Ghana, Farangitakis *et al.* (1997) in Greece, Hoare (1998) in Canada, Compha (2001) in Mali, throw some light on the impact of community-based projects relating to afforestation and greening the community through planting of trees,

TABLE 9.2

Impact of Community-based Environmental Programme: *Green Your Village*

Objectives	*Task*	*Expected Result*	*Acutal*
(1)	*(2)*	*(3)*	*(4)*
To form village green committee.	Organizing meeting of the villagers to form village green committee.	Formation of a village green committee consisting of influential and interested persons of the community to remain in charge of making the village green.	The village green committee consists of 10 members including five women members of self-help group, ward member, *Naik* (the traditional village head). The committee took a vow.to complete plantation activities within a year.
To mobilize resources for the project.	Motivating villagers to contribute for the project in terms of money and labour.	Collect money for the project from the villagers and existing village fund.	An amount of Rs.10.00 per family was collected for the purpose. As many as 36 families contributed for the purpose. Money could not be resourced from the village fund as such fund does not exist.
To establish coordination between village green committee and resource agencies including NGOs and government departments.	Inviting resource persons/ experts from forest department and NGOs; and organize discussion with the villagers.	Active involvement of the experts from the forest department, soil conservation departments, and NGOs in the project activity.	• Two members of the village green committee met the experts of soil conservation department and horticulture department at nearby town Koraput. The soil conservation department agreed to provide

			seedlings and financial assistance of Rs. 200 per nursery along with necessary technical and material help. • An expert from soil conservation department held discussion on different schemes of the department relating to plantation.
To generate awareness among the villagers about plantation, gardening and utilization of natural resources, including water and wasteland, for the purpose.	Organization of community awareness programme.	Ensure motivation of the villagers for plantation activities.	People could understand that they are surrounded by wasteland. They can easily earn their livelihood by putting little efforts such as planting fruit bearing trees like cashew nut and trees for firewood. They also expressed their interest to develop kitchen garden.
To establish a nursery for the village.	• Collection of money for the purpose. • Contribution of labour by the villagers. • Collection of seeds. • Consultation with soil. conservation department.	Establishment of a nursery inside the primary school campus.	A nursery house was constructed inside the school campus. As many as 1000 seedlings, including cashew nut, sandalwood, Nilgiri, were grown with the financial as well as technical assistance from soil conservation department.

(*Contd.*)

TABLE 9.2 (*Contd.*)

Objectives	*Task*	*Expected Result*	*Acutal*
(1)	*(2)*	*(3)*	*(4)*
To plant trees/plants in and around the village.	• Organizing village meeting and distributing the task of tree planting.	• Plantation of trees in and around the village. • Active participation of the village green committee and the villagers.	Five hundred cashew nut trees were planted in a large patch of wasteland at one end of the village. Thirty Sandalwood seedlings and two hundred Nilagiri seedlings were planted in both sides of the approach road to the village and in the school campus. Each families were assigned to adopt few plants for watering and necessary maintenance according to their convenience.
To enhance desirable attitudes and habits of the community to maintain trees/plants regularly.	Follow-up and monitoring of the programme.	Beautiful, healthy, green and productive environment.	As many as 350 plants of different types were found to survive after one year of plantation. People are interested to replant in cases of loss due to various reasons.

etc. Studies conducted in India in this area by Rammurthy and Thirumaran (2001), Kausik (2001), Khan (2002), Reddy *et al.* (2002), Goyal (2002), have also shown positive impact of community-based projects.

Based on the findings of community-based research projects conducted in India and abroad and that of the present project, it can safely be deducted that various problems, including environmental ones, can be solved at the community level utilizing its own resources—human and financial.

10. CONCLUSIONS AND EDUCATIONAL IMPLICATIONS

The major conclusions derived from the study are as follows:

(i) The resources in terms of money, materials and labour could be mobilized from the tribal inhabitants of the village under study for the promotion of their own environment.
(ii) Tribal people are receptive. They are ready to listen to functionaries who come forward to assist them for their development. Spectacular changes in interest and attitude towards environment could be seen among the tribal people after project implementation.
(iii) There is a community feeling among the tribal people. They exhibited positive enthusiasm, interest and attitude to work in group for the attainment common goal. However, the need for regular monitoring and follow-up was felt in order to maintain the level of their enthusiasm, interest, attitude and habits.
(iv) Environmental problems of all kinds, particularly those relating to land, forest, water, health and hygiene, can be solved through community-based education and community participation.

The conclusions of the study seems to have immense implications for the government in the department of Environment and Forests; community level functionaries including teachers, agricultural workers, health workers; and NGO functionaries, devoted to protection of the environment. They should realize the fact that concerns for the environment starts with one's community; people have the innate capacity to manage their environment and environmental problems; environmental problems confronting them can be overcome through their own effort with some assistance from government and non-government agencies; and the best advocates of an ecosystem are said to be the community members whose livelihood depends on the ecosystem.

REFERENCES

Adepoju, S. (2001): The Environment as a Focus of Democratic Culture; In *Connect*—UNESCO-UNEP Environmental Education Newsletter, Vol. XXVI, Nos. 1-2, UNESCO Environmental Education Sector, Paris.

Atrash, I. (1994): Children for the Protection of Nature; In *Connect*—UNESCO-UNEP Environmental Education Newsletter, Vol. XIX, No. 1, March 1994; UNESCO Environmental Education Sector, Paris.

Buchan, G. (1996): Environ School; In *Connect*—UNESCO-UNEP Environmental Education Newsletter, Vol. XXI, No. 3, September 1996, UNESCO Environmental Education Sector, Paris.

Clover, D.E. (1995): Community-based Environmental Popular Education for Adults; In *Connect*—UNESCO-UNEP Environmental Education Newsletter, Vol. XX, No. 4, December 1995, UNESCO Environmental Education Sector, Paris.

Compha, A. (2001): Combating Deforestation at Elementary School Level; In *Connect*—UNESCO-UNEP Environmental Education Newsletter, Vol. XXVI, Nos. 1-2, 2001, UNESCO Environmental Education Sector, Paris.

Dovie, D.B.K. (1995): Wildlife Awareness for School Children; In *Connect*—UNESCO-UNEP Environmental Education Newsletter, Vol. XX, No. 4, 1995, UNESCO Environment and Population Education for Human Development, Paris.

Farangitakies, G. (1997): Urban Forest of Argyroupolis; In *Connect*—UNESCO-UNEP Environmental Education Newsletter, Vol. XXII, No. 1, 1997, UNESCO Environmental Education Sector, Paris.

Goyal, S.K. *et al.* (2002): Effects of Seasonal Variations on Dispersion of Air Pollutants—A Case Study, National Environmental Engineering Residential Institute, Nagpur; In Ministry of Environment and Forests (2002): *Paryavaran Abstract*, Vol. 19, Nos. 1-2, New Delhi.

Hoare (1998): Eco-Grow Planting Activity; In *Connect*—UNESCO-UNEP Environmental Education Newsletter, Vol. XXII, No. 1, 1998; UNESCO, Education Sector, Paris.

Jerath, N. (1998): *Source Book on Environmental Issues in Technical Education* (Ed.), UNESCO and PSCST, Chandigarh.

Jessop, T. (1998): A *Model of Best Practice at Lareto Day School, Sealdah, Calcutta*, Education Sector Group, DFID (India), New Delhi.

Kausik, A. *et al.* (2001): Heavy Metal Pollution of River Yamuna in the Industrially Developing State of Haryana, Department of Science and Engineering, Gujarat

University; In Ministry of Environment and Forests (2002): *Paryavaran Abstract,* Vol. 19, Nos. 1-2, New Delhi.

Khan, A.B. (2002): Water Monitoring and Sea Water Intrusion in Kalapet, Pondicherry University, Pondicherry; In Ministry of Environment and Forests (2002): *Paryavaran Abstracts,* Vol. 19, Nos. 1-2, New Delhi.

Merriam, S.B. (1988): *Case Study Research in Education—A Qualitative Approach*, Jossey Bass, Inc.

Neamt (2002): Two Cultures for One Environment; In *Connect*—UNESCO-UNEP Environmental Education Newsletter, Vol. XXVII, Nos. 3-4, 2002; UNESCO Education Sector, Paris.

Ombe, Z.A. (1995): Environmental Education Activities in Beira; In *Connect*—UNESCO-UNEP Environmental Education Newsletter, Vol. XX, No. 3, September 1995; UNESCO Environmental Education Sector, Paris.

Potapova, T. (1995): School Children as Environment Education Teachers for Pre-School Age Children; In *Connect*—UNESCO-UNEP Environmental Education Newsletter, Vol. XX, No. 3, September, 1995; UNESCO Environmental Education Sector, Paris.

Ramamurthy, N. and Thirumaran, M. (2001): The Carbon Monoxide Levels Automobile Exhaust—A Case Study in Chidambaram Annamalainagar, Annamalai University; In Ministry of Environment Forests (2002): *Paryavaran Abstract,* Vol. 19, Nos. 1-2, New Delhi.

Reddy, R.C. *et al.* (2002): Collection, Treatment and Re-use of Treated Sanitary Wastewater—A Case Study, National Environmental Engineering Research Institute, Nagpur; In Ministry of Environment and Forests (2002): *Paryavaran Abstract*, Vol. 19, Nos. 1-2, New Delhi.

Serre, P. (1995): Getting to Know the Environment; In *Connect*—UNESCO-UNEP Environmental Education Newsletter, Vol. XX, No. 4, December 1995, UNESCO Environmental Education Sector, Paris.

Sharma, R.C. and M.C. Tan (1990): *Source-book in Environmental Education for Secondary School Teachers* (Ed.), UNESCO Principal Regional Office for Asia and the Pacific, Bangkok.

Siron, R. (1997): EE on the Banks of St. Laurent; In *Connect*—UNESCO-UNEP Environmental Education Newsletter, Vol. XXII, No. 1, 1997; UNESCO Environmental Education Sector, Paris.

Talisayon, V.M. (1990): Community-based Environmental Education; In UNESCO (1990): *Source Book in Environmental Education for Secondary School Teacher* (Ed.), UNESCO Principal Regional Office for Asia and the Pacific, Bangkok.

Timisina, T.P. (1995): Involving Teachers in Environmental Conservation; In *Connect*—UNESCO-UNEP Environmental Education Newsletter, Vol. XX, No. 2, June 1995; UNESCO Environmental Education Sector, Paris.

UNESCO (1999): *Sustainable Development Education—The Force of Change*, Paris, France.

10

Family Life Values in the Tribal Communities: An Ethnographic Case Study of the Paraja

NITYANANDA PRADHAN AND SHREELEKHA DEI

1. THE RATIONALE

The family is the basic unit of society. It refers to a group of individuals who are related by blood, marriage or adoption. The strength or weakness of any society is directly related to that of the family. The family is also a co-operate unit of interacting and inter-development personalities who have common bonds and goals, and share resources and living space. The concept of family starts with the partners in marriage, with development of relationship between newly wed couples, as they begin their future life. Their plan includes, having children, a house of their own, a regular income for necessities, children's education, etc. The family seed is sown with the birth of a child start growing. Children are born amidst the love and care of their families, parents, brothers and sisters, grand parents and other family members. Murdock (1949) proposed that a family always and everywhere fulfilled four essential functions necessary for the continuation of any human society, namely, sexual relations, economic co-operation, reproduction and socialization (Reported in UNESCO, 1988, p. 27). But many societal forces such as modernisation, working parents, liberalised codes of sexual ethics, diffusion of culture appears to be eroding the beautiful socio-cultural family values mostly in eastern countries. Recent years have seen the joint family breaking up as members move out to seek their own fortunes elsewhere. However, family members often wish to keep close ties with those at home, sending money and visiting their native place. The strength and solidarity of a society depends largely on how this basic unit performs its function. It is the responsibility of all members of a family to fulfil family obligations.

Overview of research studies and other literature related to major aspects of family life, viz., responsible parenthood, marriage, adolescent fertility, status of women; and various family life education initiative for adolescent and youth revealed that there is neglect of research studies in these areas concerning tribals, a major disadvantaged section of India. The available literature also did not reveal any initiative in the country, by the government or NGOs; to meet the family life education need of tribal youth. However, specific projects targeted at various disadvantaged groups, e.g. rural youth, slum-dwellers have reported to been implemented in the developing countries like Pakistan, Nepal, Bangladesh, Bhutan, etc., under RHI Programme supported by European Council, UNFPA and NGOs. Only two studies conducted in India by Balakrishna (1986) and Nagaich (1986) are related to family life of tribal groups. These studies, however, speak little of the ground level reality.

An important feature of most of the studies reviewed here, whether Indian or foreign, is that they belong to Knowledge, Attitude and Practices (KAP) category (e.g. Goswami, 1978; Bhargava, 1979; Sharma, 1981, Patel, 1983; World Health Organisation, 1995; United Nations, 1995; The Alan Guttmacher Institute, 1988). These studies conducted at the macro-level do not reflect the ground level realities. Most the them have used structured tools for collection of data and have deliberately tried to present the findings in numerical terms. Such findings no doubt have contributed a lot for comparative analysis of the state of affairs among the countries and even at the national or regional level but have almost no relevance when applied to a specific group. The present study, therefore, employed ethno-graphic case study research design with extensive use of the tools of qualitative research such as interviews, observation, focus group discussion and documentary analysis, so as to make the family life-related issues of the community under study more transparent and specific.

2. OBJECTIVE OF THE STUDY

The major objective of the study is: To study, in cultural context, the values in the Paraja tribal community of Koraput district, Orissa, with reference to the following aspects of their family life:

- Adolescent fertility.
- Responsible parenthood.
- Marriage.
- Status of women.

3. SEARCH DESIGN

The research design is based on the principles of ethnographic case study (Yin, 1994; Reported in Jessop, 1998). More than a simple case study, ethnographic techniques of data collection, e.g. interview, observation, documentary analysis, use of informants to study the cultural characteristics of subjects (Best and Kahn, 1995) were extensively used. Further, socio-cultural analysis in studying different variables under study, e.g., marriage, incidence of adolescent fertility, gender issues, family size, sets this study apart from other types of case study research, e.g. historical, psychological. The study, therefore, is categorised as ethnographic case study.

The case, i.e. the Paraja tribal community was selected from among the major tribal communities of Koraput district, e.g. the Paraja, the Kandha, the Soura, the Bhottada, from the point of view of the convenience of the researchers to do field work, and acquaintance with the community.

The sample for the study consisted of the sample of Paraja habitations; and the sample of key informants selected from these habitations. Six Paraja habitations, viz. Manbar, Bageipadar, Padeiguda, Deoghati, Badachindri, and Talajaniguda, were purposively selected so as to ensure representation of typical characteristics, unique characteristics, extreme characteristics and ideal characteristics (Goetz and Le Compte, 1984; Reported in Merriam, 1988). These habitations represent Paraja belonging to urban, rural and remote areas; habitations with exclusive Paraja and that inhabited by the Paraja along with other tribal as well as non-tribal communities. The key informants consisted of 574 Paraja, with varying age groups, marital status and social status; and 16 opinion leaders, including Sarpanch, Ward Members and Members of traditional Panchayat. Selection of key informants involved various sampling techniques like multi-phase sampling and incidental sampling (Aggarwal, 1988). The basic information such as literacy and education, income and savings, occupation, population, etc., were collected in respect of each and every households of the sample habitations. But the detailed information pertaining to different aspects of family life, e.g. marriage, adolescent fertility, responsible parenthood, were collected from the key informants. The tools of qualitative research such as semi-structured interviews, observation, documentary analysis, focus group discussion were used to collect data from multiple sources. The use of multiple methods of collecting data, i.e. combining dissimilar methods to study the same unit, contributed to building up a chain of evidence related to the sensitive research questions, e.g. questions pertaining to one's extra marital sexual relationship, contraceptive use. The rationale for this strategy is that the flaws of one method are often the strengths of another . . . (Denzin, 1970; Reported in Merriam, 1988, p. 69). The data were analysed mostly using qualitative techniques such as describing attitude, events, behaviour or relationships. However, simple quantitative technique such as percentage was also employed to supplement and substantiate qualitative analysis in required cases.

4. CASE PROFILE

The Paraja, otherwise called Paroja, Porja or Parja, is one of the well known major tribes of Orissa. They mainly inhabit in the districts of Koraput and Kalahandi and also found in small number in other districts such as Sundargarh, Cuttack and Mayurbhanj. The term Paraja is so broad a term that it includes, in a very loose sense of the term, a number of other communities. At times the Bonda and the Gadaba also refer themselves to be Bonda Paraja and Gadaba Paraja respectively. The tribe is mainly divided into two sections, viz. *Bada Paraja* and *Sana Paraja*. Apart from others, the major distinction between these two is that the former, following the Hindu tradition, do not eat beef or buffalo meat and observe elaborate purificatory rituals even when a cow or buffalo dies in their households, while the later eat the flesh of both these animals. Hence the *Bada Paraja* claim higher position in social ranking over their *Sana Paraja* counterparts.

Marriage is the most significant event in a Paraja's life. It is also the important ceremony in the Paraja villages. Paraja boys after attaining 16-18 years of age and girls after attaining puberty are considered fit for marriage. The Paraja have various ways of acquiring mates, viz. *Maga Baha* (marriage by arrangement), *Udlia Baha* (Love marriage), *Jhinka Utra Baha* (marriage by capture), *Paisamundi Baha* (marriage of the widows and the divorced ladies), and *Gharjwain* (marriage by being adopted as a son to the wife's father). The most common, prestigious and ideal way is marriage by arrangement (*maga Baha*).

The Paraja worship a number of Gods and deities for their wellbeing, e.g. *Danteswari, Laxmi, Landi, Jhankar Debata, Dongar Debata, Nisan Debata.* They observe many festivals round the year to mark first sowing, eating of new rice, eating of mango as well as for their enjoyment. The important ones are: *Asadhi Parab, Nuakhia, Diali Parab, Baulam Parab, Pus Parab* and *Chait Parab.* During these festivals they do not do any work but wear new dresses, take good food, dance in group and go for hunting, etc. Dance, song and music are a characteristic feature of their aesthetic life.

Rice is the staple food of the Paraja. It is supplemented by millets, maize, vegetables and other edible fruits, roots, and leaves collected from the forest. The Paraja are habituated to alcoholic drinks and beverages. Use of liquor is a customary practice in all the religious rituals, festivals, and feasts.

The Paraja villages have well organized socio-political system which functions as an independent autonomous unit. The office bearers of the village administrative structure constitute, *Jani,* the village head-*cum*-priest; *Muduli,* the de facto head of the village; *Disari,* the village medicine man-*cum*-astrologer; *Gurumain,* the priest-*cum*-witch doctor; and *Bhatanayak,* an important religious functionary.

The Paraja are primarily cultivators, but the poor sections are mostly landless labourers. Educationally they fall far behind like many other tribes. Parji is their mother tongue and language of communication among themselves.

So far the Paraja have more or less retained their own way of life which distinguish them from other tribal and non-tribal communities. Their traditional socio-political organization, marriage and kinship system, religious life, housing pattern, food habits, folk culture and world view, though have changed to some extent with changing time, still continue to function effectively.

5. ANALYSIS AND INTERPRETATION OF DATA

The data pertaining to the major family life values and ethos of the Paraja, collected from the key informants using the tools of qualitative method, e.g. interviews, observation, focus group discussion, were put to qualitative analysis under four headings, viz. adolescent fertility, responsible parenthood marriage, and status of women. However, the quantitative data collected through structured household survey schedule were used to supplement and substantiate the qualitative analysis.

Adolescent Fertility

Table 10.1 depicts the composition of adolescent Paraja by sex and marital status in respect of six case studies habitations, viz. Manbar, Bageipadar, Padeiguda, Deoghati, Badachindri, and Talajaniguda.

The results of Table 10.1 show that the adolescents (12-19 age group), in the study habitations, constitute 22.14 per cent of the total population; and as high as 61.22 per cent of them are married (45.75 per cent male and 74.19 per cent female). Interviews with adult Paraja revealed that 89.38 per cent of the male and 86.78 per cent of the female have married prior to the minimum age of marriage, i.e. 20 years and 18 years, respectively for males and females. The median age at marriage and at first birth among the adolescent mothers (15.58 and 16.68 respectively) seems to be very close and indicates that majority of them have their first child within marriage. The rate of fertility among these mothers is reported to be very high (305 births per 1000 women).

Responsible Parenthood

The Paraja society is patriarchal in nature and governed by the division of labour based on age and sex. It was, however, learnt that wife plays a vital role in Paraja family. Paraja women do more physical work. They too play major role in the management of

TABLE 10.1

Habitation-wise Composition of Adolescent Paraja by Sex, Marital Status and their Ratio to the Total Paraja Population

Name of the Habitation	*Paraja Population*	*No. and Percentage of Adolescents*						*Ratio*
		Male		*Female*		*Total*		
		Unmarried	*Married*	*Unmarried*	*Married*	*Unmarried*	*Married*	
Manbar	370	20 (47.62)*	22 (52.38)	9 (18.75)	39 (81.25)	29 (32.22)	61 (67.78)	90 (24.32)
Bageipadar	503	27 (50.94)	26 (49.06)	19 (28.36)	48 (71.64)	46 (38.33)	74 (67.67)	120 (23.86)
Podeiguda	461	33 (56.90)	25 (43.10)	16 (24.24)	50 (75.76)	49 (39.52)	75 (60.48)	124 (26.90)
Deoghati	370	24 (54.90)	20 (45.45)	10 (28.57)	25 (71.43)	34 (43.04)	45 (56.96)	79 (21.35)
Badachindri	292	21 (61.76)	13 (38.24)	09 (26.47)	25 (73.53)	30 (38.46)	48 (61.54)	78 (26.71)
Talajaniguda	380	09 (56.25)	07 (43.75)	07 (36.84)	12 (63.16)	16 (45.71)	19 (54.29)	35 (09.21)
Total	2376	134 (54.25)	113 (45.75)	70 (25.09)	209 (74.91)	204 (38.78)	322 (61.22)	526 (22.14)

*Figures in the parentheses indicate percentage.

household work such as cooking, collecting, firewood, marketing, etc.

The contraceptive knowledge and current use among the Paraja shown in Table 10.2 indicates that the Paraja women play greater role in the matters of family planning.

TABLE 10.2

Contraceptive Knowledge and Current Use Among the Married Paraja

	Knowledge of any Method (%)		*Use of any Method (%)*	
	12-19 age group	*20 years and above*	*12-19 age group*	*20 years and above*
Men	64.52	92.50	6.45	8.13
Women	82.86	93.10	5.71	24.14

It was learnt from the focus group discussion that the daughters possess higher values in the Paraja society as compared to sons from an economic point of view. Despite the higher value of daughters from the economic point of view, the Paraja mostly prefer to have a son from a socio-cultural view. In one opinion the son is the one who will inherit the family property and treasures. Another opinion held by some parents is that the son is the hope for the parents' security in their old age.

The distribution of a sample of 138 Paraja couples aged 20 years and above with varying family size (Number of children) in Table 10.3 show that majority of them (50.72 per cent) have family size

TABLE 10.3

Paraja Couples Aged 20 Years and Above by Number of Children

(N = 138)

No. of Children	*No. and Percentage of Couples*
0	9 (6.52)*
1	17 (12.33)
2	42 (30.43)
3	50 (36.23)
4 or more	20 (14.49)

*Figures in the parentheses indicate percentage.

more than two; and 42.76 per cent of the couples have desirable family size, i.e. 1-2 children.

Marriage

Marriage is one of the most important event in a Paraja's life. Marriage between the members of the same clan is prohibited as the boys and girls of the same clan are treated as brothers and sisters. Cross-cousin marriage, i.e. marrying mother's brother's daughter is preferred. Three types of marriage, viz. (i) *Maga* or *Haribol Baha* (Marriage by arrangement), (ii) *Jhinka Utra Baha* (Marriage by capture), and (iii) *Udlia Baha* (Love marriage) are followed in the Paraja community. *Maga* or *Haribol Baha* is the most ideal type of marriage and settled by negotiations. In all these types of marriage, the bride's father need not pay any dowry to the bridegroom's father. Instead the bridegroom's father is required to pay some bride-price *(Jhola)* to the bride's father. The amount of bride-price varies from place to place and depends upon the capacity of the groom's father. It is paid both in cash and kind. The wedding ceremony is held at boy's house.

It was learnt from the focus group discussion and interviews that divorce is socially permitted on the grounds of maladjustment, marital incompatibility or any other reason(s) the Village Council feel appropriate. The divorce can be initiated by either party (wife or husband) and the matter is decided in the traditional Village Council. A husband divorcing his wife pays her compensations as fixed by the Village Council and an women divorcing her husband has to return back the bride-price. Remarriage is permitted to both divorced men and women after the divorce is formally granted. Remarriage is also permitted to widows and in fact the younger brother has the right to marry his deceased elder brother's wife.

Status of Women

Women in Paraja society play an important role. Although hard works like ploughing are expected from the males and minor agricultural operations and household works from the females, most of the outside works, including marketing, collection of fuel and fodder, etc. are practically performed by the females. They too play a major role in the management of household works. Thus, the economic contribution of the Paraja women to their family seems to he higher as compared to their male counterparts. It was learnt that the girls are considered as economic assets to the family. They help their mothers in household works, e.g. cooking, taking care of younger siblings. As they become young they work almost at par with their boy counterparts. From the point of view of literacy the Paraja women fall far behind as compared to their male counterparts. Table 10.4 depicts a comparative picture of the percentage of literacy between Paraja men and women in respect of the six habitations under study.

Table 10.4 reveals that the percentages of literacy among the women are less in all the habitations as compared to men in the respective habitations. Further the percentage of women literacy in these habitations vary between 2.87 per cent and 8.96 per cent. Thus the status of paraja women from the point of view of literacy is lower as compared to their men counterparts.

TABLE 10.4

Literacy Status of Paraja Women *vis-a-vis* Men in Six Case Study Habitations

Name of the Habitation	*Percentage of Literacy*		
	Total	*Women*	*Men*
Manbar	4.76	2.87	6.79
Bageipada	6.07	3.08	9.17
Padeiguda	5.25	3.15	7.61
Deoghati	6.80	3.75	9.55
Badachindri	15.56	8.96	22.06
Talajaniguda	5.90	4.31	7.64

It was found that most of the paraja women are thin and have distended abdomen. The reasons, as revealed from the discussion with the people are: teenage pregnancy, lack of adequate space between two births, and lack of food intake during pre-natal as well as post-natal period. It was learnt that the food intake of a pregnant women is less in all nutrients as compared to that of her counterparts who is not pregnant, although a pregnant women needs more food than one who is not. However, no differential treatment between men and women is found in the matter of food.

Despite the prevalence of bride-price and higher economic contribution of daughters, the Paraja, as it happens in other societies, mostly prefer son's to daughter's. In their opinion the son is the one who will inherit the family property and look after the parents during their old age. Thus, the Paraja prefer to have sons from the socio-cultural point of view.

Incidence of early marriage and teenage pregnancy; the high rate of fertility among the women; closeness of the median age at marriage and at first birth among women; low percentage of literacy, indicate the low status of women in Paraja society.

6. CONCLUSIONS

(i) Majority of the Paraja, particularly females, marry during their adolescence. As high as 74.91 per cent of the total female adolescents surveyed are found married.

(ii) Child marriage is still prevalent in Paraja community.

(iii) Majority of the adolescent mothers have their first child within marriage. The rate of fertility among these mothers is very high (305 births per 1000 women) and the median age at marriage and at first birth (15.58 and 16.68 respectively) are very close.

(iv) Paraja society although is patriarchal in nature, wife plays a vital role in family due to her hard work, more economic contribution and greater role in family planning, etc.

(v) The majority of couples aged 20 years and above (50.72 per cent) had family size beyond two.

(vi) Young boys and girls in Paraja society are economic assets to their family. The girls, however, are valued more as compared to the boys.

(vii) Many families prefer sons to daughters primarily because he will inherit the family property and look after the parents during their old age. Those who prefer both, they like to see their first child as son.

(viii) Marriage is strictly prohibited between the members of the same clan. Cross-cousin marriage, i.e. marrying mother's brother's daughter, is the general rule.

(ix) Bride's father does not pay any dowry to bride groom's family. He instead demands bride price (*Jhola*) to the groom's family.

(x) The trend with regard to marriage practices is changing in favour of marriage by free choice as against that by arrangement.

(xi) Divorce is permitted and can be initiated by either party (wife or husband). The traditional village council decides the matter.

(xii) Remarriage is permitted to both divorced men and women as well as widows. The younger brother has every right to marry his deceased elder brother's wife.

(xiii) Women play a major role in the family from an economic view. They use to manage most of the outside works including marketing, minor agricultural operations, collection of fuel, etc. They too go to nearby towns as daily labourers.

(xiv) The economic contribution of a young girl to her family is normally higher as compared to that of a young boy.

(xv) Most of the married women seem to be weak and have distended abdomen, due to teenage pregnancy, lack of adequate space between two births, and inadequate food intake during pre-natal as well as post-natal period.

(xvi) Majority of the families prefer sons to daughters from a socio-cultural view. In their opinion a son is needed so as to inherit the family property and look after the parents, during their old age.

REFERENCES

Aggarwal, Y.P. (1988): *Better Sampling Concepts, Techniques, Evaluation,* Sterling Publishers Pvt. Ltd., New Delhi.

Balakrishna (1986): Effect of Socio-cultural Deprivation on Some Cognitive and Non-cognitive Abilities of Tribal Adolescents, Ph.D. Psy. Mag, U.: In M.B. Buch (1991b): *Fourth Survey of Research in Education* (1983-88) Ed., Vol. II, NCERT, New Delhi, p. 1427.

Best, J.W. and Kahn, J.V. (1995): *Research in Education*, 7th Edn., Prentice Hall of India Ltd., New Delhi.

Bhargava, M.A. (1979): A Study of Attitudinal and Personality Correlates of People's Acceptance of Family Planning, Ph.D. Psy. Agra, U.: In M.B. Buch (1986): *Third Survey of Research in Education* (1978-83) Ed., NCERT, New Delhi.

Goswami, P.K. (1978): A Study of the Self-Concept of the Adolescents and its Relationship with Scholastic Achievement and Adjustment, Ph.D., Edn., Agra,

U.: In M.B. Buch (1986): *Third Survey of Research in Education* (1978-83) Ed., NCERT, New Delhi.

Jessop, T. (1998): *A Model of Best Practice at Loreto Day School, Sealdah, Calcutta,* Education Sector Group, DFID (India), New Delhi.

Merriam, S.B. (1988): *Case Study Research in Education—A Qualitative Approach,* Jossey Bass Inc.

Murdock, G.P. (1949): Social Structure, The Macmillan Company, New York: In UNESCO (1988): *Family Life Education,* Package One, UNESCO, Principal, Regional Office for Asia and the Pacific, Bangkok.

Nagaich, N.K. (1986): The Effect of Home Environment and Parenting Style on Some Personality Variables—A Study of Disadvantaged Tribal Student population of Madhya Pradesh, Ph.D. Psy., D.H. SGVV: In M.B. Buch (1991): *Fourth Survey of Research in Education* (1983-88) Ed., Vol. II, NCERT, New Delhi, p. 1442.

Patel, G.K. (1983): An Investigation to Study the Extent and Patterns of Frustration of Adolescent Pupils of Secondary Schools of Ahmedabad City with Reference to Demographic Variables, Ph.D., Education, SPU: In M.B. Buch (1986): *Third Survey of Research in Education* (1978-83) Ed., NCERT, New Delhi, p. 458.

Sharma, A. (1981): Mother-Child Relationship as Function of Family Size and Socio-Economic Status Among Working Housewives of Meerut, Ph.D., Psy. Agra U.,: In M.B. Buch (1986): *Third Survey of Research in Education* (1978-83) Ed., NCERT, New Delhi, p. 458.

The Alan Guttmacher Institute (1988): Into a New World: Young Women's Sexual and Reproductive Lives, New York, p. 18: In UNESCO (1988a): *Handbook for Educating on Adolescent Reproductive and Sexual Health,* Book One, UNESCO-PROAP Regional Clearing House on Population Education and Communication, United Nations Population Fund, Bangkok.

UNESCO (1988): *Family Life Education, Package—I,* Regional Clearing House on Population Education and Communication, UNESCO-PROAP, Bangkok.

United Nations (1995): Unpublished Tabulations of Age-Specific Fertility Rates, 1990-2045; and the Sex and Age Distribution of World's Populations: The 1994 revision, New York: In UNESCO (1998) *Handbook for Educating on Adolescent Reproductive and Sexual Health Book One,* UNESCO-PROAP Regional Clearing House on Population Education and Communication, United Nations Population Fund, Bangkok.

WHO (1995): Adolescents Health and Development: The Key to the Future, Paper Prepared for the Global Commission on Women's Health, Geneva: In UNESCO (1998): *Handbook for Educating on Adolescent Reproductive and Sexual Health, Book One,* UNESCO-PROAP Regional Clearing House on Population Education and Communication, United Nations Population Fund, Bangkok.

Anthropometric Status of Child Labourers

ANJALI PATTANAIK AND HARITHA, N.

1. INTRODUCTION

The progress of growth and all-round development of a country fully depend on its children. Hence they are its most valuable assets. India being one of the developing countries must look to her children with great care in respect of their physical and educational development. In fact India is one of the most poverty stricken country but its children should not be the victims of her poverty which leads to retardation of their physical and mental development.

While observing the 10th anniversary of the Year of Child in 1989, UN approved the convention of preservation of their right to survive, health, education and protection against abuse and exploitation. Even though in Indian constitution a broad legal framework has been provided for the minimum protection of child workers, still this vulnerable section is in jeopardy.

The child labour in our country is a great problem and not favoured as it is economically unsound, psychologically in distress and physically as well as morally dangerous and harmful. In India where two-fifth of its population is in the age group of 14 years, about 111 millions of children are engaged in child labour. Child labour is a world-wide problem.

It is a fact that the basic cause of child labour is poverty, so unless and until poverty is removed, the problem of child labour cannot be eliminated. These children are employed both in organised and unorganised sectors of work either for part time or full time activities and are exploited to a delinquishing degree. As long as child labour exists educational deprivation will continue which ultimately jeopardise their all-round development.

Very few studies have been done in this respect till now. Orissa is one of the poverty stricken states of India, where 7.2 per cent children of its total child population are engaged in employment (1981 census) out of which five per cent in urban areas and 95 per cent in rural areas are working in agricultural fields and other areas to earn their livelihood. In the rural areas of the districts like Kalahandi, Koraput, Phulbani and Ganjam of Orissa state, 36 per cent of children are found in employment. Realising the importance of this social problem the present study is a step in this direction.

2. OBJECTIVES

- To ascertain the growth status of child workers;
- To trace out their health problems;
- To understand the causative factors encouraging child labour; and
- To suggest certain measures to tackle the problem.

3. MATERIALS AND METHODS

The study was carried out in the slum areas of Berhampur town in the Ganjam district of Orissa state where the samples were selected randomly comprising of 100 child labourers from both the sexes equally in the age group of 9 to 14 years.

Anthropometric status of the children was assessed by weight for age on the basis of Jelliffe's classification of malnutrition and by comparing the mean heights of the samples with the ICMR norms of heights.

Clinical signs pertaining to hair, face, eyes, lips, tongue, teeth, skin and other external characteristics arising out of nutritional deprivation were detected by a physician.

As most of the samples were illiterate, an interview method was used to collect information regarding their home environment and community background, living conditions, nature of work, working hours and causes of their employment.

The data was statistically analysed using 't' test of significance to test the significant difference between mean heights and weights of the samples and ICMR norms of heights and weights.

RESULTS AND DISCUSSION

Home Environment

Data showed that number of family members varied from 5 to 11. Their academic background were very very poor due to high population density and lack of educational facilities and only eight per cent of members had education up to primary level. Their economic status was very poor as their monthly income ranges from Rs. 150 to 600 only.

Community Environment

Their community environment was totally poor where they had a single multi-purpose room to live in. They used to get their drinking water from very unhygienic source and were habituated to use open fields for defaecation. Some of them were living on road-side to use street light and very few were using kerosene lanterns for lighting purpose.

Anthropometric Status

On the basis of weight for age the samples were classified into different degrees of malnutrition by comparing their weights for age with ICMR norms which is shown in Table 11.1. All the children were suffering from third and fourth degree malnutrition (3rd degree—36 per cent of male and 42 per cent of female; 4th degree—10 per cent of male and 12 per cent of female).

The present study shows that more number of female child labourers were suffering from 3rd degree malnutrition than their male counterparts.

TABLE 11.1

Distribution of Child Labourers According to Degree of Malnutrition

(Per cent)

Age (Years)	*3rd Degree*		*4th Degree*	
	Male	*Female*	*Male*	*Female*
9+	–	6	–	–
10+	8	10	–	–
11+	12	16	4	6
12+	4	6	4	6
13+	8	4	2	–
14+	4	–	–	–
	36	42	10	12

The mean heights and weights of the subjects are shown in Table 11.2 which shows that all children were grossly underdeveloped as compared to ICMR reference heights and weights.

It is evident from the statistical analysis that the height and weight of the child labourers were significantly lower than the ICMR reference heights and weights (at 0.01 per cent as well as 0.05 per cent level).

Clinical Manifestations

Table 11.3 in respect of clinical manifestations of the subjects shows that a great percentage of 50 per cent each male and female samples had pale and flabby; red saw fissured tongue; and other clinical signs were more or less present in the children from which it is obvious that all of them had deficiency diseases.

Nature of Work

From Table 11.4 it is clear that a highest number of children (male—1 per cent; female—45 per cent) were engaged in domestic activities like sweeping, cleaning utensils, washing of clothes and cooking. Nine per cent of children (male—8 per cent; female—1 per cent) were in agricultural activities, 7 per cent of male children were engaged in hotel work, 14 per cent of children (male—10 per cent; female—4 per cent) were engaged in other major tasks pertaining to shopping,

TABLE 11.2

Mean Heights and Weights of Child Labourers

Age (years)	Height (cm.)						Weight (kg.)					
	Male			Female			Male			Female		
	No. of samples	Mean	S.D.	No. of samples	Mean	S.D.	No. of samples	Mean	S.D.	No. of samples	Mean	S.D.
9+	–	–	–	6	105.6	5.67	–	–	–	6	17.0	1.63
10+	8	118.5	4.06	10	132.2	12.27	8	21.25	01.117	10	24.8	1.73
11+	14	127.8	8.99	18	121.6	5.85	14	23.28	4.38	18	23.0	1.14
12+	8	131.0	5.86	12	134.6	7.21	8	23.75	4.32	12	30.3	4.84
13+	10	136.2	10.09	6	139.6	9.54	10	28.6	6.99	6	28.3	1.26
14+	8	138.0	10.69	–	–	–	8	28.25	4.14	–	–	–

TABLE 11.3
Prevalence of Deficiency Diseases

(Percentage)

Clinical Manifestations	*Male N = 50*	*Female N = 50*
Hair brittle	20	31
Face-Pallor	3	18
Depigmented	11	21
Moon face	33	14
Eyes—Conjunctivitis	1	12
Bitot's spot	8	–
Lips—Angular stomatitis	6	2
Cheilosis	5	7
Tongue—pale and flabby	50	50
Red ray fissured	50	50
Teeth—Mottled enamel	7	11
Dental canes	24	36
Skin—Dry	35	29
Scaly	8	16
Follicular	2	10
Oedema	–	–
Rachitic changes		
Bow legs	22	6
Pigeon chest	14	18

TABLE 11.4
Distribution of Child Labourer According to their Nature of Work

Activities	*Male (Per cent)*	*Female (Per cent)*	*Total (Per cent)*	*Work (Hours)*
Domestic	1	45	46	3
Agricultural	8	1	9	4
Hotel works	7	–	7	10
Other major tasks	10	4	14	6
Miscellaneous	22	2	24	7

fetching water, gardening, baby care and bringing ration and 24 per cent of children (male—22 per cent; female—2 per cent) were engaged in miscellaneous works like boot polishing, garage work, selling balloons, and working in shops.

While considering the working hours in various spheres of activities where children were engaged as indicated in Table 11.4. It has been seen that 46 per cent of children (male—1 per cent; female—45 per cent) were engaged for 3 hours in domestic activities, 9 per cent of children (male—8 per cent; female—1 per cent) were engaged in agricultural activities for 4 hours, in hotel work 7 per cent of male children were engaged for 10 hours, 14 per cent of children (male—10 per cent; female—4 per cent) were engaged in other major tasks for 6 hours and in miscellaneous 24 per cent (male—22 per cent; female—2 per cent) were engaged for 7 hours per day.

Reasons for Taking Employment

It was observed that poverty was the sole cause of child labour but besides this, some other reasons were there for taking up the jobs as to supplement family income (40 per cent), for death of the bread earner (10 per cent), due to large family (15 per cent) and parental compulsion (35 per cent).

Health Facilities

These vulnerable sections were not availing any type of health facilities in their localities.

The present study reveals that all the child workers were from economically poor and illiterate family background and they were staying in very unhygienic conditions without having any proper facility of water supply, hygienic food, and housing conditions.

Their growth status proved their insufficient and unhygienic food intake resulting in various clinical manifestations and also all were suffering from 3rd and 4th degree malnutrition.

It was found that all the child workers were engaged in unorganised sectors of activities where their working hours varied from three to ten hours per day.

So far as the reasons concerned with the child labour problem, in the present context, 92 per cent of family members were illiterate for which they could not think of educating their children, otherwise those children who were engaged for three to ten hours per day could have utilised their precious time in developing their potentialities. It was also found that to supplement family income, to maintain large families, death of bread earner, and circumstantial compulsions of the parents made these children to be employed in different activities.

CONCLUSION

To conclude, it can be said that the plight of children in these unorganised sectors of activities will never allow them to become physically and skilfully fit for any sort of organised work. Even though constitutional and legal provisions are made for the protection of children against exploitation, these will not help to ameliorate this horrible child problem. This problem can be solved only when the society or community realises the ultimate fate of children.

SUGGESTION

To eliminate exploitation of child workers certain positive steps may be suggested as follows:

- Education of the employed children should be the responsibility of the employer where the expenditure can be shared by the Government and the employer.
- Children should not be employed in any hazardous work. There should be legal provisions for minimum hours of work according to their capacities.
- The skill of child worker should be enhanced by providing proper training.
- They should be provided with proper medical and recreational facilities.
- There should be a vocational training for these children where they should get a fixed amount of money to support their family till they are able to earn their livelihood independently as is implemented in 12 towns of India like Faridabad, Mirjapur, Aligarh, Surat, Jaipur, Sivakasi.

PART III

NUTRITION, CREATIVITY AND METHODS OF TEACHING

12

Nutritional Status and its Effect on Physical Development and Educational Achievement

ANJALI PATTANAIK

1. INTRODUCTION

Children are the citizens of tomorrow who would substantially and significantly contribute towards socio-economic development of a nation; and hence the physical and mental health of a child become important issues. Unfortunately enough India is one of the developing countries which has as large as 33 per cent of under-five infant mortality mainly due to malnutrition. Hunger and malnutrition are serious problems in Asia, South America and Africa which prove hazardous towards normal development of mind and body of a child. Nutrition *vis-a-vis* protein deficiency is one of the commonest factors in creating health hazards, and therefore, demands special research attention. Evidences are plenty, from the reviews of nutrition and dietary surveys/studies, particularly those of the ICMR, that 35 per cent of children do not get adequate protein in their regular diet, and alarmingly as large as 92 per cent do not get adequate calories. However, the effects of socio-cultural and environmental processes on physical and mental development of Indian children has not been extensively studied, even though it has been believed that these socio-cultural factors have a significant influence in dietary practices/food habits and quality and quantity of calorie intake in particular. Some important studies (Sen, 1976; Mohanty, *et al.*, 1988; Easwaran, *et al.*, 1972; Martin, 1973 and Udani, 1963) have established that poverty itself prevents healthy development with regard to physical status and academic performance of a child. Adverse economic condition resulting in poor house and sanitation, inadequate health care, susceptibility to disease, large family size, insufficient living space, restricted educational opportunities, unfavourable feeding and child-care practices, etc. (Cravloto, 1970; Rath, 1976; Rath, *et al.*, 1979 and Chowdhury, 1984) always lead to retarded physical and educational development and most frequently causing premature death. Nevertheless nutritional status has been regarded as most important causal factor for mental impairment in addition to social, environmental, obstetrical and genetic factors.

Children are like barometers, which reflect the nutritional status of the community. Imperatively any improvement in the quality of child life is clearly a step towards social and economic development of a country. In such a premise the objectives of the present study were formulated to:

1. ascertain the nutritional status of the children,
2. find out the factors responsible for nutritional deprivation,
3. see the effects of nutritional status on physical development,
4. ascertain the effects of malnutrition on educational achievement,
5. assess the environmental factors responsible for the physical development of the children,
6. find out the causes for poor educational performance of students, and
7. suggest measures for amelioration of this situation and improvement of the health as well as education of children.

However, the scope of the work was limited to ascertain the nutritional status of the children, particularly living in poor state like Orissa, and to find out the extent to which their physical development and educational achievement have been affected. In the backdrop of three different places of residence (urban, rural and slum) and various other variables pertaining to home and parental conditions.

1.1 Methods and Techniques

The present study, which was essentially exploratory in nature, involved school going children at three different areas—urban, rural and slum. To find out developmental status and educational achievement, the researcher selected four groups of children from each area, in the age of 6, 7, 8 and 9 years, from both the sexes.

The researcher followed questionnaire methods for ascertaining the physical development status and evaluating the students' potentialities. And one interview schedule was used for collection of information regarding the nutritional intakes and family background. The researcher used anthropometric indicators such as height (cms.), weight (kgs.), mac (cms.), chest circumference (cms.), head circumference (cms.), skinfold thickness over tricep (mm); level of haemoglobin (gm per cent) and clinical examination of signs of deficiency diseases. To measure the academic potentialities Teacher Evaluating Inventory and Academic Achievement methods were used. For the assessment of nutritional status calorie values of food consumed by the children for three consecutive days and for the data regarding home background parents of the children were interviewed using a structured schedule.

Data thus gathered were treated, scored and analysed using standard statistical procedures which helped in objective interpretation of the findings. Group means were first computed to observe gross differences in various indices. Correlation coefficients were computed to establish and ascertain the relationship between groups across various dimensions. Finally, analysis of variances was done on a few important dimensions to further examine the interactional pattern between background variables and the development of the child; and significant difference between different groups of subjects, across area and age dimensions.

1.2 Analysis and Interpretation of Data

The data pertaining to various factors affecting nutritional status, physical development and educational achievement in three different localities, across four age groups and both the sexes were analysed to find out mean differences, inter-correlations between various factors and degree of their variance.

Nutritional Status

Nutritional status of urban children was found to be better (1462.87) than that of rural children (1358.22). Slum children had poorer nutritional status (1313.08) than children of both the rural and urban areas. Children of each age group also showed a gradual increase in calorie intake (6 years—1232.19, 7 years—1337.77, 8 years—1420.13 and 9 years 1501.75) with the advancing age. And so far as sex was concerned, boys had a little more calorie intake (1389.01) than the girls (1356.9).

Level of education was found to be one of the important factors responsible for nutritional status of the child as found from its positive and significant correlation with nutritional status in case of both the sexes and different age groups except 6 years children.

It was found that the **parents' education** in urban areas was higher (27.97) than rural (11.31) and slum areas (11.27) and that might be leading to better nutritional status of urban children which was proved by its positive correlation.

Impact of **income of the family** on calorie intake of the child was found from its significant correlation in case of three areas, four age groups and both the sexes.

Monthly income of the urban families was higher (Rs. 1838.74 p.) than rural (Rs. 758.47 p.) and slum areas (Rs. 438.56 p.) which might be responsible for better nutritional status of urban children than rural and slum children.

Size of the family including children was proved to be a causative factor of affecting nutritional status. As found from the interpretation of the result, its correlation with nutritional status was found to be inverse and significant in most of the cases.

In urban families, number of children was less (2.7) than rural (3.69) and slum (3.76) families. Members in urban families were more (5.47) than rural families (4.9) but higher in slum families (6.34). It might be due to better economic condition and parents' education, food intake of urban children did not get affected as was the case for rural and slum children.

Physical Development

With regard to growth and development, urban children were of better health, status than their rural and slum counterparts, and rural children had better physical development than slum children. Also in case of different age groups, the results showed that each advancing age had better growth and development. However, boys were ahead of girls.

With regard to height, urban children were better (123.55 cms.) than rural children (117.96 cms.) and rural children were better than slum children (116.72 cms.); and for different age groups, 9 years children (128.37 cms.) were found to be the tallest. Height of 8 years children (122 cms.) was more than 7 years children (116.91 cms.) and 7 years children were taller than 6 years children (110.39 cms.). In case of both the sexes girls' height (118.62 cms.) was lower than that of boys' height (119.96 cms.).

Weight of the urban children (21.68 kgs.) was better than rural children (19.37 kgs.), and slum children (18.44 kgs.) had poorer weight than rural children. It was also found that amongst different age groups 9 years children (23.27 kgs.) had more weight gain than other age group of children. 6 years children had lowest weight (16.38 kgs.) gain than others, 7 years children's weight (18.96 kgs.) was lower than that of 8 years children (20.72 kgs.). Girls' weight (19.42 kgs.) was lesser than that of boys' (20.23 kgs.).

Mid-upper arm circumference (mac) was found lowest in case of slum children (14.36 cms.), whereas mac of urban children was highest (15.65 cms.) than rural children (14.98 cms.). Mac for 9 year children (15.61 cms.) was more than others; 8 years of children (15.05 cms.) had better mac than 7 years (15.03 cms.) and 6 years (14.32 cms.). However, in respect to both the sexes, girls' mac (15.20 cms.) was lesser than boys' mac (15.39 cms.).

Urban children's chest circumference was more (55.36 cms.) than rural (55.22 cms.) and slum children (54.40 cms.); 6 years children had the lowest (52.59 cms.) chest circumference. The chest circumference of 9 years children was the highest (57.67 cms.). The 7 years children's chest circumference (54.01 cms.) was lower than that of 8 years of children (55.57 cms.). Boys' chest circumference (55.21 cms.) was better than girls' (54.71 cms.).

Head circumference of urban children (50.11 cms.) was better than rural (49.72 cms.) and slum children (49.73 cms.). With regard to age groups upper age groups' head circumference was higher than that of lower age groups of children (9 years—50.82 cms., 8 years—49.83 cms., 7 years—49.75 cms. and 6 years—49.02 cms.).

Girls' head circumference (49.37 cms.) was lower than that of boys' (50.34 cms.).

Slum children's tricep (6.16 mms.) was the lowest compared to other two areas, whereas urban children's tricep (9.91 mms.) was better than that of rural children (7.45 mms.). Amongst different age groups 9 year children's tricep (7.5 mms.) was higher than other age groups. Children of 8 years had better tricep (8.42 mms.) than 7 years (7.45 cms.) and 6 years children had the lowest tricep (6.01 mms.). Tricep of boys (7.37 mms.) was less than that of girls (7.40 mms.).

Deficiency diseases in slum children were more (1.87) than rural (1.06) and urban children (0.21). In respect to age groups, in 6 years children deficiency diseases (1.20) were more than 7 years (1.07), 8 years (0.96) and 9 years (0.97) of children. However, girls were suffering from less (0.97) number of deficiency diseases as compared to boys (1.13).

Haemoglobin level of slum children was the lowest (81.01 per cent). It was also lower in rural children (86.69 per cent) as compared to urban children (89.45 per cent). Across age groups, 8 years children had highest (87.14 per cent) haemoglobin level followed by 9 years (85.33 per cent), 7 years (85.89 per cent) and 6 years (84.67 per cent).

Physical development of children was also found to be affected by their food intake as was evident from their significant correlations in almost all the cases.

Most of the indicators of physical development were affected by the parents' education, and in some cases their correlation coefficients were significant.

In most of the cases also, income of the family was related to physical development showing its effect on physical growth and development.

Further, size of the family was found to affect the health status of the children as found from their correlations which were significant in some cases.

Educational Achievement

So far as educational achievement was concerned urban children had the highest (TEI—47.80; AA—51.60) achievement when compared to rural (TEI—33.96; AA—35.03) and slum (TEI—28.74;

AA—28.33) children, and rural children's achievement was better than slum children.

Amongst different age groups educational achievement was better in 7, 8 and 9 years children (7 years-TEI—36.13, AA—37.34; 8 years-TEI—35.22, AA—37.17; 9 years-TEI—36.51, AA—39.76) than 6 years of children's educational achievement which was lowest (TEI—32.22, AA—31.77).

Boys' achievement was found to be better (TEI—36.13, AA—37.42) than that of girls' (TEI—33.91, AA—35.60).

The present study revealed that children having better nutritional status were rated highly and found to be securing the highest marks than the children having poor nutritional status as proved in case of children of three areas where urban children's educational achievement was better than the children of other two areas.

Parents' level of education also influenced the educational achievement of the children as found from its significant correlations in almost all the cases.

Economic condition of the family also determined the educational achievement of the children as was evident from its positive and significant correlations in most of the cases.

Educational achievement was also influenced by number of children and members in the family which was proved by their inverse and significant correlations in most of the cases.

Parental interest in the study of the children was also an influencing factor which showed a significant correlation with educational achievement in all the cases except for rural and slum children.

Educational achievement was also affected by the physical facilities provided at home for study, as was proved from their significant and positive correlations.

Children's educational provisions at homes also affected their achievement in academic career as revealed from their significant correlation.

Lastly, from the interpretation of educational achievement and physical development it was found that physical development had its effect on the educational achievement of the children as reported in most of the cases where there were significant correlations. This proved that children of better health status were doing well in their educational achievement.

In order to compare groups across age and area dimensions, and to establish the nature of relationship ANOVA was done for five important variables. For **calorie intake**, the differences between sub-groups corresponding to age were found to be very highly significant, and for other four variables the differences were non-significant. Thus it was found that the children belonging to four different age groups were very well comparable, but there was little or no difference in respect of four major background variables, viz., parents' education, family income, number of children, and number of members in the family.

Comparison across area of living (urban, rural and slum), Inter-group differences were found to be very largely significant, for all the five variables mentioned above. Hence, the four different age groups of children were different from each other in any particular area from the other two. In other words, children of three areas greatly varied both in calorie intake, and for their background variables. However, within group differences were marginal and non-significant in most cases.

2. RECOMMENDATIONS

On the basis of the above findings, the following recommendations are proposed to the Government and concerned agencies and organisations for ameliorating the existing conditions.

(a) Since none of the children was getting adequate food in their daily intake as per the ICMR recommendations as was confirmed by the findings of this study, the state and other voluntary agencies need to plan and implement development programmes for improving the nutritional status of the children in general, and those of the poor sections in particular.

(b) As the parents' education has proved to be of immense importance in improving the nutritional status, physical growth as well as development and educational performance of the children, there ought to be multipronged efforts by the state and other agencies to educate the people, especially in rural and slum areas, regarding the nutritional requirements of the children and its importance with regard to their growth and development as well as educational achievement. It is proposed that effective ways of educating the parents, who are out of formal education, could be through extension education programmes.

(c) Since economic conditions of the family has much significance in maintaining nutritional status of the children, the government *vis-a-vis* voluntary agencies may take adequate steps towards improvement of the economic status of the communities.

(d) As has been found, size of the family has negative correlation with the nutritional status, ultimately affecting the growth and development and educational achievement of the children, the family planning/welfare programmes being implemented at present should be reviewed and made more effective and attractive in order that objectives of child welfare can be actualized.

(e) Since physical development and educational achievement of the children were hampered due to lack of sufficient food and nutrition, the current school mid-day meal programme should be more effectively planned and strengthened.

(f) As educational achievement was found to have been influenced by physical development there should be a systematic and continuous school health programme, comprising of the following measures, to achieve physical, mental and social well-being of the children.

  (i) Provision for medical check up of the children,
  (ii) Remedial measures and follow-up,
  (iii) Preventive measures,
  (iv) Nutrition services,
  (v) Maintenance of mental health,
  (vi) Nutrition and health education, and
  (vii) Maintenance of health records.

(g) Further provisions may be made for good and healthy school living which includes good hygienic environment of the school with cleanliness in and out of the school premises; adequate space in the class room according to number of students; proper ventilation and light conditions; hygienically suitable drinking water provision; and facilities for sanitary latrines, etc.

3. FUTURE RESEARCH IMPLICATIONS

On the basis of the present study, and taking into consideration its limitations, the following suggestions are made which may be considered by researcher in future:

(a) Since the difference between different areas have been established through this present study, for calorie intake and other variables affecting nutritional status, physical development and academic achievement; and within group differences were marginal and non-significant; more area specific studies are required to be conducted, in order that micro-level differences pertaining to calorie intake and other associated variables can be critically examined.

(b) Though the present study had taken into consideration four different age groups, in order to highlight upon a developmental sequence and the differences thereof, the range was not perhaps adequate. Therefore, it calls for a larger range of age to be examined in respect of nutritional status, physical development and academic achievement, in order to establish further facts/variables associated with the growing child.

(c) While the present researcher conducted her study on acceptable small samples and found that the outcomes of the study were not at all affected by the size of the sample; she strongly feels that future studies should be based on larger samples, preferably selected by a stratified random sampling technique, so as to acquire more flexibility in drawing sub-samples for critical analysis.

13

Creativity: A Study of Children with Different Disabilities

ANJALI PATTANAIK

1. INTRODUCTION

Creativity is a special mental process through which an individual receives in his own ways and organises the experiences in an unusual manner with some meanings and senses. This is a unique mental process. Some persons are born with exceptional potentialities for creativities, and in some others it can be developed by giving them proper opportunities. Albert Einestein has said that "Imagination is more powerful than knowledge. The children are born with unlimited imaginations. Hence, they have ability to create untold number of fanciful illusions from birth until a child enters educational system. This creative ability increases through imagination, ingenuity and curiosity."

Hence, creativity is responsible for one's success in his different sphere of activities. Guilford has said: "Creativity is a magic word and it catches our immediate attention" (Krishnan, 1993). So this magic word 'creativity' can be promoted when a conductive and supportive environment would be provided. Thus, in the present context, it is worth an attempt to explore the creative thinking capacities in school children born and brought up in different settings with different physical capacities.

While considering the physical capabilities the researcher has attempted to find out the creative potentialities in the disabled as well as the normal group of pupils. So far as the term 'disabled' is concerned it is objectively defined as impairment of structure and functions. A disabled person means he is only handicapped which is partial but can compete with restricted range. So, this is an attempt to give a cross-analytic report on the level of creative abilities in children of different capabilities pertaining to their physical, mental and socio-cultural environment.

2. OBJECTIVES

- To assess the level of creative thinking abilities of visually impaired (VI), hearing impaired (HI) and normal pupils.
- To draw a comparative conclusion across all the three categories of examples.
- To analyse the percentile range of creative thinking across various selected sample groups.

3. DESIGN

The researcher adopted random sampling technique for the present study where 90 students were drawn in the age group of 12 to 13 years from both the sexes. The respondents were selected in equal number 30 from each category with a view to undertake a comparative analysis pertaining to creative thinking of visually impaired (VI), hearing impaired (HI) and normal children (N). The study used Baqer Mehdi's Verbal Test of creative thinking and a self-developed socio-economic status scale and school environment questionnaire.

The tests were administered to the sample giving sufficient information regarding the test materials. In case of visually impaired samples, the teachers had to write the responses. Each item pertaining to fluency, flexibility and originality was scored. The raw scores were converted into T-scores and were added up to get the total scores for each item. Finally, the mean, standard deviations of all the T-scores and t-ratios were calculated for the purpose of statistical interpretation.

4. RESULTS AND DISCUSSION

The samples of three categories were compared on the basis of their scores obtained in respect of their fluency, flexibility and originalities. And, to draw a conclusive report on the differences across all the three groups, t-test was done. The results pertaining to above aspects along with the home and school background variables have been discussed under the following sub-headings:

Home-background

Data on family background reveals that in 70 per cent of families of visually impaired (VI) and hearing impaired (HI), fathers are occupied in Government services whereas rest are the businessmen. But, in respect of normal children fathers of all the children are government servants and their income range varies from Rs. 3000 to Rs. 5000. In case of VI and HI samples 63 per cent of them are in the income range of Rs. 1000 to Rs. 3000 and rest belong to the families earning Rs. 3000 to Rs. 5000 per month. Information also reveals that none of the family members of VI and HI groups are having any such physical deformity.

School Environment

Information about school environment depicts that neither the staff structure nor the other infrastructure are according to the needs of the pupils, especially for VI and HI groups. Comparatively normal pupils have better school environment than their counterparts.

Creativity Scores in VI, HI and Normal School Children

Table 13.1 displays the mean, SD and t-ratio of creativity tests across two categories of respondents, i.e. normal and Visually impaired.

It is evident from the result analysis of Table 13.1 that normal samples have scored higher than their Visually Impaired counterparts in respect of fluency, flexibility and originality. Differences are significant at 0.001 level in all the cases.

Results of Table 13.2 depicts the mean scores, SD and t-ratio across normal and hearing impaired samples which prove that the normal groups have higher scores pertaining to all the three aspects

TABLE 13.1

Creativity Scores Across Normal and Visually Impaired Samples

Creativity		*Normal*	*VI*	*t-ratio*
Fluency	mean	49.92	32.28	7.2*
	SD	(10.04)	(8.92)	
Flexibility	mean	43.99	19.23	9.10*
	SD	(11.25)	(9.77)	
Originality	mean	19.19	204	6.35*
	SD	(14.59)	(2.73)	

*Sig. at 0.001 level.

TABLE 13.2

Creativity Scores Across Normal and Hearing Impaired Samples

Creativity		*Normal*	*HI*	*t-ratio*
Fluency	mean	49.92	30.65	8.48*
	SD	(10.04)	(7.42)	
Flexibility	mean	43.99	20.70	10.73*
	SD	(11.25)	(3.92)	
Originality	mean	19.19	2.08	6.38*
	SD	(14.59)	(1.94)	

*Sig. at 0.001 level.

of creative thinking than the hearing impaired groups and the differences are also highly significant at 0.001 level.

So far as creativity of both the disabled group of samples are concerned, the results in Table 13.3 prove that there are very marginal differences across both groups which are not at all significant.

TABLE 13.3

Creativity Scores Across VI and HI Samples

Creativity		*VI*	*HI*	*t-ratio*
Fluency	mean	32.28	30.65	0.772^{NS}
	SD	(8.92)	(7.42)	
Flexibility	mean	19.23	20.70	0.746^{NS}
	SD	(9.77)	(3.92)	
Originality	mean	2.04	2.08	0.066^{NS}
	SD	(2.73)	(1.94)	

NS: Non-significant.

Percentile Range of Creativity

The results enlisted in Table 13.4 and 13.5 reveal percentile ranges of samples pertaining to different fields of creativities, i.e. fluency, flexibility and originality.

Table 13.4 shows that in respect of normal children of 12 years of age a maximum of four number of samples have 70th to 60th percentile of fluency, whereas a maximum of nine have their flexibility level above 99th percentile, but originality is very low, i.e. only three have above 99th and 99th to 95th percentile (in each of the cases).

In case of Visually impaired respondents, fluency level starts from 80th to 70th percentile range and a maximum of four number of samples have fluency level of 10th to 5th percentile. The flexibility level of majority of samples (eight) is below 5th percentile. And, originality is nil in majority of samples (eleven).

So far as the percentile range of HI samples is concerned it is found that a majority samples (four) have secured 20th to 10th and 10th to 5th percentile ranks in respect of their fluencies. A maximum of eight have flexibility in the range of 20th to 10th percentile. And, majority pupils (eight) have no originality at all.

Similarly, the results of percentile range of creativity of 13 years of pupils across three categories of physical capacities are presented in Table 13.5 which can be interpreted as follows.

In case of normal categories of samples it is found that in respect of fluency whole sample group come within the 99th to 70th percentile range. A majority of six have fluency level of 80th to 70th percentile range followed by three pupils within the range of 95th to 90th percentile and two pupils have the highest percentile range, that is, above 99th percentile. Whereas a maximum of six number of pupils have flexibility above 99th percentile followed by four, two and one samples in the percentile range of 95 to 90, 90 to 80 and 70 to 60 respectively. In regard to originality only three samples are above 99th percentile and rest of the samples are almost equally distributed in the range of 95th to below 5th percentile.

While analysing the percentile range of creativity of VI groups it is found that the fluency level starts from 80th to 70th percentile which is secured by a maximum number of samples (four). So far as flexibility is concerned a maximum five number of pupils are below

TABLE 13.4

Distribution of Samples in Respect of their Ranges of Percentile Across Three Categories (12 Years Age) of Samples

Percentile	*Above 99*	*99-95*	*95-90*	*90-80*	*80-70*	*70-60*	*60-50*	*50-40*	*40-30*	*30-20*	*20-10*	*10-5*	*Below 5*	*Nil*	*Total*
Fluency															
Normal	1	–	3	3	3	4	2	1	–	–	–	–	–	–	17
VI	–	–	–	–	1	1	3	–	2	2	1	4	3	–	17
HI	–	–		–	–	–	1	1	2	2	4	4	3	–	17
Flexibility															
Normal	9	–	3	–	4	–	1	–	-	–	–	–	–	–	17
VI	–	–	–	–	3	2	–	1	–	2	1	–	8	–	17
HI	–	–	–	–	–	–	–	1	1	4	8	2	1	–	17
Originality															
Normal	3	3	–	1	–	1	1	1	1	2	1	2	1	–	17
VI	–	–	–	–	–	–	–	–	–	1	1	2.	2	11	17
HI	–	–	–	–	–	–	–	–	–	–	1	1	7	8	17

TABLE 13.5

Distribution of Samples in Respect of their Ranges of Percentile Across Three Categories (13 Years Age) of Samples

Percentile	*Above 99*	*99-95*	*95-90*	*90-80*	*80-70*	*70-60*	*60-50*	*50-40*	*40-30*	*30-20*	*20-10*	*10-5*	*Below 5*	*Nil*	*Total*
Fluency															
Normal	2	1	3	1	6	–	–	–	–	–	–	–	–	–	13
VI	–	–	–	–	4	1	1	–	3	2	1	1	–	–	13
HI	–	–	–	–	1	2	4	4	1	1	–	–	–	–	13
Flexibility															
Normal	6	–	4	2	–	1	–	–	–	–	–	–	–	–	13
VI	–	–	–	1	1	2	–	–	1	–	3	–	5	–	13
HI	–	–	–	–	–	–	2	2	2	3	2	–	2	–	13
Originality															
Normal	3	–	1	–	1	1	–	2	2	1	1	–	1	–	13
VI	–	–	–	–	–	–	–	–	1	–	1	1	5	5	13
HI	–	–	–	–	–	–	–	–	–	1	–	1	9	2	13

the 5th percentile followed by three numbers followed by next highest number of respondents (three only) in the range of 20th to 10th percentile. The originality of visually impaired group starts from 40th-30th percentile range (only one) and a maximum of five samples are below the 5th percentile and five samples have no originality at all.

Interpretation of percentile range of HI show that the fluency level starts from 80th to 70th percentile (only one) followed by 70th to 60th percentile (two), 60th to 50th percentile (four), 50th to 40th percentile (four), 40th to 30th percentile (one) and 30th to 20th percentile (one). Fluency of the HI pupil starts from 60th to 50th percentile range (two) and a maximum (three) samples are within the range of 30th to 20th percentile and two of them are below 5th percentile range. Originality level was very marginal with the HI group of pupils (maximum samples below 5th percentile).

CONCLUSION

The following conclusion is drawn from the analysis of the results on creativity:

- Children with normal physical capacities have significantly higher level of creativity than their Visually impaired and hearing Impaired counterparts.
- Socio-Economic Status (SES) may be an associated factor for the development of creativity as reported in earlier studies (Badrinath *et al.*, 1978, 1979; Canty, 1974; Krishnakumari *et al.*, 1986 and Gupta, 1982).
- Not only SES but school environment plays a crucial role in developing creativity.
- So far as age is concerned it has been found that there is a progress increase in creativity with the advancement of age but with a very little deviation which might be a chance factor.

However, an extensive study is needed to draw more authentic conclusion.

REFERENCES

Badrinath, S. and Satyanarayan, S.B. (1978, 1979): Correlates of Creative Thinking of High School Students, *Creative Newsletter*, 7(2), 8(1), 16-23.

Canty, R.E. (1974): The Relationship of Father Absence, Socio-economic Status and other Variables to Creative Abilities in 5th Grade Boys, *Dissertation Abstract International*, 34(7-A), 3981.

Gupta, A.K. and Sharma, S.K. (1982): Creativity, Intelligence and Socio-economic Status, *Indian Education Review,* XVII(1).

Krishnakumari, P., Lalitha and Paramaji, S. (1986): Study of Creative Abilities of Tribal Children in Relation to Their Sex and Socio-economic Status, *Journal of the Institute of Educational Research*, 8(4).

Krishnan, S.S. (1993): A Study of Creativity in Relation to Some Selected Variables, *Journal of Education Research* and *Extension*, 29(3).

14

Effect of Creative Method of Teaching English (CMTE) on Development of Creativity and Achievement—An Experiment on Secondary School Students

PRAMOD KUMAR PRUSTY

1. INTRODUCTION

The study was intended to find out the effectiveness of CMTE on development of creativity and achievement in comparison to the traditional method. Following Randomized Matched Group Pretest Post-test Design, the study was conducted on 140 Class IX students. Creativity and achievement tests were administered before and after the intervention which extended for about eight weeks. Analysis of data reported the superiority of CMTE over traditional method in developing creativity and achievement of students.

2. RATIONALE

Creativity is a highly valued ability of the civilization. It is the foremost responsibility of educational scientists to develop such human resource for multidimensional socio-individual well-being. A well-prepared creative method fertilizes the creative ideas of an individual in geometric proportion by opening its sterilizing knots. In this regards Osborn's (1957) "Brainstorming," Gordon's (1961) "Synectics," Tylor's (1961) "PASKA," Suchman's (1962) "Inquiry Training Model" and Bono's (1962) "CoRT" method are some innovations in the history of creativity and training. Wallas (1945) found preparation, incubation, illumination and verification as the sequential steps for developing creative potential. Grossman and Wiseman (1993) reported seven operating principles for enhanced problem solving. Davidow's (1995) five major ecological themes of creative intervention, Passi's (1996) "Strategic Reasoning" and Feuerstein's "Instructional Enrichment" are also some methodological advancements in developing creative talents.

There are studies reporting positive impact of training on development of creative thinking (Torrance, 1961; Prasad, 1979; Katiyar and Jarial, 1985; Singh, 1985; Show and Cliat, 1986; Burns, 1988; Ferrel, 1991; King, 1991; Coleman, 1992; Jampole, 1993; Camp, 1995; Pandian and Rengarajan, 1998). Probably there exist no study exploring the development of creativity through language training besides the study of Nandanpower (1986). Though quite a small number of study are based on effect of training on achievement no study has yet been undertaken to establish relationship among creativity, training and achievement in language studies. Hence, here, the researcher has tried to find out the effectiveness of CMTE on development of creative thinking and achievement in English language of secondary school students.

3. CMTE—ITS PROCEDURE

Creative Method of Teaching English (CMTE), is developed by the researcher as a new method of teaching English language at Secondary level. It is developed in accordance to Gordon's synectic model and is entirely different from any traditional method of teaching English language. Its instructional effect is related to development of general and subject-related creative thinking ability and its nurturant effect is related to development of achievement in English, it also intends to develop specific competencies-relating language skills.

The CMTE follows six steps of teaching a topic in a class. There will be an introduction about the topic and writer, loud reading by teacher, language drilling, comprehension test, asking divergent questions, and application test questions. More stress will be laid on asking divergent questions relating metaphors, analogies, consequences of happenings, unusual uses of things, etc. Comprehension will also be stressed on to provide the students a clear understanding and internalization of new content matters and language skills here, the teacher acts as an initiator and facilitator of divergent discussion. He will encourage active participation of all students of the class by recognizing and appreciating every type of response. Teacher should bear in mind that no response is wrong or vague. Audio-visual teaching aids should be used necessarily and appropriately to make the transaction living and interesting one.

4. OBJECTIVES

1. To find out the effectiveness of CMTE on development of students creative thinking.
2. To find out the effectiveness of CMTE on students' achievement in English.
3. To find out the relationship that exists between increase in achievement and development of creative thinking due to the impact of CMTE.

5. HYPOTHESES

H_{01} There exist no significant difference between experimental and control groups in their—

- (a) Pre-test creativity mean scores
- (b) Post-test creativity mean scores and in their
- (c) Mean gain scores in creativity

H_{02} There exists no significant difference between the experimental and control groups in their—

- (a) Pre-test Mean achievement scores
- (b) Post-test mean achievement scores
- (c) Mean gain scores in achievement

H_{03} There exist no significant relationship between creativity gain scores and achievement gain scores.

6. METHODOLOGY

(a) Design

Basically it was an experimental study and it followed randomized matched groups pre-test post-test design to test the effectiveness of CMTE. Two sections of class IX students were randomly chosen from a secondary school and the sections were assigned with control and experimental groups at random. Pre-test on creativity and intelligence were administered. The control groups were taught through traditional method and the experimental groups were taught through CMTE for eight weeks. After the intervention post-test on creativity and achievement in English were administered.

(b) Sample

The sample of the study consisted of 140 ninth graders reading in two sections of a secondary school. Each section was represented with 70 students reading in class IX and were matched on their intelligence, age and creative thinking abilities.

(c) Tools

Verbal Test on Creative Thinking by Mehdi (1973) was used to collect data on students' creative thinking ability. Intelligence of students was measured by Tondon's Group Test of Intelligence (2/70). Marks scored by students in English in Class VIII annual examination and Class IX half-yearly examination were added with the scores of Listening-Speaking English Achievement test I and II to get the pre-test and post-test achievement scores respectively. Listening-Speaking English Achievement test I and II were constructed by the investigator himself since the classroom tests were specifically designed to measure students reading and writing skills in English.

(d) Statistical Techniques

Coefficients of correlation and 't' test were used to test the significance of relationship and difference between different variables used in the study.

7. RESULTS AND DISCUSSION

Data presented in Table 14.1 stated that at pre-test stage no significant difference was found between experimental and control groups in their creativity mean scores (t = 0.4244, P > 0.01). After intervention, the post-test creativity scores showed a significant difference between experimental and control groups in their creativity mean scores (t = 9.7779, P < 0.01). The third sub-hypothesis is also refuted since the difference in mean gain scores in creativity test is found to be significant (t = 15.4309, P < 0.01). In post-test and in mean creativity gain scores, the experimental group is found to have performed better. It may be reasoned that CMTE is proved more effective than the traditional method in developing students' creative thinking ability. The analysed data accepts the H_{01}(a) and refutes H_{01}(b) and H_{01}(c). Such findings confirm that CMTE is an effective method of increasing creative talents of secondary school students.

TABLE 14.1

Means, SDs and 't' Values in Creativity of Control and Experimental Groups Relating Different Stages of Experiment

Stages of Experiment	*Groups*	*N*	*Mean*	*SD*	*t*	*Level*
PRE-TEST	Control Group	70	111.8568	27.0785	0.4244	P > 0.05
	Experimental Group	70	114.0692	34.0261		
POST-TEST	Control Group	70	117.0713	29.9690	9.7779	P < 0.01
	Experimental Group	70	176.3567	40.9297		
GAIN SCORE	Control Group	70	3.8444	9.1726	15.4309	P < 0.01
	Experimental Group	70	65.0712	31.9048		

Table 14.2 presented the data relating three sub-hypotheses of H_{02}. An overall analysis showed that the difference in mean achievement scores of control group and experimental group which was found significant at pre-test stage (t = 2.1912, P < 0.05) was not visible at post-test stage (t = 1.2481, P > 0.05). But a striking feature was observed when the mean values of those groups were compared at pre-post test stages comparatively. At pre-test stage the control group was at higher level in its mean value (m = 37.7856) than the

TABLE 14.2

Means, SDs and 't' Values in Creativity of Control and Experimental Groups Relating Different Stages of Experiment

Stages of Experiment	*Groups*	*N*	*Mean*	*SD*	*t*	*Level*
PRE-TEST	Control Group	70	37.7856	14.0057	2.1912	P > 0.05
	Experimental Group	70	32.6430	13.7631		
POST-TEST	Control Group	70	39.2854	13.8919	1.2481	P > 0.05
	Experimental Group	70	42.1431	3.1902		
GAIN SCORE	Control Group	70	1.1142	3.8809	11.9509	P > 0.01
	Experimental Group	70	10.3320	5.1574		

experimental group (m = 32.6430). But at post-test stage, although the experimental group was at higher level in its mean value (m = 42.1431) than the control group (m = 39.2851), the difference was not found statistically significant. A critical view on the range of increment of achievement score from pre-test stage to post-test stage kept the experimental group at higher order with a range of mean value increment of 9.5001 than the control group, the range of mean value increment of which was 1.4998. From this analysis, it may be proved that the experimental group had achieved significantly more in mean achievement test scores in English than of control group, although the difference at post-test stage was found non-significant. Such finding is substantiated by the third sub-hypothesis of H_{02} which found significant difference ($t = 11.9509$, $P < 0.01$) in mean gain scores in achievement test scores of control and experimental groups. Such spectacular increase in achievement scores in English of experimental group was obviously due to the impact of CMTE and the slight increment in achievement scores of control group may be due to the impact of maturation, time and interaction among participants. Hence it is experimentally proved that the CMTE is more effective in increasing students' achievement in English than the traditional method.

Table 14.3 revealed a moderate and positive coefficient of correlation ($r = 0.5332$) between gain scores in creativity and achievement. Further the 't' value proved its significance at 0.01 level of confidence ($t = 9.1765$, $P < 0.01$). Hence the third hypothesis H_{03}

TABLE 14.3
Significance of Relationship in Gain Scores in Creativity and Achievement

Variables	*N*	*r*	*t*	*Level*
Gain scores in creativity Gain scores in Achievement	140	0.5332	9.1675	P < 0.01

which stated that creativity gain score is not significantly correlated with achievement gain score is rejected. It is confirmed that growth of creativity as a result of CMTE is moderately and significantly related to growth of students' achievement.

8. MAJOR FINDINGS

1. The CMTE is more effective than traditional method of teaching English in developing creative thinking.
2. The CMTE is more beneficial than traditional methods of teaching English in improving students' achievement in English.
3. There exist significant moderate relationship between the growth of students' creative thinking ability and achievement in English as a result of CMTE.

REFERENCES

Bruce, J. and Well, M. (4th edn.) (1992): *Models of Teaching*, New Delhi, Prentice-Hall of India Pvt. Ltd.

Buch, M.B. (ed.) (1993): Fourth All India Survey on Educational Research, New Delhi, NCERT.

Burns, M.T. (1988): Music as a Tool for Enhancing Creativity, *The Journal of Creative Behaviour*, 22(1), 62-69.

Davidow, J.R. (1995): The Aims of Intervention, *Psychology in the Schools*, 31(9), 305-308.

Drevadahl, E.J. (1962): Educational Etiology of Creativity, *The Gifted Child Quarterly*, 6, 91-94.

Feldhusen, J.F. and Clinkenbeard, P.R. (1986): Creativity and Instructional Materials: A Review of Research, *The Journal of Creative Behaviour*, 20(3), 153-81.

Gehlbach, R.D. (1987): Creativity and Instruction—The Problem of Task Design, *The Journal of Creative Behaviour*, 21(1), 34-47.

Gelade, G. (1995): Creative Style and Divergent Production. *The Journal of Creative Behaviour*, 26(1), 36-53.

Pandian, C.C. and Rengarajan, V. (1998): Effectiveness of the ITM an Autonomy in Learning and Creativity of Students, *Experiments in Education*, XXVI (7), 127-29.

Raina, M.K. (1980): Creativity Research International Perspective, New Delhi, NCERT.

Torrance, E.P. (1965): *Rewarding Creative Behaviour: Experiment in Classroom Creativity*, New Jersey, Prentice-Hall Inc.

Torrance, E.P. and Myers, R.E. (1970): *Creative Learning and Teaching*, New York: Dodd, Mead & Co.

Torrance, E.P. and Safter, H.T. (1986): Are Children Becoming More Creative?, *The Journal of Creative Behaviour*, 20(1), 01.13.

15

Effect of Creative Method of Teaching English on Development of Creative Thinking of Secondary School Students

PRAMOD KUMAR PRUSTY

1. THE RATIONALE

Creativity has many-sided connotation. Some accept it as a psychological characteristic which generate reflective thinking (Torrance), while others accept such hemispheric function as divergent thinking (Garrett and Guilford). Looking the contribution of social factors in generating individual's creativity Arieti (1970) described it as a bio-social element. Describing the magnitude of product of creativity Edward de Bono (1968) ascribed it as lateral thinking and Maslow and Elliot (1970) defined it as whole brain synchronization. Creativity, in an amalgamated thought, is accepted as a process, a power and a product. Sometime it expressed from unconscious state of individual as an imagination or abstract thinking and get the concrete shape in some creative product.

As a major personality attribute creativity has relationship with intelligence, achievement, socio-economic status (SES), sex, etc. Researchers contradict in their findings relating such relationships. But all coincide on the effect of training on development of creativity of learners. Osborn's "Brain Storming." Gordon's Synectics, Bono's CoRT Method, Loznov's 'Super learning Technique' are some milestones in developing creative thinking through training. Pradhan (1990) also reported positive impact of training in developing creativity in Science. Besides Science, teaching of language is also regarded as a saturated ground of developing creative thinking among students. As such area has received little attention from the researchers, it was thought worthwhile to undertake a study to know the effect of Creative Method of Teaching English on development of creativity.

2. STATEMENT OF PROBLEM

"Effect of Creative Method of Teaching English (CMTE) on Development of Creative Thinking of Secondary School Students."

3. OBJECTIVES OF THE STUDY

1. To find out the effect of CMTE on creative thinking.
2. To find out the effect of CMTE on achievement in language skills in English.
3. To find out relation between intelligence and development of creativity through CMTE.
4. To find out the relationship between change in creativity and change in achievement as a result of CMTE.

4. HYPOTHESES

H_{01} (a) There exist no significant difference between experimental group and control group at pre-test stage in their creative thinking scores.

(b) There exist no significant difference between experimental and control group at post-test stage in their creative thinking scores.

(c) There exist no significant difference between experimental and control groups in their mean creativity gain scores.

H_{02} There exist no significant difference between control group and experimental group in their—

(a) Pre-test achievement scores in English.

(b) Post-test achievement scores in English.

(c) Achievement gain scores in English.

H03 There exist no significant difference in creative thinking scores of high-intelligence and low-intelligence group of control group and experimental group at—

(a) Pre-test stage.

(b) Post-test stage.

(c) There exist no significant difference in gain scores in creative thinking of high intelligence and low intelligence group of experimental and control groups.

H04 (a) There exist no significant difference in mean creative thinking gain scores of high-achievers and low-achievers of experimental group.

(b) There exist no significant difference between the high-creatives and low-creatives in their achievement gain scores of experimental group.

(c) There exist no relation between gain scores in creative thinking and achievement of experimental group.

5. OPERATIONAL DEFINITIONS

Creative Method of Teaching English was developed by the investigator as a method of teaching English. CMTE has the following aims—

1. To develop creative abilities—fluency, flexibility, originality and elaboration.
2. To develop achievement of students in English language skills—listening, speaking, reading and writing.

Steps of CMTE

It has six steps:

Step	*Work*	*Time allotted*
1.	Introduction about the topic and author	3 minutes
2.	Model loud reading by teacher (with silent reading of students)	7 minutes
3.	Drilling of language	5 minutes
4.	Comprehension Test	6 minutes
5.	Asking Divergent Questions	14 minutes
6.	Application Questions and Home Test	5 minutes
	Total	40 minutes

Creative thinking was that which was measured by Mehdi's Verbal Test on creative thinking which includes fluency, flexibility and originality.

Secondary School includes Class IX and X, i.e. lower secondary level.

6. SCOPE AND DELIMITATION

The study was delimited to—

(a) ascertain effect of CMTE on creative thinking,
(b) the students of Class IX, and
(c) urban secondary schools.

7. METHODS OF STUDY

The study followed the experimental design. Two designs were followed in the study. In pilot study design the CMTE was first tried out. One group pre-test post-test design was followed. The result showed a significant difference ($t = 6.0518, P > 0.01$). In the experimental design Randomized Matched Groups pre-test post-test design was followed. At pre-test stage tests on creative thinking, intelligence, SES and achievement were administered. Then the control group was taught by traditional method and the experimental group was taught by CMTE for two months by the investigator himself. Then the post-test on creative thinking and achievement were administered.

8. SAMPLE

A stratified random sample was selected.

Total Students	*Appeared in tests*	*Sample taken*
222	176	140

Groups were matched on creativity and intelligence.

Tools

Four tools were used.

Variables	*Tools*
Intelligence	Verbal Group Test of Intelligence (2/70) of R.K. Tondon
Creative thinking	Verbal test of Creative Thinking by Baquer Mehdi
SES	SES scale (Urban, Form B) by Kuppuswamy
Achievement	Annual and Half-yearly Examination marks in English.

9. MAJOR FINDINGS

1. Creative Method of Teaching English (CMTE) proved to be effective in developing creative thinking among students.
2. CMTE was also found to be effective in increasing students' achievement in English language.
3. High-intelligent students profit more than their low-intelligent counterparts from the CMTE.
4. Both creativity and achievement grow moderately as an impact of CMTE.

10. IMPLICATIONS FOR FURTHER RESEARCH

1. This method can also be used in teaching other subjects with some alteration.
2. CMTE can also be experimented in different levels of education.
3. Audio-visual aids may be incorporated in CMTE to know the effectiveness.

16

Study of the Efficacy of the Field Trip in the Teaching of Social Studies in Primary Schools

JAGANNATH MOHANTY

1. NEED OF THE PROJECT

The syllabus for Primary Schools in Orissa enunciates, "This Programme of Social Studies is quite different from all other Programmes in the syllabus in that it is not so much learning of facts, like such other disciplines as Mathematics, Literature and Grammar and Science. It is indeed not any sort of information stuffed into the child's mind, but the very formation of his character, his attitude to life-situations and personal habits. Success of this programme may be taken as the education of the child much more than knowledge of the 3 R's (Reading, Writing and Arithmetic). It wants drilling of the child in the virtues of citizenship, in civilized ways of living and in the awareness of group obligations and loyalties." However, in practice, it is found that Social Studies is taught in the way only to impart certain facts to be crammed by the pupils for passing the examination.

The important objectives of teaching Social Studies such as inculcation of the civic virtues, formation of civic habits, understanding the physical and social environment in the life-situations and training in citizenship, are not adequately realized through conventional methods, like lecturing or textbook reading, etc. It is felt essential to provide learning experiences through the study and exploration of the immediate and local surroundings. Hence, the use of Field trips as and when possible, with a view to supplementing the theoretical knowledge with practical experiences, is immensely important. Therefore, it is advisable to study the efficacy of the field trip through experiment and to ascertain its real significance for achieving the objectives of the social Studies.

2. SCOPE OF THE STUDY

The following come under the scope of this mini-experiment:

1. Only students of class III were included in the experiment.
2. Three days only were utilized for the experiment.
3. Only one topic in Social Studies was dealt in the experiment.

3. METHODS OF STUDY

The class III of the Government U.P. Schools, Unit-I, Bhubaneshwar was taken for experimentation. It was felt that experiment would be conducted under the existing set-up without creating any problems of dislocation or regrouping. Since class III has 4 sections, it was a problem to select two equal sections—equal approximately in merit and achievement of the students. For this purpose, the results in the last Annual Examination, 1972 were taken into consideration. General achievement of the students appeared was taken as criteria for grouping the students for experimentation.

Table 16.1 will show the basis for selection of the Sections B and C from among the four Sections.

It will be found from the above data that Sections B and C will be approximately comparable in achievement as well as in merit.

After selecting thte sections, Sections A and B were taken as Control and Experimental groups respectively. It was decided that teaching would be made, separately in both the groups in traditional methods with necessary teaching aids and only the students of the Experimental group would be taken on a field trip in order to give them direct experiences.

In the syllabus for class III there is a topic "Post Office," which is taught haphazardly and no attempts are made to give students proper insight and experience in the actual life situations.

TABLE 16.1

Comparison of the Sections for Selecting Approximately two Sections

Range of the percentage of marks Secured	*Section A*	*Two Sections*		*Section D*
		Section B	*Section C*	
1-20	12	6	7	4
21-40	14	23	17	22
41-60	5	2	6	6
61-80	–	1	1	–
81-100	–	–	–	–
Total	31	32	31	32

It was also thought proper to entrust the same teacher for teaching both the groups. So the experimenter himself took up that responsibility and taught both the sections. The topic was divided into two units: (1) Functions of the Post Office, and (ii) Organisation of the Post Office. Thus, excepting one variable, i.e. field trip, all other variables were the same for both the groups.

Both the groups were taught in two units about the Post Office separately in the narration-*cum*-discussion methods with adequate use of real objects and illustrations. Lastly, the students of the experimental group were taken to the Capital Post Office and introduced to the Staff-members there. The students were explained about each and every object and activity in the Post Office. They evinced keen interest and the persons dealing with different activities there explained to them with so much interest. Even the participants shared the experiences of the students and helped clarifying their own concepts as well as of their students.

3. PARTICIPANTS (HEAD-TEACHERS)

Lastly the participants, who are all experienced head-teachers of Primary Schools from different parts of the State, were requested to give their suggestions for evaluating the achievements of the students reading in Control and Experimental group. It was decided that students should be orally tested, as students had not yet acquired the skills for writing down their answers. A set of questions was prepared and finalised in the joint sitting of participants and the experimenter.

The participants were divided into 5 groups and each group was given a set of questions for collecting the oral responses from the students. Attempts were made to create rapport between the examiners and the students. Some questions had to be written on the blackboards for convenience of the students to give answers.

Each group was asked to administer the test on about the same number of students both from the experimental and Control Groups for counteracting the subjective elements. The experimenter kept himself aloof from the evaluation and was supervising the groups with a view to maintaining the same standard and uniformity in following the rules and procedure of examining the students. Hence, all possible precautions were taken for safeguarding objectivity, reliability and validity of the tests in evaluating the performances of the students.

4. INTERPRETATION OF THE DATA

The scores so collected have been tabulated as follows:

TABLE 16.2

Comparison of Scores Secured by the Students of Control and Experimental Groups Appeared in the Test

Frequency of the Scores Secured	*Control Group*		*Experimental Group*	
	Number	*Percentage*	*Number*	*Percentage*
1-20	3	10	2	8
21-40	12	40	6	24
41-60	6	20	6	24
61-80	7	23	9	36
81-100	2	7	2	8
Total	30	100	25	100

It is evident from the scores secured that the students of the Experimental group have fared better than those of the Control group. The average percentage of scores in the Experimental group is 55, whereas that in the Control group is 49 only. Similarly, the larger group of students, i.e. 40 per cent of students in the Control section have secured scores in the frequency of 21-40, whereas the larger group of students in the Experimental Section have secured scores in the frequency 61-80. It is also to be found that majority of students in the Experimental group have secured comparatively higher scores. But the majority of students in the Control group have secured lower one. Moreover, it is the general feeling of the participants that the practical or first-hand experiments of the Experimental group gained through actually visiting the Post Office and its various sections, talking to the persons engaged in the different functions of the Post Office and, so on, have made the teaching more effective and meaningful. Thus the participants became convinced of the efficacy of field-trip.

5. CONCLUSION

The objectives of Social Studies are better realized, through providing learning experience in different real contexts. The stereotyped method of teaching Social Studies by mere lecturing or reading from the textbooks in the class not only makes Social Studies dull and boring, but also it fails to make pupils realize the true worth of Social Studies. Especially in the Primary classes, students should be provided with ample facilities of gaining direct experiences through field-trip, interview, dramatisation and so on. Unless we make the teaching of Social Studies interesting and relevant to the reality, the students are not benefitted by it. Hence, teachers should supplement as well as enliven the learning experiences of students in Social Studies by arranging field-trips as far as possible. This mini-experiment is just a fact-finding study and a small action research project to ascertain the efficacy of field-trip in the teaching of Social Studies.

17

Science Education Programme in Secondary Schools

RAJASHREE MOHANTY

1. INTRODUCTION

We are living now in an age rapid changes. Science is playing a dominant role in bringing about these changes. It is no exaggeration to say that at present science influences every field of our activities. The technological advances have explored and multiplied the possibilities of affording sustenance and comforts to human beings. Thus from cradle to grave scientific discoveries and inventions have inextricably woven themselves into the fabric of human existence.

Now, it becomes very essential to be in possession of some basic knowledge of science on the part of each individual. One encounters with innumerable events and objects regularly in his/her social and natural environment which regulates the daily life. To understand these a bit manipulation of the basic knowledge in science is the prerequisite. The water we drink, the air we breath, the food we take, the shelter we undertake, the commodities we transport, the clothing we wear and in all sphere our life we face a lot of problems. To get solution to these we are bound to take assistance of knowledge which has got strong basis of science. Considering these aspects, science has been included in the school curriculum even from elementary stage so as to make human being an efficient one. In new pattern of 10 + 2 Education System, science is one of the major subjects to be taught in secondary schools. Hence, the school as well as the science teacher have immense responsibility in the changed situation particularly in teaching of science. It is proper to know the perspectives and problems of science education in our State, i.e. the state of Orissa. Hence, it was attempted to have "A Critical Appraisal of Science Education at the Secondary Level."

2. OBJECTIVES OF THE STUDY

The objectives of the study were as detailed:

(i) To make a survey of the existing provisions and facilities available for organising Science Education programme in secondary schools of Orissa.
(ii) To find out the lacunae and deficiencies in the Science Education programme which is in vogue to meet the requirement of Secondary School students.
(iii) To identify the strengths and good practices in the system.
(iv) To pool the views and suggestions of the Teachers, Supervisors and Educationist in order to suggest remedies for removal of the deficiencies.
(v) To recommend the measures for improving the Science Education programme in Secondary Schools.

3. DELIMITATION OF THE STUDY

The problem which is selected to be investigated is quite a vast one which requires enormous time, energy and financial support. Keeping these constraints in view the study has been delimited to the following:

- All the sample schools were either affiliated to Board of Secondary Education, Orissa, Cuttack or Central Board of Secondary Education, New Delhi.
- The Boys' schools, Girls' schools and Co-education schools of urban and rural background are included in the study.
- The study is restricted only to Science Education Programme conducted in the secondary schools of Orissa by the year 1995.

4. METHODOLOGY

4.1 Sample

The schools were selected on the basis of stratified random sampling. The sample thus was the systematic representation of all the Secondary Schools spread over nine districts of Orissa such as Balasore, Bolangir, Bargarh, Cuttack, Ganjam, Khurda, Puri, Sundargarh and Sambalpur. The distribution of sample has been indicated in Fig. 17.1.

However, all 12 CBSE schools were situated in urban areas and all were co-educational type. English is the medium of instruction in CBSE schools whereas Oriya, the regional language is the medium of instruction in BSE affiliated schools.

Data were collected from different personnel like Headmasters, Science Teachers and Students of higher classes of the schools,

FIG. 17.1

Showing Distribution of Sample Schools

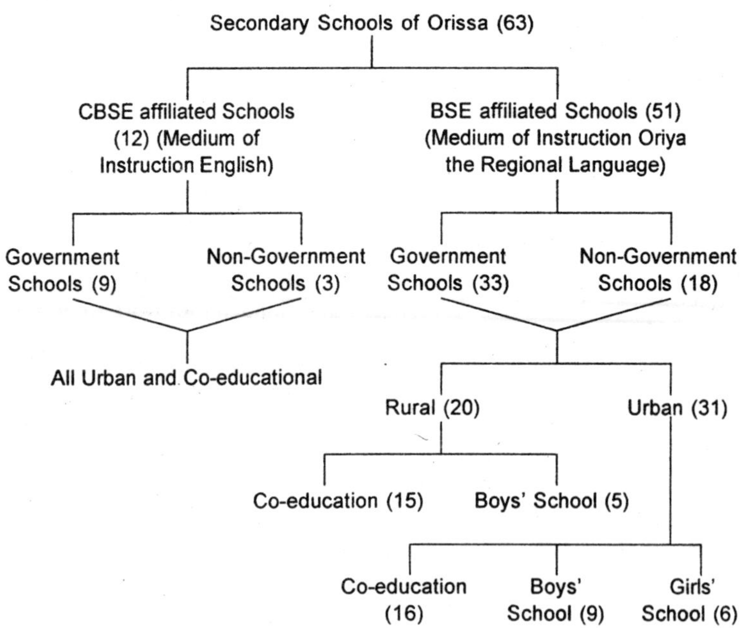

Science Supervisors working in the office of the Circle Inspectors of Schools and Educationists who were concerned about science education. Altogether 63 Headmasters, 230 Science Teachers (180 from BSE schools and 50 from CBSE schools), 500 Students (400 from BSE schools and 100 from CBSE schools), 15 Science Supervisors and Experts and 15 Educationists constituted the sample.

4.2 Tools and Techniques

A questionnaire was developed with great care to elicit information from the Headmasters about individual schools, the institutional conditions for teaching science, infrastructural facilities available at secondary level, information regarding management of school, co-curricular activities usually conducted, information regarding the finance, inspection system, time-table allotment, course content and methods of teaching. In the tool scope was provided to elicit suggestions and criticism on the existing science education programme which is in vogue in the state.

A questionnaire for the Science Teacher was developed which had two sections. The first section of the questionnaire consists of nine broad items and each time has five to seven sub-items, the items were about general information about the teachers' concerned, time table, science room facilities, science laboratory, library, teaching aids facilities, curricular and co-curricular activities, home assignments to students, evaluation process and standard of text books. The first section of the questionnaire provides information as regards to the status of science education in secondary schools whereas the second one reveals specific information as regards to the problems faced by science teachers in the school during teaching and learning situation.

Another questionnaire was developed for students belonging to both CBSE and BSE affiliated schools. Information was collected with the help of the questionnaire about different aspects such as locality of the school, science teachers, their attitude towards students, science room facilities, laboratory condition, library facility and participation in co-curricular activities, etc.

An opinionnaire for science supervisors and experts was developed seeking information as evaluation, co-curricular activities, inspection of science programmes and suggestions for their improvement.

An interview schedule for educationist was developed to elicit remarks on science syllabus, improvement of the programme, methods of teaching, physical facilities available for science practical, co-curricular activities and above all the inspection and evaluation process which were in vogue in the state.

4.3 Data Collection

The survey technique was adopted in collecting data. After the development of Questionnaires, Opinionnaire and Interview Schedule for the target groups, data were collected first hand by establishing direct contact with all the respondents' concerned.

5. MAJOR FINDINGS

The major findings of the study were as follows:

- There was dearth of trained science teachers in both physical and natural sciences in the schools as a result of which interchange of teaching of the subjects by the teachers become the common practice.
- Although sections of different classes have been opened in view of increasing number of students but the number of teachers remained the same.
- Lack of auxiliary staff was very common among the secondary schools.
- There is no science laboratory in most of the BSE schools and few of the CBSE schools.
- Chemical and other consumable materials were only met 40 per cent of laboratory requirements. But all the secondary schools of both the categories schools had some equipments, chemicals and science apparatus.
- Teaching aids were not adequately available in majority schools. Of course, some enthusiastic teachers used self-prepared low-cost and no-cost teaching aids but these were not sufficient.
- Although there were Circle level, State level, and National level competitions in Debate, Essay, Quiz and Science Exhibition, etc., but hardly few schools participated in the same, the reason being lack of communication, delayed

information and negligent attitude of educational administrators and school personnel.

- There was provision for inspection of institutions. In BSE schools science teaching is normally inspected by Inspectors of Schools and Science Experts from Board of Secondary Education, Orissa, Cuttack. Government CBSE schools were inspected by the supervisors appointed by their competent authorities. However, in some non-government schools classes were inspected by the members of managing committee who were not competent. There was no equal parameter of quality checking and supervisory work was unsatisfactory because of the negative attitude of the personnel involved.
- There were 32 theory periods available for a teacher per week for teaching science in BSE schools and absolutely no scope for conducting practical work in the time-table while a science teacher in CBSE schools got 18 theory classes with one practical class for each science branch, i.e. physics, chemistry and biology per week. It indicated the work load variation in both the categories of school.
- Course content and methodology of science teaching were almost equivalent in both CBSE and BSE schools. Methods followed by the science teachers in both the categories of schools were mostly lecture method and invariably they used text book while teaching. Rarely demonstration-*cum*-discussion and other better dynamic methods were used by the science teachers in schools.
- Deficiencies in teaching and auxiliary staff found in both BSE and CBSE affiliated schools. In the BSE school science teachers are sometimes transferred and an arts teacher substituted him. It was due to the defective transfer policy. There was lack of adequate science hands which caused serious hurdles in science teaching in many schools.
- Even some teachers do not get monthly salary regularly as they have been adjusted without financial sanction in the budget of the State.
- There were no special science library in some schools of both the categories. Hardly half of the sample CBSE schools subscribed to science magazines but these were quite insufficient.

- There were no BSE schools having Botanical gardens excepting few CBSE affiliated schools.
- There were no Science clubs and Eco-clubs in sample secondary schools.
- The participation of science teachers in co-curricular activities were far from satisfactory.
- In the CBSE courses there was provision of assessment of assignments in the evaluation system but the same provision was not in the BSE schools.
- There was not provision of monthly test in the BSE affiliated schools but most of the CBSE schools conduct monthly tests to assess the achievement of the students.

6. RECOMMENDATIONS

After a detailed study of secondary school science education problems in Orissa the following measures are recommended for its improvement.

6.1 Qualifications of a Science Teacher

- A secondary school science teacher is required to have a post-graduate degree not simply the graduate degree in science to meet the requirements of present day science curriculum.
- In-service teacher training should be compulsory for all science teaches. A teacher must attend an Orientation Course once in every five years to refresh his/her knowledge in content as well as techniques of teaching.
- An In-service Training Cell must be in operation under the disposal of Inspector of Schools at the circle level to keep liaison with organisations conducting in-service teacher training and the teachers who are to attend it. The function of cell should be to regulate in-service training of the teachers within the circle. Stringent action should be taken against the teachers failing to attend the training without sufficient reasons. A science teacher should be motivated to attend seminars, workshops, symposiums and present papers of his desires.
- Some teachers are opting to attend such courses repeatedly. There should be regulations to control the same.

- Teachers are to be motivated to conduct action research programme and make use of the result in the working situations. This has to be monitored by the above mentioned cell.
- Present transfer policy should be modified so that a science teacher of physical science or natural science can be transferred as per the requirement of the school just not as per the requirement of the teacher concerned or whim of the authority. It must be such that teaching of the school would not suffer from lack of science teacher at any cost.
- A separate cadre for science teachers need be formed to ensure better job opportunity and attract good and talented persons for science teaching.
- There must be an auxiliary staff for handling science laboratory as it is a practical subject. The number of this type of staff may be commensurated with the students' strength and sections opened in the school. They will be incharge of store/science room and laboratory.
- An academic diary should be maintained under the headings of date period, class, practicals, progress made and homework given by the science teacher.

6.2 Infrastructure Facilities

Laboratory

A laboratory-*cum*-science room is the basic requirement of the school. Steps in this direction should be taken. In science room charts, diagrams, graphs are to be displayed, fixed and laboratory equipments and chemicals are to be stored as per requirement.

Library

Attention must be given to up-grade library condition keeping in view of the needs of students and teachers. There should be reference books, magazines, journals for updating teacher's knowledge. Science books can be kept in general library but its importance should be realised by the students and teachers.

6.3 Teaching-Learning Process

Methods of Teaching

The different methods that are to be practised in schools are as follows:

Lecturer Method, Demonstration Method, etc.

Lecture-*cum*-demonstration method, observation-*cum*-discussion problem-solving, project-method, laboratory method topic and assignment methods.

Out of all the methods lecture-*cum*-demonstration, observation-*cum*-discussion methods are very much recommended for science teaching in our condition. In these methods the teacher goes on demonstrating what he says through charts, graphs, models, experiments and cinematography, etc. Lecture without demonstration a film having sound without picture and demonstration without caption.

6.4 Audio-visual Aids in Teaching

Now it is recommended that the audio-visual aids like TV, Cassette recorder, projectors, Cinematography, VCR and Radio sets should be provided to each school and be incorporated in teaching methods in all the secondary schools. Through these the demonstrations to the students are made more attractive, acceptable, lively and understandable. The students not only easily comprehend the content but also able to remember it better for longer duration. The creative potentiality of the child is also enhanced because of it.

(a) *Use of TV*

Educational Technology can be of maximum useful in the training of teachers to improve quality of teaching. The Central Institutes of Educational Technology of NCERT, New Delhi at the national level and the State Institute of Educational Technology, at the state level are expected to provide necessary expertise and know-how for effective utilisation, evaluation and feedback of ETV programmes. The INSAT is a challenging national project and its experiments with television programmes is capable of providing new light and insight into the viewing problems and conditions of the rural audience. Maximum use of it must be ensured.

(b) *Film Shows*

Scientific films are now produced by expert agencies and a good deal of research is being done before producing a scientific film. The duration is usually 1½ hours. They can demonstrate many things in a much simple way. Films can demonstrate the processes of formation of rain, formation of snow, change of season, circulation of blood and heart functioning, occurrence of solar and lunar eclipses, etc., in more details which no teacher can do in a classroom by means of pictures and charts and black-board work.

The films should be shown weekly in large congregation. The shows should be followed by classroom discussion.

6.5 Science Fairs, Exhibitions and Science Club Activities

Every school should organise science fairs at least once a year. The programme should include exhibits prepared by the students. Talks by experts, film shows on scientific topics debate and discussions, music shows, scientific plays, Quiz, etc., can also be organised. Both the teacher and pupils should cooperate and contribute towards the success of such fairs. Every school must encourage science club activities and these activities are to be assessed at State level.

6.6 Science Museum

It is very much desirable that every school should have a science museum of its own. The science teacher should encourage the students to collect materials of scientific interest and improvise some apparatus. The collection of materials relating to different branches of science and a systematic arrangement of the same should be on the basis of a co-operative and active endeavour of the teachers and the students alike.

6.7 Excursion and Tours

Learning in the classroom cannot be sufficient for a student of modern times. So excursion and visits and field trips to different places of scientific importance should be organised annually to give an opportunity to the participants to get direct and practical learning experiences in an interesting manner. Science teacher must arrange tours to Radio Station, Telephone Exchange, Gardens, Factories, Planetorium which will supplement class-room instruction. The science teacher must advise the students to collect information and note them accurately for their study to develop the habit of correct observation and recording.

6.8 Modification of Science Syllabus

Science syllabus needs to be thoroughly revised and new topics are to be included taking into consideration of the resources available in the schools and the needs of children in every three years.

6.9 Improving Supervision Work

Inspection and supervision of science teaching in the school is very essential for improving the teaching of science. The inspecting personnel should inspect the items like Science Teacher's Record, Time Table, Teacher's Diary, Scheme of Work, Note Books of Students, Laboratory Equipments and Stock Register, Science Club Activities, Science Museum, Science Library.

There should be a separate science expert post in every Inspectorate, i.e. in every educational circle in the rank of Deputy Inspector. He is needed to be incharge of supervision of science classes regularly in the circle. He may be assisted by the present science supervisor available in the office of the Inspector of schools.

6.10 Upgradation of the Text Books

The review of existing text books is felt very essential. Workshops are to be organised to develop suitable text books and agencies like NCERT, SCERT, etc., should take leadership in this regard. Both working teachers and subject experts need be involved in the programme of upgrading text book.

7. SUGGESTIONS FOR FURTHER STUDIES

The following intensive and extensive studies are suggested for further research:

1. There should be special study to be conducted on the prevailing curriculum and laboratory conditions separately to reveal the situation microscopically.
2. Science Education in Secondary Schools of Tribal areas can be taken separately to know their interest and attitude to deal with the problems elaborately.
3. A critical assessment of Evaluation in Science Education programme can be taken up.
4. Study of attitude and aptitude of science teachers and critical analysis of their qualification, working conditions in the secondary schools of Orissa is very much needed.
5. The cost effective analysis of science education programme in the state is very much essential.

18

Multi-Grade Learning—An Innovation in Primary Level Education

PRAMOD KUMAR PRUSTY

1. INTRODUCTION

Amidst numerous problems those are being faced by the primary education of the nation, the lack of required number of classroom and teacher are most challenging. It has become.a regular complain of almost all primary teachers when they confront with the question of quality dilution at primary education, that they fail to do justice to the system because a single teacher is in charge of a number of classes. Such complain, at many places, get entangled with the non-availability of logistic infrastructure, which force the teacher to make the students of more than two classes sit back to back in a single classroom, which is not at all accommodative. When these complains come up from all corners of the nation; a critical analysis into the financial and allied factors of educatiqn fails to take some tangible and concrete measures immediately, so that the foundation of our educational structure could be more consolidated and get some kind of boost in perpetuating its objectives.

On the other hand, high rate of population growth, always going on adding a good number of students belonging to 6+ age group into our primary level. Under such circumstances, when there is no sign of solving our problems at an immediate effect, we have to think of an alternative means, by which our teachers might be able to achieve their objectives amidst every odds of the system. Multi-grade learning is an innovation in this regard.

2. LEARNING, NOT TEACHING—THE BASIS OF THE APPROACH

Till now we are in the conventional track of education. As the harbingers of the system, our teachers have been showing their authoritarian attitude in teaching. They teach students with rods, creating fear and supressive measures. Accordingly the students, being afraied of the red-eyed teacher, show submissiveness and try in cramming the matter, uttered by the teachers. Teachers have strong belief that they are to teach and the students are to learn without any question.

In multigrade learning, authoritarian teaching environment has to be substituted by democratic, flexible and liberal learning situation. Learning (not teaching) will go on most informal way and through interest generating activities. Teacher will be there not to teach but to facilitate the learning of the learners. Learning facilitators (teachers) should be dynamic flexible and open to take up emerging challenges of the classroom. It can be conducted outside classrooms through activities. Teachers have to change their own attitude-relating learners. They should realize that students always come to class with a good quantum of experience, knowledge, and information. It is not an empty vessel. Teacher cannot teach new things. Rather, he should help him/her in knowing more things. So teachers have to proceed from known to unknown.

3. TYPES OF ACTIVITY—AN OVERVIEW

Activities transacted in the classroom may be divided into three types, such as Learning Activity, Practising Activity and Evaluative Activity. Such difference show that the activity which intend to transmit some new knowledge, concept, theme, or information through transaction of new topic/content is called as learning activity. After learning some new concept, it is also the duty of the teacher to see that students are practising the learned activities.

Such use and re-use of learning activities when performed in the classroom by the help of the teacher is called practising Activity. The activities given to students to measure their achievement are evaluative activities. Those activities are initited by the teacher and no facilitation is required by the teacher as is needed in learning and practising activities. Hence, the role of teacher as facilitator is maximum at learning activity. In practising activity, his/her role is comparatively minimised to a jam-clearer or problem-setter, and in evaluative activity, he acts either as participant or non-participant observer.

4. STEPS OF MULTI-GRADE LEARNING

There are eleven sequential steps to work out the multi-grade learning at primary level of education. The steps are discussed as follows:

(i) Selecting the Activity and Subject-content

Made in consideration of here, the teacher has to select the activity. Such selection should be the number of classes present in a classroom. If there are students of three classes, the classes should be alloted different activities separately. If number of classes will be more than three, accordingly either practising activity or evaluative activity will be given to more than one class. It is because, teacher will get more time to devote for learning activity than other activities, those naturally require less time for facilitation of the learning activities. After selecting the activity, the subject and content (topic) should be selected for transaction.

(ii) Initating Warm-up Activity

All students should be instructed to be assembled irrespective of class and age. They should be instructed to stand up in a circle. Some physical exercise (may be walking clockwise and anti-clockwise as per instruction of the teacher or singing any song with action as shown by the teacher) be conducted to break the ice of students. Such activity will make the students psycho-physically alert and their sence organs will be made fully receptive to the learning activities. The effectiveness of such motivating technique mostly depends on

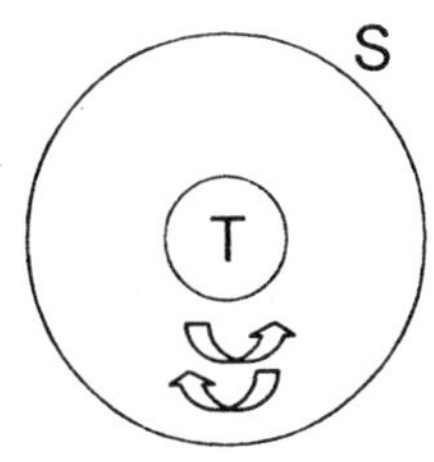

T—Teacher
S—Students

Clockwise, and
Anti-clockwise movement

the active performance of the teacher and his devotion in making situation more playful and amusing. Such activity can be conducted either inside or outside the classroom, looking at the logistic availablity.

(iii) Making Groups for Activity

While students were to practise the warm-up activities combinedly, they were to stand up and utter symbolic words (as per suggestion of the teacher) to be identified into required groups. Here, the teacher should try to his/her level best not to disclose it to any class of the students. The selection of symbolic words should be made in consideration of the classes, subject selected to be tought and the local culture, language, literature, etc. To facilitate the process similar subject be selected to be transacted in all classes. For example, if language is to be transacted in three classes simultaneously, the pupils of class I, II and III may be asked to speak out Fakirmohan/ Vyasakabi; Baladev/Kabisurya; and Laxmikanta/Kantakabi respectively for interesting and easy identification. If possible, teacher should tactically separate the students into three different classes. Taking separate names three separate groups be formed (class-wise as shown below) for conducting the activities. The groups be made sit face to face as stated in step II or by any other feasible design like circle (O) and semi-circles (Θ).

Step I

Symbol	*Class*	*Symbolic word*
●	Sts. of Class I	Fakirmohan
□	Sts. of Class II	Baldev
○	Sts. of Class III	Laxmikant

Step II

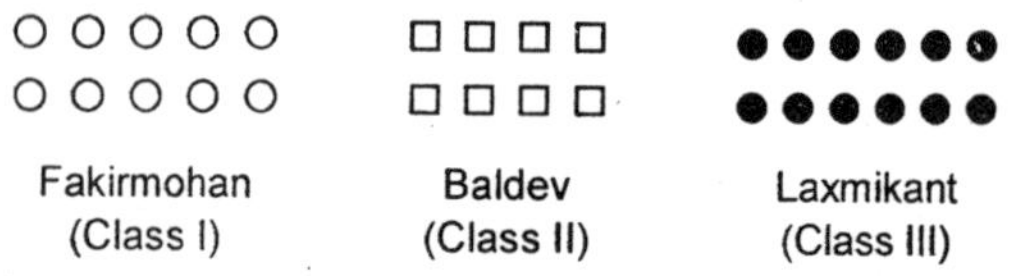

○ ○ ○ ○ ○	□ □ □ □	● ● ● ● ● ●
○ ○ ○ ○ ○	□ □ □ □	● ● ● ● ● ●
Fakirmohan (Class I)	Baldev (Class II)	Laxmikant (Class III)

(iv) Distributing Activities Among Groups

After dividing the students into three separate groups, the teacher has to specify different activities to various groups. Here, the teacher should start from the group which will perform the learning activity. Then other two groups are to be entrusted with practising and evaluative activities. By this, the teacher has to give less time for the practising and evaluative groups and comparatively more time to the group for which learning activity is sanctioned. It is because learning activity naturally needs more time to transact the new content matter to the learners.

(v) Providing Information to Group

Informations which are framed to be supplied to the students, facilitators and evaluators of such learning activities should be short, simple and clear. Language used in giving such information should be lucid and easy to be understood by all students. In case of any difficulty of understanding, the teacher should be there to help the learners. In possible cases, written information should be supplied to the learners.

(vi) Watching and Assisting in the Activity

The teacher should never try to teach rather he should try to help the learners in accomplishing his/her expected learning behaviours. As maximum stress is given on student's self-expression and utilization of own potentiality, so the teacher should always try to explore his/her inherent attributes and encourage him/her to progress independently. As facilitator of learning activity, he should keep vigilant watch on student's performance. Giving the clue of activity, the teacher has to see the cumulative growth of their learning experiences. Wherever and whenever the students get entangled with some problems, teacher should actively show the way out.

(vii) Providing Support Service

Since self-learning and auto-activity of the learner is stressed on in this process of learning the support service in the form of learning materials, audio-visual learning aids and electronic media (when and where required) play a significant role in knowledge development. Therefore, it is the duty of the teacher to see and provide as much material support as he can. The learning materials should be logical, simple to be understood and meaningful to explain the contents before the learners. As far as possible the teacher should either collect or prepare locally available no-cost low-cost learning materials. Students should be made engaged in the preparation of such aids, whenever they have interest and time. Overall, before coming to classroom the teacher should have collected all the necessary learning materials for the topic and present those as per the sequence of the activity.

(viii) Deciding Time Limit

Since the process is activity-based and activities are to be entirely performed by the students with active facilitation of the teacher, the conventional time limit of 40/45 minutes per period is not at all applicable here. Activities will generally take more time to be completed. So no sign of hastyness be shown by the teacher. Still, an overall distributions of period may be made to complete the topics of the subject and accordingly plan be kept in mind that in a learning activity the students should achieve full mastery over the concept. Activity may be repeated whenever required (in case of MAL and LAL students).

(ix) Discussion on the Process of Activity

At the end of each activity, a discussion be made by the students on the sequence of the activity. Such discussion of students should be synchronized by the teacher to make the students aware of the means (steps) of such activity. The teacher should solicit students' suggestion by which the activity could have been performed in a better way which would have benefitted students much better. Such discussion will develop a mental set within students for creative problem-solving. The students should write-up the processes for future reference and such writing should include task objective, process of activity, role of learning material, and result.

(x) Procedure of Participatory Evaluation

In this approach, the procedure of evaluation is most important to measure the effectiveness of our activity. Activity may be of any type (either learning or practising or evaluative), but the evalution should be conducted first by the learner himself/herself. The self-evaluation score should be compared through peer-group evaluation and then by the teacher. This process will strengthen the mathematical and evaluative attitude of the learner. The teacher will only consolidate the peer-group evaluation by correcting the minor errors. In each stage of evaluation, learner, peer-group members and the teacher will actively participate through discussion and analysis. Teacher may frame sub-groups for such activities.

Paradigm of Participatory Evaluation

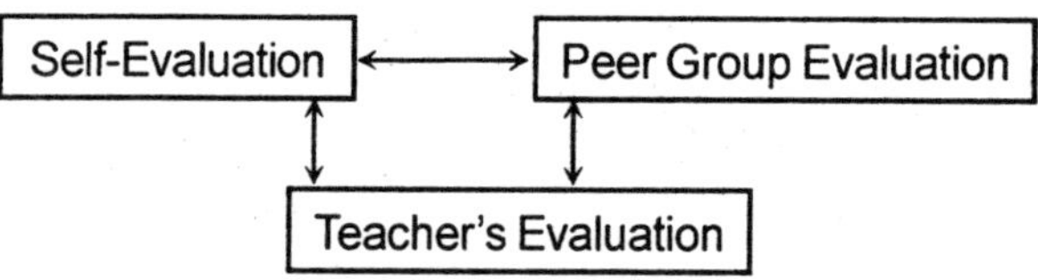

(xi) Role of Motivational Technique

This learning process is entirely child-centred. Working with children and sensitising children to work are two different things. Unless and untill students feel that the work is interesting and enjoying, they will never attend it. So, it is the duty and responsibility of the teacher to make the process motivating and interesting to that students will be envolved in the activity. During the activity when students gradually go on step by step, some motivating tips (an encouraging smile; patting on back of student; saying good, very good, 'go on' , right, you are on the right track clapping for group success, etc.) be given to them from time to time. It will accelerate their interest for learning. Here the expression of body language of the teacher is most important.

5. PREPARATION OF ACTIVITY-CENTRED CURRICULUM AND TEACHER'S HANDBOOK

In order to make this process of learning more effective, there is a need of well-prepared curriculum which is based on activities. Unless there is a well-developed activity-based curriculum, teachers would not be able to transact the contents perfectly. On the other hand, teacher's handbooks are to be developed accordingly to guide them towards perfection.

Since these activities are new in their nature, active co-operation of the parents, teachers and of the community is needed urgently. It is because, the out-school environment plays very important role to develop student's attitude towards such activity-based play-way learning. Unless the community is mobilised to support this new approach the process will not yield full benefit.

6. MAJOR FINDINGS

In conclusion, it can be said that this process of learning can also be tried out on different subject and classes. Expertiseness and vibrant zeal of the teacher is most urgent for the success of the activity. Teachers are to be trained on the line and materials are to be developed thereof.

19

Effect of Super Learning Technique (SLT) on Development of Creative Thinking

PRAMOD KUMAR PRUSTY

1. RATIONALE

Super Learning is a technique developed by Dr. Georgi Lozanov, a Bulgarian doctor and psychiatrist. This method is developed on the basis of Indian Raja Yoga and on some principles of Bulgarian Yogic culture. Experiments conducted in USSR, USA and Bulgaria by Lozanov, Ostander and Schroeder (1979) proved its effectiveness in developing the activity of the whole brain in general and the activity of left brain in particular. But no study has yet been undertaken in foreign lands relating effectiveness of Super Learning Technique (SLT) on development of left hemispheric function, more specifically on the development of creative thinking. In India as reported by Passi and Prabhu (1997), not a single study has been undertaken relating its effectiveness either on left hemispheric or right hemispheric function.

Hence, the researcher has undertaken the study to know how far the 'Super Learning Technique' is beneficial for developing creative thinking.

2. STATEMENT OF PROBLEM

The problem is stated as EFFECT OF SUPER LEARNING TECHNIQUE (SLT) ON DEVELOPMENT OF CREATIVE THINKING.

3. SCOPE AND LIMITATIONS

This was an experimental study to find out the effect of Super Learning Technique (SLT) on development of creative thinking. The study was delimited to the following:

(i) The experiment was conducted on the secondary level students.
(ii) History was the subject to be taught to students during the intervention.
(iii) Super Learning Technique (SLT) was regarded as independent variable whereas creative thinking and achievement will be regarded as the dependent variables in the study.

4. OBJECTIVES

(i) To find out the difference in creative thinking scores of boys and girls as an effect of Super Learning Technique (SLT).
(ii) To find out the effect of Super Learning Technique (SLT) on development of creative thinking,
(iii) To find out effect of Super Learning Technique (SIT) on achievement in History,
(iv) To find out the relationship between intelligence and development of creative thinking as an effect of Super Learning Technique (SLT),
(v) To study the rate of development of achievement scores in History in relation to levels of intelligence, and
(vi) To find out the relationship between change in creative thinking scores and change in achievement test scores as an effect of Super Learning Technique (SLT).

5. HYPOTHESES

H_{01} (a) There will be no significant difference between boys and girls in their mean creative thinking scores at pre-test stage.

(b) There will be no significant difference between boys and girls in their mean creative thinking scores at post-test stage.

(c) There will be no significant difference between the boys and girls of the experimental groups in their gain scores in creative thinking tests.

H_{02} (a) There will be no significant difference between the experimental and control groups in their pre-test creative thinking mean scores.

(b) There will be no significant difference between the experimental and control groups in their post-test creative thinking mean scores.

(c) There will be no significant difference between the experimental and control groups in their mean gain scores in creative thinking.

H_{03} (a) There will be no significant difference between the experimental and control groups in their pre-test mean achievement scores.

(b) There will be no significant difference between the experimental and control group in their post-test achievement mean scores.

(c) There will be no significant difference between the experimental and control groups in their mean gain scores in achievement test.

H_{04} (a) There will be no significant difference in creative thinking mean scores high intelligence group and low intelligence group at pre-test stage.

(b) There will be no significant difference in creative thinking mean scores of high intelligence group and low intelligence group at post-test stage of—
(i) Control group, and (ii) Experimental group.

(c) There will be no significant difference in the gain scores in creative thinking of high intelligence group and low intelligence group of—
(i) Control group, and (ii) Experimental group.

H_{05} There will be no significant difference in the gain scores in achievement in History of high intelligence group and low intelligence group of experimental group.

H_{06} (a) There will be no significant difference in mean creative thinking gain scores of high achievers and low achievers in History achievements test scores of the experimental group.

(b) There will be no significant difference between mean achievement gain scores in history of high creative and low creative groups.

(c) There will be no significant correlation between creative thinking gain scores and achievement gain scores.

6. OPERATIONAL DEFINITIONS

(A) Super Learning Technique (SLT)

Super learning is a technique of learning which builds up the link between consciousness and unconsciousness to produce super-consciousness. This state of mind is regarded as Alpha Level which absorbs and retains all knowledge, information, etc. It is developed by Dr. Georgi Lozanov and is accepted as mean to accelerate learning.

This technique has following two phases:

Phase I: The Mind Calming Session.
Phase II: The Memory Session.

Phase I: Mind Calming Session

It has four steps:

Step 1: Relaxation

Simple Exercise was used to relax the mind by releasing the body tension.

Step 2: Visualization

Meditation was used as a means of visualizing calm and peaceful scenes. It was to develop concentration by erasing worry and distractions.

Step 3: Affirmation

It was to Know Thyself or to develop self-concept with optimistic thoughts like, 'I am intelligent', 'I am creative', 'I can do this', 'I remember it perfectly', etc.

Such affirmation was always in present tense, positive, short and simple. It should not accept any doubt or hesitation.

Step 4: Breathing Exercise

The children were breathing exercise as per following rules.

Inhale	–	1	2	3	4	5	6	7	8
Hold	–	1	2	3	4	5	6	7	8
Exhale	–	1	2	3	4	5	6	7	8
Pause	–	1	2	3	4	5	6	7	8

Phase II: The Memory Session

Topics of History were to be taught in this phase. This phase has two steps.

Step 1: Teaching Session

Topics were taught to students. Divergent questions will be asked to students and the teacher will give divergent meaning and uses of a thing to the students to develop their critical thinking abilities. The teacher was encouraged new thoughts among students and instigate them to generate such thoughts.

Step 2: Remembering Session or Practising Session

The students could be encouraged to remember the things taught to them. During remembering activity recorded sound of flute with 60 beats/minutes were given in the background. These activities should be conducted in closed eyes.

(B) Creative Thinking

Guilford defines creative thinking as divergent thinking (Guilford,

1957), Garrett accepts it as hemispheric function (Garrett, 1976) and Edword De Bono defines creative thinking as lateral thinking (Bono, 1967). Many psychologists explained it as the product of whole brain synchronization and characterised by fluency, flexibility, originality and elaboration. But, here, creative thinking refers to the scores obtained through the administration of Mehdi's Group Test on creative Thinking (Verbal).

(C) Intelligence

Psychologists accept intelligence as convergent thinking (Guilford, 1957), abstract thinking (Terman, 1960), ability of analysis and synthesis (Spearman, 1904) and capacity relating reasoning, thinking and effective environmental adjustment (Wechsler, 1958). Here, intelligence is defined as the scores obtained from Tondon's Verbal Group Test of Intelligence (2/70).

(D) Achievement

Successfulness of individuals in different fields of life is generally accepted as their achievement. In the field of education, students' scholastic performance or success is regarded as their academic achievement. Here, achievement refers to the scores obtained by students in the achievement test on History administered by the school and developed by Orissa Secondary School Teachers' Association (OSSTA).

(E) Secondary School

In connection to implementation of National Policy on Education—1986, in Orissa, the secondary level of education consists of Lower Secondary Level (Class IX and X) and Higher Secondary Level (XI and XII/+ 2 Level). Here, the secondary school will refer to the classes IX and X, i.e. the lower secondary level and the experiment will be conducted on ninth class students.

(F) History

In Orissa, History has been taught as a school subject from primary level onwards. Sequentially it includes the Local History, Regional

History, History of the State, National History and World History keeping pace with the development of students and progress of classes. In this study, ninth class students will be taught the topics included in the history book of ninth class published by the Board of Secondary Education, Orissa.

7. METHODS OF THE STUDY

Sample

Two sections of students reading in class IX were chosen for the study at random. The participants were divided into control group and experimental group at random.

Tool

Verbal Group Test of Intelligence of R.K. Tondon (2/70), Verbal Group Test on Creative Thinking of Baqur Mehdi and Achievement Test on History developed by the Orissa Secondary School Teacher's Association (OSSTA) was used to measure the variables like intelligence, creative thinking and achievement in History respectively.

8. MAJOR FINDINGS OF THE STUDY

The analysed and interpreted results reported the following major findings. The major findings were stated according to the objectives of the study:

8.1 Super Learning Technique (SLT) was effective enough in developing creative thinking of secondary school students.

8.2 Super Learning Technique (SLT) was very much effective in increasing academic achievement of students in history.

8.3 Super Learning Technique (SLT) was equally effective for high-intelligence and low-intelligence groups in developing their creative thinking. Level of intelligence had no significant impact on development of creative thinking as an impact of SLT.

8.4 Super Learning Technique (SLT) was not affected by levels of intelligence in developing students' academic achievement. Thus, SLT is equally effective for high-intelligence and low-intelligence groups in increasing their academic achievement in history.

8.5 The effect of Super Learning Technique (SLT) on development of creative thinking and academic achievement was almost equal and significant. The rate of growth of creative thinking and academic achievement as an effect of SLT was at same sequence. The relationship of such growth was high positive and significant.

8.6 Boys and girls both were equally benefited from SLT in developing their creative thinking.

8.7 Boys were benefited more than girls from Super Learning Technique (SLT) in developing their academic achievement in history.

9. IMPLICATIONS OF THE RESEARCH FINDINGS

There is a unanimous agreement on the contribution of creative thinking in developing creativogenic society (Arieti, 1976). Formal education has become a major means of generating creative thinking among students through teaching various subjects. Accordingly, psychologists and educationists have developed several methods of teaching for development of creative thinking. Like Gordon's Synectics (1961), Osborn's Brainsterming (1957), Taylor's PAKSA (1961). Lozanov's Super Learning Technique (SLT) has been proved its effectiveness in varied fields and in almost all western countries. The major findings of the present study reported the significance of SLT in developing creative thinking and academic achievement. It has also reported the significant influence of sex as a variable to influence SLT to be more effective for boys in developing academic achievement. Therefore, on the ground of above findings, the following implications were suggested on the study:

9.1 Super Learning Technique (SLT) can be used at secondary level of any school of urban area to develop creative thinking of students. Since the school, where SLT was experimented fulfils all characteristics of every type of school SLT can be used in all the schools with full success. Therefore, the secondary school teachers, educational administrators and planners should try to use SLT at secondary level.

9.2 At the present time, when learning history has created a sort of phobia among students and history departments of Orissa has been experiencing a desert-like situation, effectiveness of super learning on history has given the solace. Therefore, Super Learning Technique of learning history should be widely used in secondary schools of India, so that students' achievement will be increased and a sort of moral courage will be boosted among them to learn history with high sportiveness.

9.3 Innovative learning materials should be used at maximum rate and those should be made in eye-catching formula to create an impression in memory of the students. So, the teachers should be trained in that line to make SLT more effective in developing supra learning ability among learners.

9.4 Since 60 beats super learning music was found very much effective for rhythmic presentation and memorisation of information and learning themes and our Indian schools are practising prayer classes and some specific schools are practising meditation and alike activities, more stress be given on mass prayer and rhythmic presentation of learning matters with music. If tryst will be made to develop topic-based presentation of learning themes with music that would exert significant effect on learning of students.

9.5 Teachers, parents, educational supervisors should take due care to create a strong self-concept or self-confidence of attaining everything. In spite of their failure, they should be encouraged positively and at every time teacher should have motivating and encouraging attitude and interest to develop a positive and optimistic mental-set among learners. A positive mental-set always develops a wining personality, i.e. the need of SLT.

9.6 At no cost, students should be left tension-ridden either physically or mentally. So teachers, parents, siblings and counsellors should work hard to release such tensions through simple physical exercises and with visualization of peaceful, calm and energizing situations. The prayer classes or just before the starting of classes of the day breathing exercise at least of five minutes along with meditation with slow baroque music/slow music of flute would be profitable for releasing tension and increasing concentration, those are required for super learning.

9.7 Teachers should be trained relating development of super learning frame and converting the conventional topics into super learning frames with clear statement of learning objectives and major and minor learning themes thereof. Teacher Training Institutions, Institutes of Advanced Studied in Education, Regional Institutes of Education, NCERT, etc., should take initiative in developing super learning packages and developing training packages on super learning.

9.8 Curriculum constructors of teacher training courses should include SLT in teacher training courses of study and curriculum planners of school education should be trained on the line of super learning by which they will include topics in that direction.

9.9 Students, Teachers, Teachers' Council, Parent-Teacher Association (PTA), Mother Teacher Association (MTA), Village Education Committee (VEC), the Counsellors and Inspectors of Education need to be made aware first of the significance of SLT, so that the congenial environment would be available for application of SLT in the classroom. It is because, a fertile soil always infuses greater success for SLT.

9.10 Student-teacher relationship should be cordial, democratic and motivating. Students should be given immense freedom for expressing their open-ended thoughts and teacher should be in positive mind to organise the ill-organised thoughts of students. Teacher should provide free, encouraging, playful and failure-bearing teaching-learning environment to facilitate the effectiveness of SLT.

9.11 Super learning is not influenced by students' levels of intelligence in developing creative thinking and achievement in history. Therefore, the teacher should not be worried much for the low-intelligent students. But some care be taken for high-intelligent group if they need to excel their performance.

9.12 Both boys and girls performed equally in developing their creative thinking being influenced by SLT. So teacher should not be discriminative inside the class on the ground of sex. But when boys scored better in academic achievement than girls, it is required for the teacher to be careful for girls on the ground of achievement. Therefore, during teaching some care must be taken by the teacher in treating boys and girls. Overall, teachers should be impartial and democratic for both the sexes.

9.13 Overall tryst be made by the teachers to use SLT in perfect manner so that students learning will be progressed with super speed. Teachers should be involved in to feedback and feedback review activities of learning session which will rectify students' faults and lead their learning to success.

10. RECOMMENDATIONS FOR FURTHER RESEARCH

It has been stated in rationale of the study that though super learning has been widely and profitably used all over the world, in India, it has no use in its original form. But India has an old tradition of yoga and meditation which is the base of super learning technique. Nowadays we also have a number of institutions those have made meditative practices the part and parcel of their educational activities. Still India lacked the materialistic use of the yogic technique. In this regard this study is an attempt of initiating research on Super Learning Technique (SLT) in India. Being successful in proving effectiveness of SLT in developing creative thinking and academic achievement, the present research has opened the divergent fields of possibilities where research may be conducted.

10.1 Super Learning Technique (SLT) can be experimented on small group of students in the learning of few topics in one or two subjects.

10.2 The effect of SLT can be studied on any school subject or on a number of school subjects through learning those subjects by SLT.

10.3 Super learning may be tried out at different levels of education starting from primary through higher education.

10.4 It may be studied on different types of education such as, general, technical, professional, medical, defence, etc.

10.5 Super Learning Technique can be used on development of learning of children of special needs and exceptional qualities like handicaps, learning disables, gifted, mentally retarded, slow learners, etc.

10.6 Super Learning Technique may be used to enhance managerial competency of educational administrators—Headmaster, Principals, Vice-Chancellors, Directors, etc., to bring solution to increasing problems of the system.

10.7 Comparative studies may be undertaken on the system of group prayer and other religious practices and super learning technique (SLT) at any level of education.

10.8 As an extension of the present study, such effectiveness of SLT can be measured in relation to development of achievement scores of other subjects.

10.9 Repeated Measures Design, Replications and multi-group designs may be used to study the effectiveness of SLT on achievement in specific subject or on a number of subjects.

10.10 The effect of Super Learning Technique (SLT) may be studied on different behavioural characteristics of the person.

10.11 Cross-cultural studies may be conducted to compare the effectiveness of SLT in varied situations and also on different or same subjects and levels.

10.12 Effect of Super Learning Technique (SLT) may be studied on development of memory, retention, intelligence, attitude, cognitive abilities, perception and related psycho-educational variables.

10.13 Effect of Supper Learning Technique can be compared with the effect of other techniques like brain storming, synectics, PAKSA, Reverse learning, CMTE, CMTS, etc., to ascertain their level of effectiveness.

10.14 Effect of Super Learning Technique (SLT) may be compared between performances of urban and rural students and between different types of schools under varied administration.

10.15 The relation of SLT with that of students' examination stress and development of academic performance can also be studied at different levels of education and on the basis of achievement on different subjects.

Design of the Study

This was an experimental study. Randomized groups pre-test post-test design was used to find out the effect of SLT on development of creative thinking. Creative thinking, achievement, and intelligence were regarded as dependent variables whereas Super Learning Technique (SLT) was the independent variable of the study.

At pretest stage tests on intelligence, creative thinking and achievement were administered. Then the control group was taught through traditional method and the experimental group was taught through Super Learning Technique (SLT). After intervention programme, tests on creative thinking and achievement were administered to both the groups.

References

Lang, D. (1984): *Charisma*, London: Blond and Briggs Ltd.

Ostander, S. and Schroeder, L. (2000): *Super Learning*, New York, Dell Publishing Group.

Passi, B.K. and Prabhu, S.H. (1997): Stress-free Super Learning, *The Progress of Education*, LXXI (7), 146-51.

Toffler, A. (1982): *The Third Wave*, New York: Bantam Books Inc.

Wonder, J. and Donovan, P. (1984): *Whole Brain Thinking*, New York, Ballantine Books.

PART IV

LEARNING THROUGH MEDIA

20

A Study of the Educational Implications of Community Television Programmes

SUBASH CHANDRA PATRA

1. INTRODUCTION

With the tremendous advances in human knowledge and the rapidly changing conditions of modern life; it has become important for every person in the society to constantly strive to keep pace with these advances in knowledge and to pursue a life-long education. Countries all over the world have experienced an increasing demand for education at all levels and for all categories of learners. With a view to meeting this challenge, attention has been given to the application of communication technology.

Television being a versatile and dynamic communication medium performs these tasks with brilliance and efficiency. It functions like a catalyst extending children's experience, introducing effective education, equalising educational opportunities, improving efficiency and productivity. Exposing distant or unreachable happenings to us in the form of recorded or live telecasts with visual imagery, not only it helps for the development of creative thinking and acquaintance with contemporary knowledge but also widens our mental horizon to a great extent. Evidence accumulated from various studies conducted in different countries suggest that television can exert considerable influence on the life style of young and old and can inculcate positive attitude and moral values to them.

India today is on the threshold of a new era of development and has to respond to challenges in energy, health, agriculture, protection of environment and the establishment of her industrial base and economic productivity. National integration and education, both formal and non-formal. In order to meet these national challenges, the role of science and technology is very important. As information and communication are the basis of education, educational systems through communication technology, particularly television definitely plays a decisive role in order to face the manifold challenges India faces.

In India, television entered into the field of education in an experimental basis in 1959, in Delhi, under a project aided by UNESCO to produce and transmit social education programmes. This was followed by School Education project which was launched in 1960. There were composite programmes of one hour duration and the aim of telecast was to present enrichment programmes and also a series of programmes having a bearing on the prescribed school syllabus. But a more planned and comprehensive TV project called "Delhi School Television Project" was launched towards the end of 1961 with 360 TV sets for the benefit of 20,000 students of secondary classes. With this small beginning the TV services continued to develop in Delhi for more than a decade.

Up to 1965, the main purpose of Delhi TV was for community viewing and for educational programmes for school children, but later on regular general service was started and in 1967 a pilot rural TV project was designed to telecast agricultural information. TV services went beyond Delhi in 1972 by opening new station and relay centre in other cities of India.

India entered the satellite era in 1975. The SITE Project was in operation for a year during 1975-76 having the basic objective of utilisation of TV for social change and national cohesion with priority for primary education. At the same time ISRO set-up a transmitter at Pij for the people of Gujarat. In 1976, TV set-up in India was delinked from AIR and given the name of Doordarshan. The expansion of TV network has been phenomenal with the launching of INSAT-IB in 1983. TV facilities rapidly expanded and during certain periods the country got everyday a new transmitter.

Doordarshan has a three-tier primary programme service, the National, the Regional and the Local. In the National Programme, the languages used are mostly Hindi and English focusing on communal harmony and National integration. Regional service originates from state capital emphasises the developmental project of Government. The local programmes are area specific and focus upon local issues.

Since its inception Doordarshan has been telecasting messages of social relevance, developmental activities, ideas of National Integration and the like. All Doordarshan Kendra regularly put out programmes in their general transmission for the benefit of rural audience in their service areas. These programmes which occasionally included entertainment of rural taste covered various other aspects of development like family welfare schemes, community development, animal husbandry, functional literacy, etc. Apart from these, Doordarshan takes a major effort to generate awareness about proper upbringing of children, the neglected and destitute, victimised and exploited child labour, delinquents and drug addicts, the handicapped, drop out and the discriminated girl child. Problems of infant mortality, diseases and malnutrition are also highlighted and instruction on child care, health and hygiene, nutrition, immunisation, child spacing and family planning and the other needs of infant and growing children are telecast at specified times.

This study intends to cover the community TV programmes produced by Doordarshan Kendra and other such agencies with special reference to the various aspects of programmes assessment of quality and quantity from the point of view of the requirement of the target audience and the effective utilisation of the programmes by the audience. The rationale of the study, the statement of problem, objectives, sample, major findings, recommendation and suggestions for further research are presented below.

2. THE RATIONALE OF THE STUDY

With the rapid expansion of television in India, there is a growing concern among educators, social scientists and media planners to explore the potential of the medium for educational and development purposes. A sustained co-operative working between the educationists and related media specialists is required to make systematically planned TV programmes for education and development of unknown and uneducated audience. Together they can produce and make available programmes that exploit the dynamics of television. Both the groups of professional must work to implement the basic guidelines for quality programming in a spirit of mutuality and creative open communication.

It is evident through related literature in the previous chapter that though a number of studies have been made by a number of scholars in India as well as in Orissa on educational television programmes, so far specific attempts have not been made specially to study the Community TV Programmes produced by Doordarshan with special reference to their production, quality, value and utilisation for the audience.

In such circumstances it seems worthwhile to study the educational implication of community TV Programmes with special reference to various aspects of programme production and to provide feedback for the qualitative improvement and effective utilisation of the programmes by the target group in fulfilling their requirement and expectation.

3. TITLE OF THE STUDY

The present study entitled as "A study of the Educational Implications of Community Television Programmes."

4. OBJECTIVES

The following objectives were formulated for the study:

1. To find out the strengths and weaknesses of the community television programmes.
2. To study the adequacy and appropriateness of such programmes for the community development.
3. To find out the effect of Television viewing in terms of gain in knowledge, comprehension, skill, interest, etc., of the audience.
4. To know the extent of awareness among the people about the importance and role of TV in community development.
5. To suggest suitable measures for improving the programmes.

5. DEVELOPMENT OF TOOLS

The investigator developed two different data gathering tools.

1. Questionnaire.
2. Observation Schedule.

6. SAMPLE

The sample for the present consisted of 320 men and women viewers of three districts in Orissa. Total 28 villages and 4 towns were selected at random for the purpose. Besides this total 10 veteran experts from the various section of the society were requested by the investigator to remark and give their valuable suggestions. The questionnaire was administered on the total sample of 320 respondents and the observation schedules were given to the 10 experts for observation of CTV Programme.

7. PROCEDURE OF DATA COLLECTION

The investigator collected data by personally contacting the respondents. He developed rapport with the respondents and convinced them about the purpose of administering the questionnaire. The respondents were requested to provide reliable information. The instructions of the questionnaire were made clear to them.

The experts were requested to observe the programmes and give their valuable views with reference to the extent of emphasis, on knowledge, understanding, application skill, attitude interest and appreciation objectives of the community TV Programmes. Their opinion were also sought with regard to the adequacy, and appropriateness of various aspects of the community TV Programmes, in the observation schedule supplied to them.

The data were collected through the following steps:

1. Preparation of tools.
   A. One questionnaire for general public to collect their views with regard to the effectiveness of community TV Programmes.
   B. An observation schedule for the experts to give their views and suggestions after watching the CTV Programmes.

2. Pre-administering activities.
   A. Selecting the 28 villages and 4 towns at random.
   B. Identifying and recording the names of 320 males and females.
   C. Developing close interaction with them.
   D. Requesting 10 experts consisting of media person, academician, educated and social conscious persons.
3. Administering the questionnaires and observation schedules.
4. Scoring and Evaluation.
5. Sequential arrangement of data.

8. METHOD OF ANALYSIS OF DATA

The data were analysed by employing content analysis of the CTV Programmes. Views of the experts were also incorporated in the analysis for the qualitative improvement of various aspect of CTV Programmes. The quantitative data were analysed by finding out the frequency of responses against each item in the questionnaire for the respondents and converting them into percentage.

The discussion was illustrated by diagrams wherever necessary.

9. MAJOR FINDINGS

The major findings of the study have been presented under the following headings:

(I) Findings from Audience's responses.
(II) Findings from suggestions of the Respondents.
(III) Findings from experts' observation.
(IV) Findings from suggestions of the experts.

(I) Findings from Audience's Responses

1. The programmes selected for CTV Programmes were from 11 subject areas such as Agriculture, Cultural (entertainment), Health and Hygiene, Family Welfare, Patriotic Song, Women's Programme, Child Development, Literature, Employment news and Games and Sports out of which 27

per cent were related to agricultural development, and 22 per cent were related to entertainment of audience.

2. According to a large majority (93 per cent) of the respondents, the programmes were interesting whereas according to 7 per cent the programmes were otherwise.
3. About one-third (32 per cent) of the respondents liked the CTV programmes for entertainment purposes, 28 per cent for up-to-date agricultural knowledge and 12 per cent for general awareness.
4. As regards the clarity of voice, a large majority (88 per cent) of the respondents mentioned that the voice was clear throughout, however, according to 12 per cent of the respondents, it was not clear.
5. Majority (60 per cent) of the respondents opined the speed of the delivery was normal whereas about one-third (34 per cent) of the respondents felt that the delivery was little bit quicker and the remaining 6 per cent of the respondents marked the speed of the delivery as slow.
6. As high as 81 per cent of the respondents remarked the pictures of CTV programmes as lively and clear, but to 19 per cent, sometimes the picture were not clear.
7. Real objects were widely used in 47 per cent of the programmes.
8. In 15 per cent of the programmes no visuals were used excepting verbal communications.
9. In almost all the programmes style of presentation was good.

(II) Findings from the Suggestions of the Respondents

1. According to 23 per cent of the respondents, the real objects should have been used in visuals, i.e. these viewers have wanted documentary type of programmes which are produced about the actual situation of the community.
2. About 6 per cent of the respondents suggested for enhancement of the duration of the programmes, on the other hand 3 per cent have pleaded for reduction of duration.
3. It was suggested by 4 per cent of the respondents that direct telecast be made in some of the programmes.
4. Participation of farmers, artisans, etc., in the programmes were suggested by 4 per cent of the respondents.

5. Lack of synchronisation of visuals with the commentaries was pointed out by also 4 per cent of the respondents.
6. About 3 per cent of the respondents pleaded for use the local language in the programmes.

(III) Findings from Experts' Observation

1. Most (83 per cent) of the programmes were produced by Doordarshan Kendra. Only 17 per cent of the programmes were produced by sponsored agencies.
2. Programmes having the duration between 21 to 25 minutes were found in 28 per cent of the CTV Programmes. Only 1 per cent of the Programme was above 30 minutes duration.
3. The theme of the subjects was well explained in 50 per cent of the Programmes, satisfactorily in 46 per cent of the programmes and not so well in 4 per cent of the programmes.
4. Regarding the objectives of the programmes it was found that Knowledge objectives (64 per cent), Interest objectives (70 per cent) and Understanding objectives (59 per cent) were given much emphasis in most of the programmes, but Skill, Attitude and Appreciation objectives were not emphasised at all in most of the programmes. Application objective was given emphasis to a great extent in about one-third (33 per cent) of the programmes and to some extent in considerable percentage (43 per cent) of the CTV Programmes.
5. The experts mentioned that 38 per cent of the programmes were presented through narration, format Demonstration and discussion formats were adopted equally in 21 per cent of the programmes. Further 22 per cent of the programmes were presented through documentary format and 19 per cent with musical features. Drama and dance formats were adopted in 1.5 per cent of the programmes, whereas only in 11 per cent of the programmes quiz or question answer format was adopted.
6. Most of the agricultural and health programmes were presented through discussion and quiz format. Chorus with musical feature was very much appropriate for development of aesthetic sense and patriotic feeling among audience.

7. There was no such hard or fast rule in adopting a specific format. However, as opined by experts formats used in different programmes were appropriate in almost all the programmes.
8. Wide use of real objects were found as high as in 41 per cent of the programmes which was highly appreciated by the experts.
9. In 44 per cent of the programmes, the visual aids used were very adequate while in 48 per cent adequate and in 1.2 per cent inadequate.
10. In majority (66 per cent) of CTV, Programmes picture was clear throughout whereas some time it was not clear in 34 per cent of the programmes.
11. As regards the selection of performers, it was proper to a great extent in 39 per cent of the programmes and proper to some extent in 61 per cent of the programmes.
12. Audio was clear throughout during telecast in most (85 per cent) of the programmes. Only in 15 per cent of the programmes it was not clear sometimes due to bad transmission or fault in equipments.
13. In a large majority (76 per cent) of the programmes the speed of the delivery was normal, however, it was quicker in 22 per cent of the programmes. Only in 2 per cent of the programmes the speed of the delivery was found slow.
14. As high as 74 per cent of the programmes were presented at a level suitable to the audience. But 22 per cent of the programmes were presented at a higher level and 2 per cent of the programmes presented below the level.
15. It was found from all the programmes that, information contained was 65 per cent whereas the percentage of entertainment was 35 per cent.
16. It was also found that language used in the programmes was very much appropriate in 53 per cent of the programmes whereas appropriate to some extent in 47 per cent of the programmes for the public of that particular age.

(IV) Findings from the Suggestions of the Experts

1. According to 7 per cent of the experts duration of time in the programme should be longer.

2. Synchronisation of audio with video was suggested by 4 per cent of the experts.
3. According to 41 per cent, more use of real object would be better.
4. More participation of farmers, artisan, etc., was advocated by 25 per cent of the experts.
5. It was suggested by 26 per cent of the experts to present the programmes by interviewing concerned officials.
6. More emphasis on burning issues was demanded by 11 per cent of the expert.
7. It was also suggested by 10 per cent of the observers not to repeat any programmes.

10. RECOMMENDATION OF THE STUDY

On the basis of major findings and suggestions of the respondents and experts, the following recommendation has been made for improving the existing scenario:

1. As it is demanded by experts, due weightage should be given to the theme of burning issues besides the various topics of social development.
2. Duration of the programmes should be judiciously decided at the time of production of programmes.
3. At the time of planning due weightage should be given to various objectives for producing suitable community TV programmes.
4. Since at present a large number of CTV programmes are being sponsored by outside agencies more weightage should be given to the CTV programmes with developmental themes and messages at the time of selection.
5. The formats like dramatisations and quizzes should be more used for CTV programmes.
6. Since visuals were felt inadequate in many programmes more visuals, relating to real object, development sight, places of interest should be utilised adequately.
7. Utmost care should be taken for synchronisation of audio with video aspect in the programmes.
8. Necessary steps need for improving the clarity in picture and clarity of sound in the programmes.

9. Programmes should be produced and telecast according to the level of audience—psychological, emotional and awareness level.
10. Local issues and language should be given prominence in CTV programmes for making them effective and appealing.
11. Adequate participation of the audience such as farmers, artisans, concerned officers, subject specialists should be provided in CTV programme for their better reception.
12. In order to cares the attention of the adult audience it is essential to produce interesting programmes with reasonable quantum of entertainment so that the hard core messages can be well-received.

21

The Effect of Radio Interventions on the Language and Cognitive Development of Pre-School Children

AMARENDRA PRASAD BEHERA

1. SIGNIFICANCE OF THE STUDY

Provision of free and compulsory education to all children until they complete the age of 14 years is a Directive Principle of Indian Constitution. Since 1950, determined efforts have been made towards the achievement of this goal. Over the years there has been a very impressive expansion in the provision of educational facilities and enrolment. As a result of which universal provision of educational facilities has been substantially achieved at the primary stage. Besides a number of innovative programmes have continued to be accorded priority for the same.

However, the Universalisation of Elementary Education (UEE) in its totality is still an elusive goal and much ground is yet to be covered. Also dropout rates continue to be significant, retention of children in schools is low and wastage considerable. The dropout rate is 38 per cent at primary stage and 53 per cent at upper primary stage. Despite increased participation of girls gender disparity still exists (only 42.8 per cent of enrolment at primary stage and 38.9 per cent at upper primary stage).

At the juncture, it is worth-mentioning that Early Childhood Education (ECE) is very crucial input towards the UEE. In the total spectrum of human development early childhood years, i.e. 3-6 years that represent the most critical period of life during which the foundation of cognitive, socio-emotional language and physical-motor competence is laid (Bloom, 1964). But in our country organised education of the child below primary school age did not, until very recently receive the attention it deserved.

From the history of pre-school education it is relevant that the concept of infant schools was introduced in India by British Missionaries in the later part of 18th century when such schools were set-up in the Western and Southern part of India. In the pre-independence period all these efforts were confined to voluntary sector and received the support from the government. During the post-independent period, the movement for education of young children drew great support from the private and voluntary sectors.

Realising the crucial importance of rapid physical and mental growth during early childhood years, a number of Early Childhood Care and Education (ECCE) centres were started particularly after the National Policy on Children (1974). Of those, Integrated Child Development Services (ICDS) Scheme is the leading one. Launched in 1975, with 33 projects on an experimental basis, ICDS (Integrated Child Development Services) scheme is currently the biggest programme of Early Childhood Development. Under ICDS, a package of services, including supplementary nutrition, immunisation, health check-up, referral services and non-formal pre-school education is provided to the children below six years. However, non-formal pre-school education is imparted to the children in the age group 3-6, who years attend the pre-school (Anganwadi) for three hours a day. The main function of the pre-school component is to satisfy the curiosity of the child rather than follow any rigid learning curriculum. Children are taught songs, stories and games. Pre-school activities are conducted by the Anganwadi Worker (AWW) who is selected from the community and considered as a multiple agent of change.

Although the AWW is considered as the key person and torch bearer in the success of ICDS scheme but, due to less qualification and dearth of pre-school literature and activities with them they often face difficulties to organise the pre-school activities continuously for three hours a day.

Keeping in view the above points radio programmes for young children are being developed and broadcast by All India Radio. These programmes are theme-based and have educational and entertaining value. Also all the Anganwadi workers have been provided with radio sets for listening of these programmes and supplementary guide books having pre-broadcast, broadcast and post-broadcast activities.

In this regard, very little information is available about how much can an ordinary field worker (Anganwadi worker) make use of these radio programmes and materials in her routine work. Is the radio broadcast have any impact on the young children? Do they listen to the programme regularly? Being encouraged by the above queries the researcher was interested to conduct a systematic study for assessing the usefulness of radio broadcast for young children.

In the light of the above background the problem for the study is stated as under:

"THE EFFECT OF RADIO INTERVENTION PROGRAMME ON THE LANGUAGE AND COGNITIVE DEVELOPMENT OF THE PRE-SCHOOL CHILDREN."

2. OBJECTIVES OF THE STUDY

(1) To study the effectiveness of the Radio Intervention Programme on the language development of the pre-school children.
(2) To study the effectiveness of the Radio Intervention Programme on the cognitive development of the pre-school children.
(3) To study the effect of Radio Intervention Programme on the language development of pre-school children in relation to their age, sex and socio-economic status (SES).
(4) To study the effect of Radio Intervention Programme on the cognitive development of pre-school children in relation to their age, sex and SES.

3. HYPOTHESES OF THE STUDY

(1) The Radio Intervention Programme will have a positive effect on the language development of pre-school children.
(2) The Radio Intervention Programme will have a positive effect on the cognitive development of pre-school children.
(3) The effect of Radio Intervention Programme on the language development of pre-school children will differ significantly at different age levels.
(4) The effect of Radio Intervention Programme on language development of pre-school children will not differ significantly with difference in sex.
(5) The effect of Radio Intervention Programme on the language development of pre-school children will differ significantly with different SES levels.
(6) The effect of Radio Intervention Programme on the cognitive development of pre-school children will differ significantly at different age levels.
(7) The effect of Radio Intervention Programme on the cognitive development of pre-school children will not differ significantly with difference in sex.
(8) The effect of Radio Intervention Programme on the cognitive development of pre-school children will differ significantly with different SES level.

4. DELIMITATION

(1) The study is delimited to the Thanesar block of the Kurukshetra district (Haryana) only.
(2) The study is further delimited to the Anganwadi children (3 to 6 years) including boys and girls.

5. DESIGN

As per the requirements of the study "Randomized Groups, Pre-test-Post-test design was followed.

6. SAMPLE

In all 100 pre-school children of 3-6 years (Boys and Girls) were included in the final sample. Further, 10 Anganwadi Centres of the Thanesar Block (Kurukshetra, Haryana) and 10 children were selected from each Anganwadi randomly. Equal number of Anganwadi Centres (five each) were included in the experimental and control group.

7. TOOLS USED

To study the effectiveness of the Radio Intervention Programme on the language and cognitive development of the pre-school children the following tools were used for the collection of data:

(1) Language Development Test developed by NCERT.
(2) Cognitive Development Test developed by NCERT.
(3) Socio-economic Status Scale developed by S.P. Kulshrestha.
(4) Monitoring Proforma, adopted by the investigator.

8. STATISTICAL TECHNIQUES USED

After the treatment and the post-test the performance of the experimental and control groups was to be compared on language and cognitive development. The following statistics were used for this purpose:

(i) Means and S.Ds. of different groups.
(ii) 't' test for measuring the significance of difference between the groups.

In addition to that the data was also represented graphically by drawing bar diagrams.

9. MAIN FINDINGS

On the basis of the analysis, interpretation and discussion of results as given in the previous chapter the following main findings regarding the effect of Radio Intervention Programme on the language and cognitive development of pre-school children have emerged out of the present study.

• Language Development

(1) The Radio Intervention Programme has a positive effect on the **listening comprehension** of the pre-school children.

(2) The Radio Intervention Programme has a positive effect on the **vocabulary** of the pre-school children.

(3) The Radio Intervention Programme has also positively affected the overall **language development** of the pre-school children.

In general the gains of the experimental group in language development are not only significant but much higher than the control group.

• Cognitive Development

(1) The Radio Intervention Programme has a positive effect on the **awareness of the immediate environment** of the pre-school children.

(2) The Radio Intervention Programme has a positive effect on the **awareness of the cultural heritage** of the pre-school children.

(3) The Radio Intervention Programme has a positive effect on the development of **concept of colour and shape among pre-school children.**

(4) The Radio Intervention Programme has a positive effect on the **sequential thinking** of the pre-school children.

(5) The Radio Intervention Programme has also positively affected the **overall cognitive development** of the pre-school children.

In general the gains of the experimental group in cognitive development are not only significant but much higher than the control group.

• Language and Cognitive Development Differentials in Pre-School Children with Respect to Age, Sex and SES

¤ *Age*

(1) The Radio Intervention Programme has not been found to be differently affecting the language development of the pre-school children at different age levels.

(2) The Radio Intervention Programme has not been found to be differently affecting the cognitive development of pre-school children at different age levels.

¤ *Sex*

(1) The Radio Intervention Programme has not been found to be differently affecting the language development of pre-school boys and girls.
(2) The Radio Intervention Programme has not been found to be differently affecting the cognitive development of the pre-school boys and girls.

¤ *SES*

(1) The Radio Intervention Programme has not been found to be differently affecting the **language development** of the pre-school children at different SES levels.
(2) The Radio Intervention Programme has not been found to be differently affect the **cognitive development** of the pre-school children at different SES levels.

10. EDUCATIONAL IMPLICATIONS

From the present study it is evident that radio as an effective audio aid is capable of providing valuable assistance to the Anganwadi Workers in the non-formal pre-school setting under ICDS by presenting worthwhile information and learning experiences simultaneously to a large number of students.

Hence, in many ways the findings of the present study can be beneficial in strengthening the non-formal pre-school education component under ICDS. The finding can be useful for the young children, the Teachers/Anganwadi Workers who handle the young children, the ICDS functionaries, teacher training institutions and the policy makers as well.

In the absence of a structured and prescribed syllabus for the non-formal pre-school education component under ICDS such radio programmes can more effectively and frequently be used by the Teachers/Anganwadi Workers for conducting the non-formal pre-school activities in the Anganwadis. Even the daily three hours non-formal pre-school activities can be based on the specific themes of the radio broadcast. By which the same theme can be recapitulated/ repeated in one way or the other by conducting pre-broadcast and post-broadcast activities.

In the absence of a well-sequenced material and printed textbooks the content of the radio broadcast can be printed along with the pre-broadcast and post-broadcast activities and supplied as guide books to the Teachers/Anganwadi Workers. So that the Teachers/Anganwadi Workers can prepare themselves to conduct the pre-broadcast and post-broadcast activities.

It has already been discussed earlier that each radio programme is in a magazine format and of 15 minutes duration keeping in view the pedagogical considerations, each programme includes conversation, song, story, drama, games, riddles, music and sound effects and fun/humour in it. Hence the programmes can arouse interest, increase attention span and develop language and cognitive skills among the young children. The present study therefore, strengthens the use of all such activities in organising the pre-school education. Therefore, such programmes should be a regular feature of the All India Radio, so as to help enhance the language and cognitive development process of the young children and strengthen the ability of the teachers by providing worthwhile information, which are useful in our daily life.

As the content of the radio programme are researched well before its production and subsequent transmission so the Teachers/ Anganwadi Workers can get authentic information which is useful for them as well as for the young children they handle.

Also the findings of this study can be equally useful for the other ICDS functionaries, i.e. programme officers (P.Os.), Child Development Project Officers (CDPO's) and Supervisors and the Teacher Educators of the Pre-school Teacher/Anganwadi Workers' Training Institute who can always train the Pre-school Teachers/ Anganwadi Workers by keeping in view the mental, physical, social and psychological need of the young child. Also there is a need to train the Pre-school Teachers/Anganwadi Workers about the process of conducting pre-broadcast and post-broadcast activities either in the pre-service or in-service training.

The findings of the present study can also be beneficial for the policy-makers who in turn may try to strengthen the pre-school education component in ICDS by allocating additional funds and planning more such radio broadcast in future.

11. SUGGESTIONS FOR FURTHER STUDY

The results of the present study threw a valuable light on the usefulness of the radio broadcast in the language and cognitive development of the young children. But the present study is based on a sample from a limited geographical and socio-cultural areas. For a wider generalisation a study can be undertaken covering a wider geographical areas and different socio-cultural context.

In the present study only the pre-school children enrolled in the Anganwadi Centres were studied. A comparative study of the children enrolled in the Anganwadis and in private schools can be made. Similarly, the children of remote, tribal and backward areas may be studied which might be helpful for future planning.

Only two dependent variables, i.e. language development and cognitive development were studied under the present study. Some more dependent variables, i.e. social development, emotional development, etc., may be included in the future studies.

Keeping in view the higher dropout rate and emphasis on quality education at primary level the findings of the present study throw a hint to investigate if similar benefits can be extended to primary level also. This needs to be studied.

The present study is limited to investigating the effect of Radio Intervention on the language and cognitive development of pre-school children only. The similar study can be conducted on the effect of radio interactive strategy on the development of pre-school children and primary school children.

Also some follow up studies may be conducted to know about the retention and achievement of the children of the present study, while.they are in primary grades. Unlike radio, the effect of other educational media, i.e. Television and Computers may be studied.

22

Study of the Effectiveness of Educational TV Programmes for Primary Schools

SADASIBA MAHARANA

1. INTRODUCTION

In recent years, Television is being utilised increasingly by developed as well as developing countries to meet the growing demand for education and to improve and enrich instruction. In India, television entered into the field of education in 1959, but it started systematic telecasting of educational programmes for primary school children after the successful launching of INSAT-1B in 1983. Now the project under INSAT is functioning in six states of the country, viz. Andhra Pradesh, Bihar, Gujarat, Maharashtra, Orissa and Uttar Pradesh. In Orissa, the project started operating in three districts, viz. Bolangir, Sambalpur and Dhenkanal. Now it has been extended to other districts of the state on small scales.

Since the functioning of educational television in Orissa, very few studies have been conducted on the effectiveness of the educational television programmes. Hence, a good deal of doubt remains as to how their potential is to be fully utilised. Again with the successful functioning of INSAT system, it is envisaged that educational television would be utilised more and more for the purpose of qualitative improvement and quantitative expansion of primary education. In such circumstances, it seems worthwhile to study the effectiveness of educational television programmes and to provide feedback for its effective utilisation.

The present study entitled "A CRITICAL APPRAISAL OF THE EFFECTIVENESS OF EDUCATIONAL TELEVISION PROGRAMME AT PRIMARY SCHOOL LEVEL IN ORISSA." It has been undertaken with a view to providing valuable suggestions for better planning and organisation of the educational system in general and effective utilisation of educational television programmes in particular. The findings of the study will help in effective planning, production, utilisation and evaluation of educational television programmes.

2. OBJECTIVES OF THE STUDY

The following objectives were formulated for the study:

1. To study the effect of ETV programmes on primary school children in terms of
   - Academic Achievement
   - Attitude towards school, and
   - Motivation in learning
2. To study the effect of intervention programmes, i.e. post-telecast discussions to be conducted by teachers along with educational television programmes on primary school children in terms of
   - Academic Achievement
   - Attitude towards school, and
   - Motivation in learning
3. To provide feedback to planners and producers on different aspects of educational television programmes.

3. HYPOTHESES

The following hypotheses were formulated keeping in view the objectives of the study:

1.1 Children exposed to ETV programmes in schools will have higher academic achievement than those who are not exposed to such programmes.

1.2 Children exposed to ETV programmes in schools will show more favourable attitude towards school than those who are not exposed to such programmes.

1.3 Children exposed to ETV programmes in schools will have higher motivation in learning than those who are not exposed to such programmes.

2.1 Children exposed to ETV programmes in schools along with intervention programmes will have higher academic achievement than those who are exposed to ETV programmes without intervention.

2.2 Children exposed to ETV programmes in schools along with intervention programmes will show more favourable attitude towards school than those who are exposed to ETV programmes without intervention.

2.3 Children exposed to ETV programmes in schools along with intervention programmes will have higher motivation in learning than those who are exposed to ETV programmes without intervention.

2.4 Children exposed to ETV programmes in schools along with intervention programmes will have higher academic achievement than those who are not exposed to ETV programmes.

2.5 Children exposed to ETV programmes in schools along with intervention programmes will show more favourable attitude towards school than those who are not exposed to ETV programmes.

2.6 Children exposed to ETV programmes in schools along with intervention programmes will have higher motivation in learning than those who are not exposed to ETV programmes.

4. METHOD AND PROCEDURE

Design

The study was conducted through pre-test, post-test control group design. There were three groups in the study, two experimental groups and one control group. In these two experimental groups two types of treatments were given. Under treatment I, children were exposed to educational television programmes without intervention programmes. Under treatment I, children were exposed to educational television programmes along with intervention programmes that is post-telecast discussions by the teachers with the students. For this purpose teachers were provided with brief training and guidelines in advance. These schools were also visited by the investigator to see if the activities are properly conducted by the teachers. In this way there were three groups in the study, viz.

1. Experimental group-I (ETV without intervention group).
2. Experimental group-II (ETV with intervention group).
3. Control group (Non-ETV group).

5. SAMPLE

Keeping in view the nature of the study, paucity of time and intensity of work, it was decided to conduct the study in one of the districts of the state, covered under INSAT project, namely, Bolangir. As the study intends to find out the effectiveness of educational television programmes at primary school level in terms of children's academic achievement, attitude towards school and motivation in learning, it was felt essential that the study should be conducted in those primary schools where ETV programmes were regularly shown to the children. For this purpose a list of TV schools in functional order was obtained from the Office of DIs. Again a questionnaire was also administered to all these schools to gather up-to-date information regarding ETV utilisation and maintenance. On the basis of the data gathered through the questionnaire a list of TV schools having equal status was prepared and a sample of 14 TV schools for two experimental groups (7 each) were selected randomly. Comparable Non-TV schools in the nearby areas, were listed in consultation with the DIs and a sample of 7 Non-TV schools were drawn randomly for control group. In this way a total of 21 primary schools were taken as sample schools for the study.

The sample of children selected for the study was confined to the children of Class IV of these selected schools. As the number of children in three groups did not differ much, it was decided to equate the number of children in three groups for convenience in computational analysis, by dropping the excess children randomly. Finally, 120 children in each group and a total of 360 children in three groups were retained for analysis.

6. TOOLS AND TECHNIQUES

The following tools and techniques were used for collecting data for the study:

1. Raven's Coloured Progressive Matrices.
2. Achievement tests in three school subjects, namely, General Science, Mathematics and Social Studies.
3. Attitude towards School Inventory.
4. A questionnaire on utilisation of ETV in Primary Schools.
5. Interview schedule to get feed back from teachers on different aspects of ETV programmes.
6. Guidelines for intervention programmes.

7. ANALYSIS OF DATA

The data gathered through different tools and techniques were analysed in the light of the objectives of the study. Hypotheses formulated in the light of first two objectives of the study were examined to ascertain significance of the differences on criterion variables under different treatments. For this purpose, Analysis of Covariance and 't' test were used to study the difference in post-test scores between treatment groups after adjusting for the initial difference in pre-test scores. Besides the analysis of covariance, pair-wise comparison for different treatment groups were made to study the difference between ETV and Non-ETV group, ETV with intervention and ETV without intervention and ETV with intervention and Non-ETV group. Analysis of variance was also used for comparing the three groups on intelligence. The difference was found not to be significant and the three groups were found to be well equated on intelligence for the purpose of analysis.

As regards the third objective of the study responses obtained through the interview schedule from teachers of experimental schools were analysed descriptively.

8. FINDINGS OF THE STUDY

The analysis of results of the present study in respect of first two objectives led to the following findings:

1. The academic achievement of children exposed to educational television programmes was higher than those not exposed to educational television programmes. Out of the three comparisons made in three school subjects, two have reached the level of significance. In Mathematics the difference was not significant, though the result was in positive direction and in favour of ETV group.
2. The academic achievement of children exposed to ETV programmes along with intervention programmes was higher than those exposed to ETV programmes without intervention programmes and to those not exposed to ETV programmes.
3. The attitude of children exposed to ETV programmes was found more favourable towards school than those not exposed to ETV programmes.
4. The attitude of children exposed to ETV programmes along with intervention programmes was found more favourable towards school than those not exposed to ETV programmes. But the difference between the children exposed to ETV programmes without intervention programmes was found not significant, even though the result was in positive direction and in favour of ETV group with intervention programmes.
5. The children exposed to ETV programmes showed higher motivation in learning than those not exposed to ETV programmes.
6. The children exposed to ETV programmes along with intervention programmes showed higher motivation in learning than the children exposed to ETV programmes without intervention programmes and the children not exposed to ETV programmes.

In respect of the third objective of the study that is to provide feedback to planners and producers on different aspects of ETV programmes and their utilisation, the suggestions made by the teachers are presented as under.

(1) The ETV programmes should be syllabus-oriented and based on local language and environment.
(2) More syllabus-based programmes should be produced on General Science, Social Studies, Mathematics and Mother tongue.

(3) Dubbing programmes should be prepared with much care. Otherwise it should not be used for primary school children.

(4) ETV programmes should be self-contained and easily understandable.

(5) Formats like dramatisation, feature-based and documentary films be given more weightage in the ETV programmes. Lecture format should not be used for children's programmes.

(6) Demonstration programmes should have more close-ups and be slow-paced to enable children observe the steps minutely for better comprehension.

(7) Frequent repetition of the programmes should be avoided (as it discourages children's participation). There should be a transmission policy keeping in view the scheme of work of the school, to facilitate better co-ordination between classroom teaching and programme transmission.

(8) The language of the programmes should be simple and easily understandable.

(9) Support-materials like programme schedule and teacher guidance notes should be provided to the teachers much before the transmission of programme, for effective organisation of pre- and post-telecast activities.

(10) The remuneration for TV-user teachers should be given regularly in time and more monetary incentives than the present rate should be given to teachers.

(11) The TV-user teacher's training should be given to all the untrained user-teachers and there should be regular orientation and motivation of user teachers.

(12) Separate TV set should be provided for community viewing, and the responsibility for operating that set should not be given to the user-teachers (as that disturbs the normal teaching work of the user-teachers and sometime creating anomalies among villagers).

(13) Steps should be taken for obtaining full co-operation of the Deptt. of Electricity for ensuring supply of electricity during the time of telecast and refraining them from quick disconnection of the electricity on account of delayed or non-payment of electric bills.

(14) Steps should be taken for quick repair of TV sets in case of any mechanical defect or disorder.

(15) The supervisory staff should visit the schools from time to time for supervision of the utilisation;

To sum up, it may be said that the results of the study establish the effectiveness of educational television programmes in the process of education of primary school children, especially when they are strengthened by teacher's post-telecast discussion.

To better harness the medium towards this end, in Orissa, certain organisational aspects along with its planning and production need to be taken care of in the light of the suggestions made by teachers.

If care is taken for all aspects mentioned above, it is hoped that ETV will definitely prove its effectiveness in bringing qualitative and quantitative improvement in primary education in Orissa.

23

An Evaluative Study of ETV Programmes Under INSAT

Jagannath Mohanty and Prafulla Kumar Naik

After the success of SITE in 1975-76, India decided to have a multi-purpose satellite of her own. The Indian National Satellite (INSAT-1) system represents India's first step towards this direction. Finally, INSAT-1A was launched in April 10, 1982. But it failed after it worked for a short while in September, 1982 due to certain technical snags that developed in it. The second one INSAT-1B was successfully launched on August 30, 1983. The INSAT Project is mainly intended for rural audience in order to speed up the national development through television programmes. The educational television programmes constitute an important component of the whole system.

Sambalpur was one of the districts covered under SITE during 1975-76 and after a break of about 2 years the TV facility was made available under Terrestrial Transmission in 1978. This district is comparatively backward and it is expected that there will be improvement of education in this district with the help of ETV programmes, which are telecast from 10.30 a.m. to 11.15 a.m. Now, there are 237 TV sets working in various schools of the district and are being operated by the custodians being appointed from among the primary school teachers.

NEED OF THE STUDY

Since priority is being accorded to the INSAT Project, the production and utilisation of ETV suitable for the students is given due importance. With a view to creating interest among the students as well as teachers, it is imperative to produce quality programmes and for this, qualitative assessment of ETV programmes being telecast is felt essential. This study was conducted for appraising the quality of the ETV programmes being telecast in the Samabalpur district.

OBJECTIVES

The following objectives were kept in view for the study

(i) To identify the strength and weakness of the programmes.
(ii) To know the extent of suitability of these programmes from the psychological needs and conditions of the clientele.
(iii) To consider the adequacy of the programmes from methodological point of view.
(iv) To see how far the programmes are suitable for the children from their language and cultural background.
(v) To suggest steps for improving the programmes.

SCOPE

The ETV programmes numbering 29 telecast during the month of September 1983 were studied. Out of these programmes, 14 were produced by Central Institute of Educational Technology, NCERT, New Delhi, and the remaining 15 by Doordarshan Kendra, Cuttack. Every working day ETV programmes were telecast for two age-groups, i.e. 5-8 and 9-12. Out of the programmes under review 15 were meant for the 5-8 age-group and the rest 14 for the 9-12 age-group.

LIMITATIONS

Although the investigators were interested to view the programmes in school situations and tried their best to do the same, they had bitter experiences of not being able to view the programmes due to non-operation of the TV sets. Therefore, in order to avoid such disappointment, the programmes were viewed in a home situation without any external interruption and intervention. However, in this method of observation, there was lack of immediate feed-back from the students and the teachers which would have been possible in school situations. Thus the data collected through personal observation by the ETV programmes constituted the main problem of the study.

ANALYSIS AND INTERPRETATION

The date-wise as well as age-group-wise programmes viewed are stated in Table 23.1 along with the agency of their production.

It is evident from Table 23.1 that 15 programmes were produced by Doordarshan Kendra, Cuttack and 14 by CIET, NCERT, New Delhi.

TABLE 23.1

Date-wise distribution of ETV Programmes during September, 1989

Date	*Title of the Programmes*		*Agency*	
	Age-group (5-8 years)	*Age group (9-12 years)*	*DDK*	*CIET*
1.9.83	Surya Sakal Shaktir Adhar	Janasebaka Swasthya Paridarsak	DDK	
2.9.83	Bal-Jagat Nehru Smarak Sangrahalaya	Story of Man (Man Learns Farming)		CIET
7.9.83	Story—I and II	Food (Balanced Diet)		CIET
9.9.83	Bal-Jagat Rail Paribahana Sangrahalaya	Story of Man (Indus Valley Civilisation) Part-I		CIET
13.9.83	Graha Nakshyatra Desh	Jana Sebak (Chikitsaka)	DDK	
16.9.83	Bal-Jagat (Banijya Mela Buli Dekhiba)	Story of Man (Indus Valley Civilisation) Part-II		CIET
19.9.83	Mahabharata Kahani	Bigyana Katha, Alok-III	DDK	
20.9.83	Amasarirara Yantrapati	Janasevak Pasu Chikitshaka	DDK	
21.9.83	Story—I and II	Food in Different Regions		CIET
23.9.83	Bal-Jagat Palli Shobha	Story of Man, Modern Civilisation		CIET
26.9.83	Mahabharata Kahani	Bigyana Katha: 1. Alok 2. Gyana Bigyana	DDK	
27.9.83	Ama Sarirara Yantrapati	Atri O Tapta Pani	DDK	
29.9.83	Mahabharata Kahani	Pani (water)	DDK	
Total	15	14	15	14

Table 23.1 also reveals that out of 29 programmes 15 were meant for the age-group 5-8 years and 14 were for the age-group 9-12 years.

Theme

On theme-wise analysis it is found that there were 5 programmes in Life Science, 5 in Physical Science, 6 in Civics, 3 in History, 2 in Geography, 2 in Mythology, 6 in Folk Culture and 1 in Life Sketch. On the whole, it is evident that there are 10 programmes in Science, 10 in Social Studies, 2 in Mythology and 1 in Folk Culture.

It is thus found from Table 23.2 that more programmes have been imparted in Science and Social Studies and more or less similar in Folk Culture where as remarkably less in Mythology and Life Sketch. It may, however, be pointed out that subjects like mathematics, drawing and biography have not been given due weightage.

TABLE 23.2

Theme-wise Distribution of ETV Programmes

Date	*Science*		*Social*	*Studies*	*Geography*	*Mythological*	*Folk Culture*	*Life Sketch*
	Life Science	*Physical Science*	*Civics*	*History*				
1	*2*	*3*	*4*	*5*	*6*	*7*	*8*	*9*
1.9		1	1					
2.9				1				1
7.9	1						2	
9.9			1	1				
13.9		1	1					
16.9				1			1	
19.9		1				1		
20.9	1		1					
21.9	1						2	
23.9			1		1			
26.9	1	1				1		
27.9	1		1					
29.9		1					1	
Total	5	5	6	3	1	2	6	1

Format

Analysis of data regarding format of presentation of ETV Programmes has revealed that mostly the programmes have been presented through features, dramatisation, talk or narration and demonstration.

It is evident from Tables 23.3 that 4 (14 per cent) programmes have been presented through dramatisation, 19 (66.5 per cent) through features, 3 (10.5 per cent) through demonstration and 3 (10.5 per cent) through simple talks or narration supported with visuals. It may be inferred that majority of the ETV programmes have been presented through features which are found to be popular.

TABLE 23.3

Format-wise Distribution of ETV Programme

Date	*Dramatisation*	*Feature*	*Talk or Narration*	*Demonstration*
1	*2*	*3*	*4*	*5*
1.9.83	1	3		
2.9.83		2		
7.9.83		3		
9.9.83		2		
13.9.83		2		
16.9.83		2		
19.9.83	1			1
20.9.83			1	1
21.9.83		3		
23.9.83		2		
26.9.83	1	1		1
27.9.83		1	1	
29.9.83	1		1	
Total	4	19	3	3

It is evident from Table 23.4 that outside shooting was done in 14 programmes, graphic with animation in 2 programmes, graphic without animation in 10 programmes, real object in 7 programmes and life-shots in 10 programmes, and models in 5 programmes. However, it is interesting to note that in 14 programmes outside shooting has taken place.

Visuals (Qualitative)

The visuals may be adequate and useful, but if they are not lively and clear, they will not serve any purpose to the desirable extent. Therefore, qualitative analysis of the visuals used in ETV programmes has been made and the findings have been tabulated below.

TABLE 23.4

Quantitative Analysis of Visuals used in the ETV Programmes

Date	*Graphics*			*Model*	*Object*	*Life-shots*	*Pupil partici-pation*
	With Animation	*Without Animation*	*Outside Shooting*				
1	*2*	*3*	*4*	*5*	*6*	*7*	*8*
1.9.83			1			1	1
2.9.83		2	1				
7.9.83		2			1		1
9.9.83	1		2		1		
13.9.83			2	1		1	
16.9.83			1	1	1	1	1
19.9.83		1		1	1		1
20.9.83		1		1			
21.9.83		3	1		1	1	
23.9.83			2		1	1	1
26.9.83	1		1	1		3	2
27.9.83		1	2			1	
29.9.83			1		1	1	1
Total	2	10	14	5	7	10	8

From Table 23.5 it is found that in 26 (90 per cent) programmes visuals were fully clear and in case of 3 (10 per cent) programmes visuals were partly clear whereas visuals were fully lively in 26 (90 per cent) programmes, partly lively in 1 (3 per cent) programme and not at all lively in 2 (7 per cent) cases. It is heartening to find that the highest percentage of ETV programmes were having visuals both clear as well as lively.

Voice

It is experienced that voice of the ETV programmes was effective and interesting. Analysis of data regarding voice from Table 23.6 showed that in case of 27 (93 per cent) programmes voice was quite distinct whereas in 2 (7 per cent) programmes, it is partly distinct. It is thus found that in majority of the programmes there was the clarity of voice. As regards speed, it is found that in case of 27 (93 per cent) programmes speed was normal.

TABLE 23.5

Qualitative Analysis of Visuals used in the ETV Programme

Date	*Clear*			*Lively*		
	Fully	*Partly*	*Not at All*	*Fully*	*Partly*	*Not at All*
1.9.83	12			1		1
2.9.83	1	1		2		
7.9.83	3			3		
9.9.83	2			1		
13.9.83	2			2		
16.9.83	2			2		
19.9.83	2			2		
20.9.83	2			2		
21.9.83	2	1		3		
23.9.83	1	1		1	1	
26.9.83	3			3		
27.9.83	2			2		
29.9.83	2			2		
Total	26	3		26	1	1

TABLE 23.6

Analysis of ETV Programmes According to Clarity and Speed of Voice

Date	*Clarity of voice*			*Speed of voice*		
	Distinct	*Partly distinct*	*Indistinct*	*Normal*	*Quick*	*Slow*
1	*2*	*3*	*4*	*5*	*6*	*7*
1.9.83	2			2		
2.9.83	2			2		
7.9.83	3			3		
9.9.83	2			1	1	
13.9.83	2			2		
16.9.83	2			2		
19.9.83	2			2		
20.9.83	2			1	1	
21.9.83	3			3		
23.9.83	2			2		
26.9.83	2	1		3		
27.9.83	2			2		
29.9.83	1	1		3		
Total	27	2	0	27	2	0

Defects and Deficiencies

On the basis of the analysis of data and close observation of the ETV programmes, the following defects and deficiencies were found which need be done away with for improving the programmes. The defects and deficiencies found in these 29 ETV programmes have been classified into five categories: (i) Language, (ii) Theme, (iii) Visuals, (iv) Methodology, (v) Synchronisation.

Language

Since language is the vehicle of ideas and emotions, utmost care should be taken in writing suitable scripts for the ETV programme. But such defects were found in a number of programmes. These defects are in connection with pronunciation on standard of language.

Theme

Subject-matter or content is also an important factor that contributes to the effectiveness of ETV programmes. Sometimes the programmes are over-loaded with content which is not at all desirable for the children's assimilation. Content of some programmes was either above or below the level of the age-group for whom the programme was intended. The programme *Bal Jagat* (Rail Paribahan Sangrahalaya) was loaded with so much of facts and figures that students of this age-group (5 to 8 years) would naturally lose interest and the impact would fall fiat. So also, the programme, Ama Sarirara Yantrapati, was highly loaded for the students of this age-group.

Visuals

Since visuals constitute an important component, of the ETV Programmes, the quality of visuals greatly determines the quality of programmes. But in four programmes the visuals were found unsatisfactory. For example, in the programme "Mahabharatara Kahani" (Part VII) on 26.9.83 which was presented through Geetinatya and the visuals of Droupadi Bastraharan could have been shown to enrich the programme to a great extent, in programme "Pallishobha" on 23.9.83 visuals shown were not clear and in the programme

"Manabara Kahani." Ajira Duniya (Part 1) on the same day the visuals of a cow moving in the city street, the farmer wearing a Dhoti and Panjabi were felt inappropriate and the visuals of INSAT-1 was not shown though referred in the programme: *Bal Jagat* (Rail Paribahan Sangrahalaya) on 9.9.83 and in the programme "Graha Nakshyatrara Desh" on 13.9.8.3 the visuals seemed inadequate.

Methodology

The ETV programmes must be presented methodologically according to the principles of psychology as well as pedagogy in order to be effective in communicating learning experiences to the students. But, in case of at least 3 programmes adequate care has not been taken in this regard. For example, in the programme *Bal Jagat* (Rail Paribahan Sangrahalaya) on 9.9.83 the content was not psychological for the students of age-group, 5-8 years. It was very difficult to understand that there was no description regarding the function of different parts of the engine and seemed quite confusing. In the programme 'Ama Sarirara Yantrapati' on 2.0.9.83 the length of the content was heavily loaded with teaching points which seemed improper. So also, in the same programme on 27.9.83, the presentation of teaching points was not systematic, and the words, viz., "engine," acid, peritonium, chilly, etc., used by the presentor, were not in conformity with the principles of psychology, for such a programme specially designed for the students of small group.

Synchronisation

Synchronisation is a vital consideration for making the ETV Programmes interesting as well as effective. But, in case of at least 2 programmes produced by CIET, defects in synchronisation, viz., (i) Verbal, and (ii) action have been quite evident.

FINDINGS

(i) Out of the total 29 ETV programmes 14 were meant for the age-group 9-12 years and 15 for age-group 5-8 years, 15 programmes were produced by Doordarshan, Cuttack and 14 by the CIET, NCERT, New Delhi.

(ii) Uniformity has been found to be maintained on the weightage of the programme under the heads: Science and Social studies. But adequate weightage has not been given on the subjects like Mathematics, Patriotism, Folk-culture, Mythology, Drawing and Biography.

(iii) Majority of the ETV programmes have been presented through features which are found to be quite popular.

(iv) The visual like outside shooting, graphic without animation, real subjects, graphic with animation, life-shots, models and pupils participation have been utilised in most of the ETV programmes.

(v) In most of the ETV programmes visuals have been found to be clear and lively.

(vi) In the majority of the programmes there is clarity of voice and normalcy of speed.

(vii) In few of the ETV programmes defects have been found in pronunciation and standard of language, i.e. 'Nehru Smaraka Sangrahalaya' on 2.9.83 and 'Ama Sharirar Saniraja Yantrapati' on 27.9.83.

(viii) A few programmes were too much loaded with content or teaching points resulting in loss of interest and attention of learners, e.g., *Rail Paribahana Sangrahalaya* on 9.9.83 and *Ama Sarirara Yantrapati* on 27.9.83.

(ix) In some programmes visuals were found to be inadequate, e.g., *Rail Paribahana Sangrahalaya* and *Pallisobha.*

(x) Adequate care has not been taken in making ETV programmes as methodological as possible.

SUGGESTIONS

On the basis of the above findings, the following suggestions may be given for improving the quality of the ETY programmes.

(1) Adequate weight age should be given on the production of programmes in Mathematics, Drawing, Patriotic and Mythological subjects Folk culture and Biography.

(2) The formats like dramatisation, features, and demonstration with real objects should be used for presentation of ETV programmes as far as possible.

(3) The visuals like graphic with animation, life-shots and outside shooting should be used as far as possible.

(4) Pupils' participation should be encouraged to the optimum extent.

(5) Clear and lively visuals should be utilised adequately through ETV programmes.

(6) There should be clarity of voice and normalcy of speed in the ETV programmes.

(7) The pronunciation and standard of language used should be made free from errors.

(8) The ETV programmes should not be overloaded with teaching points in order to make the children interesting as well as instructive.

(9) In the production of the ETV programmes, the principles of psychology and pedagogy should be followed to make the learning effective.

(10) Proper care should be taken for synchronisation both verbal as well as action in the ETV programmes.

(11) For sustaining pupils' interests different formats should be used on a particular day for presenting the programmes.

(12) Both action and music in One Act-Play and Dance-drama should be taken care of in order to make the ETV programmes more effective.

(13) To make the ETV programmes interesting and appealing the familiar topics and incident should be chosen.

(14) All care should be taken to explain different steps followed in Science experiments and practical projects in a logical sequence.

(15) Attempts should be made to dub the programmes in Oriya language from other languages taking into care the synchronisation difficulties.

24

Educational Television Programmes for the Age-group 9-11 Years: An Appraisal

JAGANNATH MOHANTY AND SADASIBA MAHARANA

Now-a-days Television is considered a popular and potential medium of instruction in almost all the countries of the world. It has excelled other modern teaching aids by virtue of its both audio and video potentialities. It is enriched with unlimited resources of visual aids which are generally not available in schools, particularly rural primary schools. It also provides instruction in a number of areas which is generally not possible on the part of the ordinary classroom teacher. So both for quantitative expansion and qualitative development of education, at every level and for all categories of learners, TV has a unique contribution to make. Further, the visual input provided through TV undeniably makes a deep impression on the minds of the children. It motivates, creates interest and draws attention of children towards learning.

NEED OF THE STUDY

Realising the importance of TV instruction in the future social structure, the Government of India introduced TV in the field of school education during the early 1960's on a small scale. In March

1961 it was introduced in the field of primary education for the first time by the Delhi Television Centre. In the year 1975 a remarkable project, namely, Satellite Instructional Television Training was started by the Union, Government for one year covering about 2400 rural primary schools in six States of the country.

Following the encouraging results of the SITE project, the Government started telecasting educational television programmes through INSAT-1B from 15 October 1983. The programmes which are presently being telecast for rural primary school children are mainly for general enrichment. Much importance is now being given to the production aspects of these programmes in order to make them suitable for rural audience.

It was, therefore, considered necessary to provide feedback to the producers of ETV programmes regarding different aspects of these programmes through empirical studies. Hence, the present study.

Objectives

The present study was undertaken with the following objectives:

1. To point out the suitable and unsuitable aspects of the ETV programmes.
2. To find out the adequacy and appropriateness of ETV programmes.
3. To suggest steps for removing the defects.

Scope

Since ETV programmes for elementary school children are being produced both by CIET (NCERT) and Doordarshan Kendra (Cuttack), the investigators took interest in studying the ETV programmes of these production centres, telecast during the month of January 1986. The study is exclusively based on the programmes meant for the children in the age-group 9 to 11 of Orissa.

A sample of 18 programmes (Table 24.1) was taken for this study.

It is evident from Table 24.1 that out of the total 18 programmes taken for study, nine programmes belong to DDK (Cuttack) and nine to CIET (NCERT).

TABLE 24.1

Sl. No.	Title of the Programme	Day	Date	Production Centre
1.	Itikili Mitikill	Thursday	2.1.86	DDK, Cuttack
2.	Ayatana	Friday	3.1.86	CIET, NCERT
3.	Doorata	-do-	-do-	-do-
4.	Ama Biswa	Monday	6.1.86	DDK, Cuttack
5.	Ama Rajyar Aranya Sampad	Tuesday	9.1.86	-do-
6.	Akalabya	Thursday	9.1.86	-do-
7.	Bapujee	Tuesday	14.1.86	-do-
8.	Mana Chitra Kan?	Wednesday	15.1.86	CIET, NCERT
9.	Sajiba O'Nirjiba	Thursday	16.1.86	DDK, Cuttack
10.	Byayana (Part III)	Monday	20.1.86	-do-
11.	Hariki Jitiba	Wednesday	22.1.86	CIET, NCERT
12.	Adha Chantha	Friday	24.1.86	-do-
13.	Darpana	-do	-do-	-do-
14.	Budhia Kia?	Monday	27.1.86	DDK, Cuttack
15.	Ojana Mapa	Wednesday	29.1.86	CIET, NCERT
16.	Golak	-do-	-do-	-do-
17.	Kia, Kana, Kahinki	Thursday	30.1.86	DDK, Cuttack
18.	Naksa Ankana	Friday	31.1.86	CIET, NCERT

LIMITATION

The study is confined to the ETV programmes meant for the children of 9 to 11 years of age of Orissa. Again, the study is based on the direct observation of the investigators of the out-of-school situations, because of certain unavoidable difficulties like failure of electricity and disorder of TV sets. But the investigators made occasional discussions with the school teachers regarding the programmes.

METHODOLOGY

In this study Direct Observation Method was used for the collection of data. The observation schedule prepared by the investigators was in keeping with the objectives, content, format, visuals, voice, language, pace, synchronization, etc., of the ETV programmes.

ANALYSIS AND INTERPRETATION

The data collected about the ETV programmes are analysed and interpreted on the following lines.

Objectives

Since the investigators found that no programme brief was provided to the TV schools before telecasting the programmes, no clear-cut information was made available regarding the instructional objectives of the programmes. That is why the investigators assessed the ETV programmes in the light of some assumed objectives like knowledge, understanding and application. To what extent the assumed objectives have been emphasized in the ETV programmes is shown in Table 24.2.

TABLE **24.2**

Distribution of ETV Programmes According to Their Emphasis on Different Assumed Instructional Objectives

Extent of Emphasis / *Objectives*	*No. of Programmes to a Great Extent*	*Percentage of Programmes*	*To Some Extent*	*Per cent*	*Not at All*	*Per cent*
1	*2*	*3*	*4*	*5*	*6*	*7*
1. Knowledge	1, 2, 3, 4, 5, 6, 7, 8, 9, 10, 11, 12, 13, 14, 15, 16, 17, 18	100	Nil	–	Nil	–
2. Understanding	2, 3, 4, 8, 9, 12, 13, 15, 16, 18	56	1, 5, 6, 7, 10, 11, 14, 17	44	Nil	–
3. Application	2, 3, 8, 9, 13, 15, 16, 18	44	1, 4, 5, 7, 10, 12, 14	39	6, 11	17

Table 24.2 shows that all the programmes emphasized 'knowledge' objective to a great extent. As regards 'understanding' objective, 56 per cent of the programmes emphasized this objective to a great extent and 44 per cent to some extent. 'Application' objective was emphasized to a great extent in 44 per cent of the programmes, to some extent, in 39 per cent of the programmes and not at all in 17 per cent of the programmes.

It is evident from the above analysis that all the programmes were mainly knowledge-oriented, though other objectives were not neglected entirely.

Content

Content plays an important role in making ETV programmes relevant and effective. It fulfils the need of the children and helps in bringing desirable changes in their behaviour.

Table 24.3 gives a clear idea regarding the coverage of content areas in the ETV programmes taken for the present study.

TABLE 24.3

Distribution of ETV Programmes According to the Content Areas

Content Areas	*No. of Programmes*	*Percentage*
Folk Culture	1, 6, 11	17
Arithmetic	2, 3, 12, 15, 16	28
General Science	4, 9, 13	17
Geography	5, 8, 18	17
History and Civics	7	5
Physical Education	10	5
General Knowledge	14, 17	11

It is observed from the table that most of the school subjects received due weightage in the ETV programmes, excepting a few like Literature, Arts and Aesthetics, etc.

TABLE 24.4

Distribution of ETV Programmes According to the Adequacy of Content

	Over-loaded	*Adequate*	*Inadequate*
No. of programmes	1, 5, 7, 17	2, 3, 4, 6, 8, 9, 10, 11, 12, 13, 14, 15, 16, 18	Nil
Per cent	22%	78%	Nil

Adequacy of Content

Regarding the adequacy of content it is found that about 22 per cent of the programmes were over-loaded with content and in about 78 per cent, the content was adequate.

Format

In the present study seven different formats were used for the programmes. Table 24.5 shows the distribution of ETV programmes according to different formats.

TABLE 24.5

Distribution of ETV Programmes According to Different Format

Sl. No.	Format	No. of Programmes	Percentage
1.	Feature	8, 11, 12, 13, 15, 16, 18	40
2.	Discussion with Demonstration	4, 9	11
3.	Narration with Aids	5, 7, 14	17
4.	Dramatization	1, 6	11
5.	Cartoon with Animation	2, 3	11
6.	Demonstration	10	5
7.	Quiz	17	5

It is evident from the above table that Feature format was adopted in 40 per cent, Discussion with Demonstration in 11 per cent, Narration with Aids in 17 per cent, Dramatization in 11 per cent, Cartoon with Animation in 11 per cent, Demonstration and Quiz in 5 per cent of the programmes.

This shows that Feature format found suitable and attractive at the primary level is given much importance in most of the programmes. Dramatization is not given due weightage though it is felt appealing and attractive and as reported by some school teachers other formats like Narration with Aids, Quiz and Discussion formats were found unattractive and ineffective in maintaining discipline. So more emphasis should be given to Feature and Dramatization formats.

Visuals (Quantitative)

Visuals, the main elements in a format, help to a great extent in making a programme effective and attention-drawing. The visuals used in the ETV programmes taken for the study are given in Table 24.6.

TABLE 24.6

Sl. No.	*Visuals*	*To a Great Extent*		*To Some Extent*		*Not at All*	
		No. of Programmes	*Per cent*	*No. of Programmes*	*Per cent*	*No. of Programmes*	*Per cent*
1.	Activities	1, 2, 3, 4, 6, 12, 13, 14, 15, 16, 18	61	8, 9, 10, 11	22	5, 7, 17	17
2.	Two-Dimensional	14	5	4, 5, 7, 8, 9, 12, 17, 18	44	1, 2, 3, 6, 10, 11, 13, 15, 16	51
3.	Three-Dimensional	4	5	5, 9, 12, 13	22	1, 2, 3, 6, 7, 8, 10, 11, 14, 15, 16, 17, 18	73
4.	Real Objects	1, 2, 3, 8, 11,12, 13, 14, 15, 16	55	5, 6, 7, 9, 17	28	4, 10, 18	17

It is evident that Activities and Real Objects were used widely in a number of ETV programmes, whereas two-dimensional and three-dimensional aids were not used in most of the programmes.

Visuals (Qualitative)

As it is important to use an adequate number of visuals in programmes, it is also equally important to give attention to the use of these visuals in an effective way. Otherwise they will not serve the purpose to the desirable extent. Hence the need of qualitative assessment of visuals. Table 24.7 gives a clear picture about the qualitative assessment of ETV programmes.

Table 24.7 indicates that in about 67 per cent programmes the visuals were fully clear, and in 61 per cent of programmes these were lively. In 28 per cent of the programmes these were partially lively.

TABLE 24.7

Distribution of ETV Programmes According to the Use of Visuals

Sl. No.	*Fully*		*Partially*		*Not at All*	
	No. of Programmes	*Per cent*	*No. of Programmes*	*Per cent*	*No. of Programmes*	*Per cent*
1. Clear	2, 3, 4, 5, 8, 9, 10, 12, 13, 15, 16, 18	67	1, 6, 11, 14, 17	28	7	5
2. Lively	4, 5, 6, 8, 9, 10, 12, 13, 14, 15, 18	61	1, 2, 3, 11, 16 17	34	7	5

Voice

Voice plays an important role in ETV programmes. Unless voice is clear and its speed normal, it will make the entire programme ineffective and fruitless.

As regards the voice of the ETV programmes taken for study it is found that in about 78 per cent of the programmes voice was distinct and in 22 per cent of the programmes it was partially distinct. Similarly, in 89 per cent of the programmes it was found at a normal speed and in about 11 per cent of the programmes it was a little bit quicker. In this regard Table 24.8 gives a clear picture.

TABLE 24.8

Distribution of ETV Programmes According to the Clarity and Speed of Voice

	Clarity of Voice			*Speed of Voice*		
	Distinct	*Partially Distinct*	*Indistinct*	*Quick*	*Normal*	*Slow*
No. of Programmes	2, 3, 4, 5, 7, 9, 10, 11, 12, 13, 14, 15, 16, 18	1, 6, 8, 17	Nil	7, 17	1, 2, 3, 4, 5, 6, 8, 9, 10, 11, 12, 13, 14, 15, 16, 18	Nil
Per cent of Programmes	78	22		11	89	

Language

As regards the language aspect of the ETV programmes, it is found from the present study that in about 17 per cent of the programmes two languages (Hindi and Oriya) were used. But in other programmes only one language (Oriya) was used.

Pace

Except 17 per cent of the programmes (No. 1, 7, 17) which were presented a bit speedily, all other programmes were presented quite normally.

Synchronization

In about 11 per cent of the programmes (No. 8, 11) synchronization defect was evident.

Disturbances During Presentation

While collecting the data the investigators found transmission disturbances at the time of presentation of more than 50 per cent of the programmes.

Findings

The main findings of the present study are given below:

1. No clear-cut prior information has been provided to the ETV schools regarding the programmes and their objectives.
2. As regards realization of the objectives it is found that knowledge objective has been realized in all the programmes and in most of the programmes understanding and application objectives have been realized to a great extent.
3. Except a few content areas like Literature and Arts and Aesthetics, all other content areas have been given due weightage.
4. Some of the programmes (about 22 per cent) were found over-loaded with content.
5. Feature and dramatization formats were found more interesting and attractive, whereas narration with aids, quiz and discussion formats were found ineffective.
6. In most of the programmes different visuals have received their due place. But as regards the qualitative aspects of the visuals in some of the programmes (about 28 per cent) these were found partially clear and indistinct and in about 34 per cent of the programmes these were found partially lively.
7. In some of the programmes (about 22 per cent) voice was found partially clear.
8. In about 17 per cent of the programmes the use of two languages (Hindi and Oriya) was also found unsuitable.
9. Regarding the pace of the programmes it was found that about 17 per cent of the programmes were presented a bit speedy.
10. Synchronization defect was observed in about 17 per cent of the programmes.
11. Transmission disturbances were observed during the telecast of more than 50 per cent of the programmes.

SUGGESTIONS

The following suggestions may be given in the light of the major findings:

1. Programme briefs and other necessary information regarding different programmes should be provided to each ETV school before telecast of the programmes.
2. Adequate attention should be given to the production of content areas like literature, arts and aesthetics.
3. Attempts should be made to avoid over-loading of content.
4. More emphasis should be given to feature and dramatization formats.
5. Attempts should be made to make the visuals clear, distinct and lively.
6. Clarity and speed of voice should be made appropriate.
7. Transmission disturbances should be reduced to the minimum.

REFERENCES

Central Institute of Educational Technology, NCERT, New Delhi, Programme Briefs for ETV Programmes, 1985-86.

Mohanty, J. and Behera, S.C., "Teacher Education Programmes under INSAT," *EPA Quarterly Bulletin*, Vol. 8, No. 1-2, April-July, 1985.

Mohanty, J. and Behera, S.C., "Television Teacher Education Programmes: A Critical Analysis," *Journal of Indian Education,* NCERT, New Delhi, March, 1986.

Mohanty, J. and Behera, S.C., "TV Teacher Education Programmes under INSAT: An Appraisal," *JIE*, Vol. I, NCERT, New Delhi.

Mohanty, J., *Educational Broadcasting: Radio and TV in Education*, Sterling Publishers, New Delhi, 1984.

Mohanty, J., "Education Television Programmes under INSAT," *Educational Quarterly*, Ministry of Education, January, 1983.

Mohanty, J., "INSAT for National Development," *Orissa Review*, Home (P&R) Department, Orissa, Nov.-Dec., 1983.

Singh, J. and Singh, A.K., *A Study to Assess the Needs of the Primary School Children of Orissa for ETV,* NCERT, New Delhi, 1984.

25

ETV Programmes for the Children in the Age Group of 9-11 Under INSAT

JAGANNATH MOHANTY AND SADASIBA MAHARANA

Television, one of the modern mass media is going to play an important role in the expansion and improvement of education in the developing countries of the world. It has its novelty and vitality over other mass media. It arouses curiosity, draws attention, creates interest and above all, motivates children for learning. That is why, it becomes one of the important means for child education all over the world. Today in India, the ETV Programmes for elementary school children are being telecast under INSAT-IB to six States like Andhra Pradesh, Bihar, Gujarat, Maharashtra, Orissa and Uttar Pradesh.

The programmes, which are presently being produced are intended for rural audience and for general enrichment. These are not according to grades, but are produced and telecast keeping in view the elder and the younger age-groups. So there are separate programmes for children of 5 to 8 years and 9 to 11 years old, with a duration of 20 minutes for each group. The programmes are daily telecast for five days a week, Monday through Friday, from 10.30 A.M. to 10.50 A.M. for younger age-group and from 10.55 A.M. to 11.15 A.M. for older age-group. Out of these five days, Doordarshan

Kendra, Cuttack produces programmes for three days—Monday, Tuesday and Thursday and CIET, NCERT, New Delhi produces programmes for two days—Wednesday and Friday.

At present, through INSAT-IB, the elementary school children of only three districts of Orissa, namely—Bolangir, Sambalpur and Dhenkanal are getting benefits from these programmes.

NEED OF THE STUDY

It is only after the successful launching of INSAT-IB in August 1983 that systematic ETV programmes for elementary school children started in Orissa. So these programmes are at the formative stage of their development. Again these programmes are produced from two different centres—from DDK, Cuttack and from CIET, NCERT, New Delhi. The DDK, Cuttack productions are originally in Oriya language, but the CIET, NCERT productions are originally produced in Hindi and being dubbed into Oriya language for the children of Orissa. All these programmes aim at enriching the elementary education. In order to enrich and strengthen the elementary education, sound supplementary ETV Programme must be produced. Without proper feedback through systematic study, it is not possible on the part of the producers to produce suitable and sound ETV Programmes. At such a developmental stage a qualitative assessment of the ETV Programmes is felt essential for knowing their suitability for the target audience. Hence, the need of the study.

OBJECTIVES OF THE STUDY

The following objectives were kept in view for the present study:

(1) To know the strengths and weaknesses of the ETV programmes.
(2) To study the extent of suitability of these programmes for primary school children.
(3) To suggest remedial measures.

SCOPE OF THE STUDY

The ETV Programmes produced by both DDK, Cuttack and CIET,

NCERT for the children of age-group 9 to 11 for the districts of Bolangir, Sambalpur and Dhenkanal during the month of December 1985 were studied for the purpose. A sample of 15 programmes were taken for this study, which are given in Table 25.1.

TABLE 25.1

Sl. No.	*Title of the Programmes*	*Day*	*Date*	*Production Centre*
1.	Bijyan Katha (Tapa Shakti)	Monday	2.12.85	DDK, Cuttack
2.	Lanthan	Wednesday	4.12.85	CIET, NCERT
3.	Kahinki O' Kipari (Tapa O Tapaman Jantra)	-do-	-do-	-do-
4.	Patriotic Song-Chorus (Sare Yahanse Achha)	-do-	-do-	-do-
5.	Darpana	Friday	6.12.85	-do-
6.	Barsa Kana?	-do-	-do-	-do-
7.	Patriotic Song (Solo) (Sare Yahanse Achha)	-do-	-do-	-do-
8.	Swasthya O' Swasthya Rakshya (Byayam-Part-III)	Monday	9.12.85	DDK, Cuttack
9.	Ama Rajyar Aranya Sampada	Tuesday	8.12.85	-do-
10.	Sarala Jantrapali	Wednesday	11.12.85	CIET, NCERT
11.	Chasi Bhaire	Thursday	12.12.85	DDK, Cuttack
12.	Patriotic Song Chorus (Mo Gaon)	-do-	-do-	-do-
13.	Chhai	Friday	13.12.85	CIET, NCERT
14.	Patriotic Song Chorus (Sare Yahanse Achha)	-do-	-do-	-do-
15.	Kia, Kana, Kahinki Quick	Thursday	19.12.85	DDK, Cuttack

For the present study as shown in Table 1.9 programmes were taken from CIET, NCERT, Production and 6 programmes were from DDK, Cuttack production.

LIMITATIONS

Due to certain practical difficulties like disorder of TV sets and failure of electricity, it was not possible on the part of the investigators to observe ETV Programmes always in school situations. So the investigators observed these programmes out of school situations and occasionally discussed with the school teachers about the programmes.

Thus, the study is mostly based on personal observation of the investigators.

METHODOLOGY

The study is based on the Direct Observation Method. For the purpose, the investigators prepared on observation schedule and collected the data accordingly. The Scheduled was prepared keeping in view the following aspects of the programmes—objectives, content, format, visuals, voice, language, synchronisation.

ANALYSIS AND INTERPRETATION

After collecting the data the investigators found that there was no earlier information from the production agencies regarding the objectives of each programme. So the investigators assessed other aspects of the ETV Programmes in light of the following assumed objectives—knowledge, comprehension, Application, skill and Interest. Table 25.2 gives a clear picture of each programme emphasising these assumed objectives.

It is found from Table 25.2 that in 80 per cent of programme knowledge objective has been emphasized so a great extent and in 20 per cent of programmes it has been emphasized to some extent. As regards comprehension objective 40 per cent of programmes emphasized to a great extent, 20 per cent to some extent and 40 per cent not at all. But in 60 per cent of programmes application objective has been emphasized to some extent and in 40 per cent not at all. In 7 per cent of programmes efforts have been made to improve the skills to a great extent and in 60 per cent of programmes to some extent. But in 35 per cent of programmes no attempt has been made to improve skills. It is also found that about 67 per cent of programmes tried to create interest to a great extent, but about 33 per cent of programmes tried to create interest to some extent.

Thus it is evident that no one programme in the sample realized the assumed objectives fully. It might be due to several factors which are being discussed under the following heads.

Content

As regards the contents of the programme in the sample about 47

TABLE 25.2
Distribution of Programmes According to Objectives

Sl. No.	*Knowledge*	*Comprehension*	*Application*	*Skill*	*Interest*
1.	1	1	2	2	1
2.	1	1	2	2	1
3.	1	1	2	2	1
4.	2	3	3	2	2
5.	1	1	2	2	1
6.	1	1	2	2	1
7.	2	3	3	3	1
8.	1	3	2	1	1
9.	1	2	2	3	1
10.	1	2	2	3	2
11.	1	2	3	3	1
12.	1	3	3	2	2
13.	1	1	2	2	1
14.	2	3	3	2	2
15.	1	3	3	3	1

(1) stands for "to a great extent."
(2) stands for "to some extent."
(3) stands for "Not at all."

per cent of the programmes were from General Science and 27 per cent of the programmes were devoted to developing patriotic feeling among children. Besides, other 26 per cent of the programmes were equally distributed for physical Education, Geography, Agriculture and General Knowledge.

But one thing worth nothing here is that 20 per cent of the programmes were over-loaded with content thus resulting in poor assimilation of facts and information. Another thing is that except General Science, no other school subjects had received their due weightage in ETV Programmes.

Format

Format plays an important role in communicating meaning and motivating children for learning. In the sample under study 40 per cent of the programmes were produced with feature format and 20 per cent with chorus. Besides, these, in 40 per cent of programmes other formats like Narration-*cum*-Demonstration, Narration with real objects and pictures Demonstration, Group dance, Quick and sole action formats were taken for presentation. In this regard Table 25.3 gives a clear picture.

It is found from Table 25.3 that most of the programmes from General Science content were presented through feature format and all the programmes, in patriotism were through chorus except programme No. 7, which was presented through a sole performance. But other programmes were presented through different formats like Narration-*cum*-Demonstration; Group Dance and Quiz. Among all these formats feature format is found quite popular.

TABLE 25.3

Programmes According to Formats

Sl. No.	*Format*
1.	Narration-*cum*-Demonstration
2.	Feature
3.	Feature
4.	Chorus
5.	Feature
6.	Feature
7.	Sole play
8.	Demonstration
9.	Narration with real objects and pictures
10.	Feature
11.	Group Dance
12.	Chorus
13.	Feature
14.	Chorus
15.	Quiz

Visuals

In order to make the ETV Programmes interesting, attractive and effective, a number of visual aids should be used in the programmes. But it is found from the present sample that nearly 73 per cent of programmes used activities to a great extent, 20 per cent of programmes to some extent, 7 per cent of programmes not at all. In 27 per cent of programmes two dimensional aids have found place to some extent but in 73 per cent of programmes not at all. Similarly in 40 per cent of programmes three dimensional aids found place to some extent and in 60 per cent of programmes not at all. It is also found that in 33 per cent of programmes Natural Scene/Real objects have found place to a great extent, in 20 per cent of programmes to some extent and in 47 per cent of programmes not at all. Table 25.4 provides a clear picture of visual used in different programmes.

It is evident from Table 25.4 that except programme No. 6, no other programme had given equal weightage to all the visuals.

TABLE 25.4

Programmes Using Various Types of Visuals

Sl. No.	*Activities*	*2-Dimensional*	*3-Dimensional*	*Natural Scene/ Real Objects*
1.	1	3	2	1
2.	1	3	3	1
3.	1	3	3	1
4.	1	3	3	3
5.	1	3	2	1
6.	2	2	2	2
7.	1	3	3	3
8.	1	3	3	3
9.	3	2	2	2
10.	1	3	2	2
11.	1	2	3	3
12.	1	3	3	2
13.	1	3	3	3
14.	2	3	3	3

(1) stands for "to a great extent."
(2) stands for "to some extent."
(3) stands for "Not at all."

Voice

Voice plays an important role in ETV Programmes in communicating ideas and meaning to students. So the voice should be distinct and the speed of the voice should be normal in order to be suitable to the grasping capacity of the children.

It is found from the present study that in 80 per cent of programmes the voice was distinct and in 20 per cent of programmes it was partially distinct. As regards the speed of the voice it is found that in 80 per cent of programmes the speed was normal and in 20 per cent of programmes it was little bit quicker. Another noticeable thing is that in about 33 per cent of programmes occasional disturbances of sound were there during the presentation, which, resulted in poor co-ordination of facts and loss of interest. In some of the programmes adult voice was heard in case of a child's character.

Language

Since language is the means of communication, it should be appropriate to the children of primary school in order to make ETV Programmes effective. But as found from the present study 20 per cent of programmes, particularly those, which were produced by CIET, NCERT for developing patriotic feeling were communicated directly through Hindi language. Thus, it is found difficult on the part of small children of Orissa to grasp any meaning from these. Again in same of the dubbed ETV Programmes the original Hindi language was heard occasionally during presentation. Besides in about 73 per cent of programmes effort had been made to present the content through Oriya language.

Synchronisation

Out of the total sample, in 40 per cent of the programmes lack synchronisation was evident. Since the programmes produced by CIET, NCERT had been dubbed into Oriya language from Hindi language, lack of verbal synchronisation was found more or less in most of these programmes.

MAJOR FINDINGS

After analysis and interpretation of the data, the investigators obtained the following findings:

(1) Out of the total fifteen ETV Programmes meant for the children of the age-group 9 to 11 years, 6 programmes were produced by Doordarshan Kendra, Cuttack and

9 programmes were produced by CIET, NCERT, New Delhi.

(2) More weightage has been given to Science subject. No other subjects of primary school like Mathematics, Social Study, Drawing, Biography have received that much of importance in ETV Programmes.

(3) As regards the objectives, knowledge in 80 per cent comprehension in 40 per cent skill in 7 per cent and interest in about 67 per cent programmes are likely to be realised to a great extent, whereas application in 60 per cent and skill in 60 per cent of programmes are likely to be realised to some extent.

(4) 20 per cent of programmes were found overloaded with facts resulting in poor assimilation.

(5) Majority of the ETV Programmes have been presented through feature format, which are found to be quite popular.

(6) In 73 per cent programmes activities and in about 33 per cent of programmes Natural/Real objective have found place to a great extent. Two dimensional graphics in about 27 per cent and three dimensional visuals in 40 per cent of programmes have found place to some extent.

(7) In most of the ETV Programmes visuals have been found to be clear and lively.

(8) In majority of the Programmes the voice was distinct and the speed was normal. But in 20 per cent of programmes the speed was little bit quicker and in about 33 per cent of programmes, there were occasional disturbances of sound during presentation resulting in poor co-ordination and loss of interest and attention.

(9) All the programmes produced by CIET to develop patriotic feeling were presented through Hindi language, which are not found to be appropriate to small children of Orissa. Again in some of the dubbed programmes the original Hindi language was heard occasionally.

(10) In 40 per cent of the dubbed programmes verbal synchronisation was found to be defective.

(11) No earlier information about the objectives and programme was given to the teachers.

SUGGESTIONS

On the basis of the above findings, the following suggestions may be given for improving the quality of the ETV Programmes:

(1) Adequate weightage should be given to other subjects of primary school like, Mathematics, Social Study, Drawing, Biography, etc., besides Science.

(2) Care should be taken to provide information about the objectives and notes on the programmes in advance for facilitating pre- and post-broadcast activities.

(3) In order to avoid over-loading of facts due care must be taken to present a reasonable amount of content in each programme.

(4) Since the dubbed programmes are found to be ineffective, efforts should be made to produce original programmes in Oriya Language. Otherwise adequate care should be taken to avoid lack of synchronisation.

(5) Adequate attention should be given in selecting appropriate format, preference should be given in feature format, which is found to be more interesting than others.

(6) Clear and lively visuals should be given place adequately in ETV Programmes in order to make them interesting and understandable.

(7) The programmes should be presented with normal speed, so that the children can get adequate time to understand the facts clearly.

(8) Adequate weightage should be given on the skill and application objectives in the production of programmes.

(9) The programmes need be presented in the voice appropriate to the character.

26

Impact of Educational Television on the Competency of Elementary School Teachers

SURESH C. BEHERA

1. INTRODUCTION

Television, being a multi-dimensional medium of communication, possesses unique qualities and capabilities for influencing education. It is a versatile and dynamic audio-visual device which broadens the intellectual horizon of both the teachers and students from time to time. The proper use of educational television provides new incentives for students to assume more responsibility for learning. It is also a fact that effective teaching through television demands more preparation and assistance of more specialised personnel than does conventional instruction. Kinder (1959) observes:

> Television has literally captured the country. Its expansion has been much more dramatic than that of radio or the automobile. It has become an important part of our way of life, so much so that it is difficult to say whether it is a luxury or necessity (p. 59).

Educational television has the potentiality of creating interest and motivation in both children and adults. It also facilitates training of teachers: the student-teacher or any other teacher observes good and experienced teachers in action and imitates various aspects of teaching and teaching skills. It has already proved its effectiveness and supremacy in teaching subjects like agriculture, science, geography, oceanography, etc.

Educational television makes educational opportunities equal throughout the country. The students in rural and deprived areas of the country, where educational resources are not available, get the same quality of education as their counterparts in the urban centres. The best teacher is equally available for every student (Mohanty and Behera, 1985; Behera and Panda, 1987). Thus television bridges the gap between the poor and the rich, the privileged and the under-privileged, the ruralites and the urbanites. The expansion of educational television or the instructional television coverage is irresistible and its impact is immeasurable. Now-a-days, television is already being used in schools more widely in almost all advanced countries of the world.

Supports in respect of the positive role played by educational television are plentily available in scholarly literature. Research studies concerning the impact of ETV on teacher's learning were conducted by Akutsu *et al.* (1978), Bostick (1984), Choat, Griffin and Hobart (1986), Torres (1984), Noguez (1976), Ghiassi (1978) and Taglides (1984). Some studies were also conducted in India by Agrawal (1978), Sukla, Singh and Batra (1978), Rahman (1977) which were pertaining to the development of teachers' knowledge and attitude as a result of the impact of ETV.

The impact of ETV on classroom learning was also found out by some researchers like Chau and Schramm (1977), Childers and Ross (1979), Scott (1956), Greenstein (1959), Ogawa (1960), Murray (1972), Greenhill (1959), Gordon (1960), Barrington (1964), Stickell (1963), Dublin and Hedley (1969) and Cronbach (1975). These studies indicated that learning of school subjects and various skills was possible through educational television rather than face-to-face teaching-learning process. Similar studies were conducted in India by Neurath (1966), Sukla and Kumar (1977), Rahman (1977), Aghi (1977), Kanade (1982), Seth (1983), Singh and Singh (1983), and Mohanty (1986) who reported changes in behaviour and cognitive development of primary school children and changes in attitude and teaching strategies of teachers as a result of exposure to television.

The literature pertaining to impact of ETV has been studied at length by the present researcher, but no work in Indian situation which had a direct bearing on the present study was found out. Hence, the review was necessary in identifying the present problem and developing insight into various aspects of the same with special reference to the impact of ETV on increasing teachers' competency, particularly their knowledge, understanding and application in content areas and classroom interaction.

2. NEED

For the sake of qualitative improvement in education of the primary children in general and the teachers in particular, broadcasting of ETV programmes was started since October 15, 1983 under INSAT-IB. The programmes cover six states of the country, i.e. the rural and backward areas of Andhra Pradesh, Bihar, Gujarat, Maharashtra, Orissa and Uttar Pradesh. In Orissa, it covers three districts, viz., Bolangir, Dhenkanal and Sambalpur. The elementary schools of the rural and backward regions which are deprived of getting all sorts of modern facilities pertaining to teaching have been provided the educational programmes under INSAT ETV service.

Besides the children's programmes, a very specific programme for the teachers is telecast on every weekend. But both the programmes have aimed at bringing about a change and improvement in the methodology of teaching (CIET, 1984-85). The rural schools do not find any scope and opportunity of using the AV aids and modern equipment and apparatus in teaching due to paucity of funds. For example, while teaching science, the teacher adopts the textbook method in lieu of experimental method. That is because there are no such laboratory facilities available in any elementary school of the rural areas.

To update and upgrade the teachers' knowledge, understanding and their application skills, the Central Government have earmarked to spend adequately towards teacher education programmes at the state and national level, short-term training courses of the district level and distance education programmes through radio and television and printed materials. Among them, the most important medium is television because it carries the picture along with the messages to the doorsteps of the teacher. The teacher education programme which is now telecast under INSAT is an example.

This chapter is an attempt to unravel the impact of ETV (both children and teacher) programmes on the competency of the teachers of the elementary schools. Since there was no such type of study available especially in Indian situation, it was deemed an essential project to be undertaken by the researcher.

3. OBJECTIVES

The following were the objectives of the study:

(i) To study the impact of ETV on the competency of the teachers of elementary schools in terms of:
   (a) knowledge, understanding and applications in content areas, and
   (b) classroom interaction between teachers and students.

(ii) To assess the attitude of the teachers towards ETV programmes.

(iii) To identify the problems of the teachers with respect to the utilisation of the ETV programmes.

(iv) To suggest measures for improvement of the quality of the programmes.

4. HYPOTHESES

The following hypotheses were formulated for the present study:

(i) The teachers exposed to ETV have a better grasp of knowledge, understanding and application in relevant content areas than the teachers not exposed to ETV.

(ii) The teachers exposed to ETV interact more favourably with students by accepting their ideas and feelings than the teachers not exposed to it.

(iii) The teachers exposed to ETV put more questions to students in the classroom than those not exposed to it.

(iv) The teachers exposed to ETV enable the pupils to initiate talk more than the teachers not exposed to it in classroom interaction.

(v) The teachers exposed to ETV have a favourable attitude towards ETV programmes.

(vi) The teachers exposed to ETV have problems with respect to the utilisation of the ETV programmes.

5. METHODS

The design of the study incorporates both survey as well as field experiment. The socio-educational status of the school in which television operates was determined by a case study approach.

A *Quasi-experimental design* was adopted to measure the impact of ETV programmes on the competency of the teachers in respect of their knowledge, understanding and application in content areas and the interaction in the classroom situation. The quasi-experimental design adopted for the field study is the strongest of all evaluation strategies for drawing inferences in order to establish casual relationship between independent and dependent variables.

5.1 Sample

In the present study, the sample was selected in four phases:

(i) *Selection of Schools:* Out of 230 TV schools of four educational districts of Sambalpur, 25 schools were chosen randomly keeping the teacher's age, qualification, teaching experience and intelligence in view. An equal number of 25 non-TV schools were selected randomly as a control group for the sample.

(ii) *Selection of Teachers:* Two teacher custodians were selected from each of the 25 TV schools thereby leading to a total sample of 50 teachers. In case of non-TV schools, the teachers who were teaching the classes of IV and V were included in the sample. Hence, two teachers were selected from each of the 25 non-TV schools of the same four educational districts giving a total figure of 50 teachers.

(iii) *Selection of Students:* A sample of 20 students of class V were selected randomly from each of those 25 TV schools and 25 non-TV schools. Hence, the total number of the sample size of students was 500 from TV schools and 500 from non-TV schools.

(iv) *Selection of Inspecting Officers:* For this investigation, 25 inspecting officers like District Inspectors and Sub-Inspectors were selected randomly from those four educational districts.

5.2 Tools

The following tools and techniques were used in the present research for the collection of data:

(i) Competency-Based Achievement Test (CBAT).
(ii) Flander's Interaction Analysis Categories (FIAC) technique.
(iii) Opinionnaire.
(iv) Feedback Schedules.

5.3 Procedure

As per the sample of the study, data were collected from 25 TV schools and 25 non-TV schools of Sambalpur revenue district of Orissa State. First of all, the TV schools where the programmes were regularly utilised were located. In the second phase, the teachers of the said TV schools were properly matched with those of non-TV schools where the classes were running without ETV programmes. An intelligence test by Cattell and a questionnaire eliciting the background information of teachers were administered to them. At this stage, 40 TV schools and 42 non-TV schools were undertaken. In the TV schools, two TV user-teachers were requested to respond to the test materials. But in the non-TV schools, those teachers who were teaching the students of classes IV and V were requested to respond to the questionnaire and the intelligence test. In this way 80 teachers from TV schools and 84 teachers from non-TV schools came under the purview of the study.

In the third phase, proper matching was done by the researcher on the basis of the teacher's age, educational qualification, teaching experience, intelligence and residential status of both the types of schools. After the (matching, 50 teachers of 25 TV schools and 50 teachers of the 25 non-TV schools were finally retained.

During 1986-87 session, ETV programmes were telecast from 7th July 1986 to 28th February, 1987. Since this study was experimental by nature, all sorts of precautionary measures were undertaking by the researcher. The experimental schools (TV schools) were teaching the students throughout the session along with the ETV facilities whereas the control schools (non-TV schools) were not having the said facilities.

In the fourth phase, the competency-based achievement test which was developed on the programme contents was administered to the teachers of both the type of schools after the telecast of programmes. Again, the FIAC was administered to study the classroom teacher behaviour of all the teachers of both the categories. Besides this, an opinionnaire and a feedback schedule was administered to the TV user-teachers to know their attitude towards ETV Programmes, and problems and suggestions with respect to the improvement of ETV programmes respectively. Another feedback schedule had been administered to 25 inspecting officers of the educational districts and they were requested to respond to the items of the schedule as this would be used for research purpose only.

6. DATA ANALYSIS AND INTERPRETATION

The obtained data were analysed through the application of ANOVA and 't' test to see whether significant differences existed between the teachers of TV and non-TV schools pertaining to their achievement and interaction. To assess the attitude of the teachers towards ETV programmes and to identify their problems and to pool their suggestions with respect to ETV utilisation, quantitative analysis was undertaken.

The findings of the study are presented in three distinctive sections as follows.

6.1 Impact of ETV Programmes

The obtained results of impact of ETV programmes on the competency of teachers were analysed in terms of their knowledge, understanding and application in various content areas and their classroom interaction with students that are presented in Tables 26.1 to 26.4.

(i) *Teachers' Knowledge, Understanding and Application*

It was found from the analysis that significant difference existed between the teachers of TV schools and non-TV schools pertaining to their knowledge, understanding and application in the covered content areas as a whole.

TABLE 26.1

Result of Two-way Analysis of Variance

Sources of Variance	*df*	*SS*	*MS*	*F-ratios*
Teachers	1	371.86	371.86	51.00**
Competency	2	10288.97	5144.49	705.69**
Interaction	3	48.45	24.23	3.32*
Within sets	294	2144.72	7.29	

*p < .05.
**p < .01.

TABLE 26.2

Result of 't'-Test on Competency

Differences	*Mean difference*	*t-ratios*
On knowledge of TV and Non-TV teachers	2.68	4.96**
On Understanding of TV and Non-TV Teachers	2.90	5.37**
On Application of TV and Non-TV Teachers	1.10	2.04*

*p < .5.
**p < .01.

TABLE 26.3

Mean, S.D. and 't'-ratios of CBAT of Experimental and Control Schools

Sample of Teachers	*N*	*Mean*	*SD*	*SED*	*t-ratios*
Experimental (TV)	50	41.00	6.71		
Control (non-TV)	50	34.60	6.90	1.36	4.71*

*p < .01.

TABLE 26.4

Mean, S.D. and 't'-ratios of different Behaviour Ratios of Experimental and Control Groups

Ratios:	*TRR*		*TOR*		*FIR*	
Groups:	*Exptl.*	*Control*	*Exptl.*	*Control*	*Exptl.*	*Control*
Sample	50	50	50	50	50	50
Mean	42.70	35.10	38.40	34.80	45.80	40.20
SD	7.35	7.34	5.00	6.20	12.78	11.36
SED		1.47		1.12		2.42
't'-ratios		5.17**		3.21**		2.31*

*p < .05.
**p < .01.

From the result of ANOVA (Table 26.1) the F-ratio of teachers was significant ($p < 0.01$) suggesting significant difference between the teachers of the exposed and non-exposed groups. Since the mean score of the exposed teachers was higher than that of their counterparts in control schools, it was felt reasonably certain that the ETV had a significant effect on the achievement of teachers (Table 26.3).

The F-ratio for competency was highly significant ($p < 0.01$). Hence, 't'-test was applied to locate the possible combinations in which the significance was lying. Table 26.2 suggests that there existed a significant difference pertaining to knowledge gained in content areas of the teachers of the exposed and non-exposed groups. So far as understanding was concerned, TV teachers had significant differences from that of non-TV teachers. Moreover, on application dimension, the TV teachers exhibited significant differences from that on non-TV teachers ($p < 0.05$). Since the mean scores of the experimental group were more than those of control group on the three dimensions of competency, viz., knowledge, understanding and application separately, it could be stated the ETV played a significant role in enhancing the above competencies of teachers of TV schools. The F-ratio for interaction between teachers and their competencies was significant at 0.05 level, and hence there existed significant differences among the treatments.

(ii) *Teachers' Classroom Interaction*

It was found from the analysis of Teacher Response Ratio (TRR), Teacher Question Ratio (TQR), and Pupil Initiation Ratio (PIR) that significant differences existed between the teachers of TV and non-TV schools (Table 26.4).

The computed 't'-ratios for TRR, TQR ($p < 0.01$ each) and PIR ($p < 0.05$) showed that teachers of TV schools were completely different from those of non-TV schools relating to the teachers' responses and reactions to the feelings and ideas of their pupils, teachers' used of different types of questions, and pupils' responses and initiations during the process of interaction. Since the mean scores of the teachers of TV schools were more than those of their counterparts of non-TV schools in the three ratios given above, it was concluded that the teachers of TV schools were highly response and reaction-oriented to the feelings and ideas of pupils, asking more relevant questions during different stages of interaction and enabling the pupils to initiate talk more than the teachers of non-TV schools. This was possible due to the significant impact of ETV in their classroom performance.

6.2 Attitude of the Teachers towards ETV

It was revealed from the analysis of the opinions of teachers that almost all of them responded positively to the statement, i.e. students and teachers came to know many new things through ETV programmes. As high as 92 per cent of the teachers opined that ETV had been conducive to teaching and development of teachers' knowledge and general awareness. Ninety per cent of teachers responded that ETV was not a waste of children's time and did not interfere with the school work. An equal number of respondents opined that ETV was helpful in the development of knowledge and understanding of teachers and that of rural children.

Hence, it can be concluded that teachers exposed to ETV programmes did have a positive and favourable attitude towards its uses, and suitability like format, programme contents, visuals, voice and languages used in the process.

6.3 Teachers' Opinion on Problems of ETV Utilisation

The opinion of the teachers on the problems pertaining to adequate and proper utilisation of ETV programmes brought out remarkable inferences on how to plan to prevent the continued problems. This pointed to mechanical disorder to TV sets; failure of electricity; unsuitable time slot, particularly for the teacher programmes; inadequate duration of the teachers' programmes; insufficient remuneration to teacher custodians; lack of proper user-teachers' training and supply of support materials; lack of enrichment of programme contents; etc.

7. DISCUSSION

It is evident from the results that ETV had a greater impact on the knowledge, understanding and application of the TV school teachers in some specified and covered content areas. Moreover, it influenced the teachers to develop the level of knowledge and understanding and strengthen their ability to apply the gained knowledge and understanding in their real life situations, i.e. in course of their classroom interaction.

Since knowledge and understanding were treated as the most important cognitive dimensions of improving the various abilities and skills, at this stage, this got reflected by the teachers in their classroom interaction through applicat[illegible]hich was connoted as a transition between the above two. The gained result of the experimental teachers, in case of application, was contributed by their knowledge and understanding as a result of classroom interaction.

The exposed teachers got their levels of knowledge and understanding enhanced, and the ability to apply those knowledge and understanding increased in their real classroom situations through adopting modern and innovative approaches to teaching, textbooks of primary classes, in-service teacher education programmes and the formats adopted by a teleteacher in the ETV medium. But unlike them their counterparts of the non-exposed group, as discussed above, did not obtain those facilities relating to ETV, besides the textbooks and in-service teacher education programmes. The facilities they obtained relating to their improvement of knowledge and understanding and enhancement of the techniques of application in real situations were obviously limited. Therefore, the teachers of TV schools were found to have gained more knowledge, understanding and application in the specified content matters than the teachers of non-TV schools due to the exposure to ETV.

8. SUGGESTIONS FOR IMPROVEMENT

The following suggestions for improving the quality of ETV programmes and their effective utilisation at the elementary school level were offered by more than 70 per cent of the teachers and inspecting officers:

- ETV programmes should be mostly based on syllabus/ curriculum/textbooks of the students.
- The content of the teacher programmes should be based on content enrichment, new discoveries, teaching science and methodology.

- The visuals on teaching activities and three-dimensional aids should be made clear and the language should be simple, lucid and easily understandable.
- Visuals should be got synchronised with the voice of the commentator and *vice-versa*.
- The programme schedule and teacher's guidance notes should be sent to teachers sufficiently before time of telecast so that pre- and post-telecast activities would be conducted properly by them.
- The duration of teacher programmes should be enhanced for 20 minutes to 45 minutes.
- The remuneration of TV user-teachers should be enhanced up to Rs. 100 per month.
- The TV user-teacher's training should be organised regularly to upgrade their knowledge and skills.
- The TV set which remains mechanically out of order should be repaired or replaced immediately and there should not be any interruption of power supply during the time of telecast.
- The local teachers and students should be given the opportunity to participate in the production of ETV programmes, so that they would be encouraged to utilise such programmes effectively.

On the basis of the above findings, the following recommendations are offered under four heads, i.e. planning, production, utilisation and evaluation in order to strengthen the potentiality of ETV medium and promote its meaningful utilisation.

8.1 Planning

- As the teachers exposed to the medium were found to show better competency, it becomes essential that more attention should be paid towards teachers' competency-oriented programmes like the series of Air, Water and Light, Earth and Sky, Living Together and Democracy.
- Since the teachers exposed to ETV were found to have gained greater competency relating to their knowledge, understanding and application, it is recommended that more competency-based teacher programmes in content enrichment series, e.g., Human Body, Nutrition and Management,

etc. should be produced and telecast to enable the teachers to augment and enhance their competency.

- As the interaction effects and the competency of TV teachers proved to be significantly different, it is evident that the knowledge, understanding and application had a bearing upon the teachers. Therefore, the ETV programmes (both for children and teachers) should be produced with adequate ideas and objects in order to enhance the knowledge and understanding of teachers and their skills and abilities of application.
- Since the teacher responses and questions, and pupil initiated behaviour of the teachers showed significant improvement in classroom interaction, more ETV programmes should be produced with group discussion and teacher's talk to students.
- Since a large chunk of teachers revealed positive and favourable attitude towards the uses and suitability of ETV programmes, more number of programme capsules should be produced with novelty of facts and variety of treatments so that it would create interest and appreciation among the teachers who are at least interested in viewing the programme.
- As has been found out that ETV programmes for children on *Veer Balak* series and *Nitikatha* series were produced and telecast in less number, effort should be made by the programme planners towards selecting more programme contents with reference to the needs and requirements of the target audience.
- So far as the teacher programmes were concerned, a small number of teachers (56 per cent) responded to the effectiveness of programmes based on new discoveries. Hence, adequate number of teacher programmes on new discoveries, content enrichment, teaching methodology and science should be produced with proper planning, so that the authenticity and effectiveness of the programmes would be increased.
- Quite a small number (14 per cent and 16 per cent) of teachers opined that the language used was largely difficult in case of the programmes for children and teachers respectively. Hence, language as a part of programmes planning, should be made easy, simple and comprehensible.

8.2 Production

- The quality and clarity of visuals were found poor and unattractive. Therefore, the production agency should utilise the visuals which are clear and qualitative.
- It is also recommended that reasonable time should be given to the viewers to watch the visuals minutely in case of experiments of science-based programmes.
- Since the formats like features and dramas were mostly liked by children, more programmes should be produced with the above format for them.
- As the formats of teacher programmes on features and lectures with the support of visuals were found to be useful and suitable, efforts should be made by the producers to encourage the ETV programmes having the above formats for teachers.
- It has been found out that most of the programmes were filled with distinct voice along with its normal speed. Therefore, it is recommended that the ETV producers should obtain the voice of the characters and commentators distinct and clear, and speed of voice be normal.
- Since the lack of synchronisation of voice with visuals and *vice-versa* often affected the effectiveness of the programmes, it is recommended that utmost care should be taken while preparing the dubbed version of the programmes.
- The school teachers and students should be given the opportunity to participate in the production of ETV programmes, so that they would be encouraged to utilise such programmes effectively.

8.3 Utilisation

It has been mentioned by a majority of teachers that the programmes could not be utilised properly for mechanical disorder of TV sets, failure of electricity and lack of space in the classroom. Therefore, it is recommended that the administrators and higher authorities of ETV system should pay adequate attention and initiate appropriate remedial action.

- Since the duration of teacher programme is only 20 minutes, it should be enhanced up to 45 minutes.
- As high as 82 per cent of TV user-teachers were of view that they were not getting proper training in relation to ETV utilisation. The TV user-teachers' training should be organised regularly to upgrade their knowledge and skills.
- It is a fact that adequate and appropriate support materials like the programme schedules, teacher guidance, notes, etc., are often not made available to the user-teachers. Therefore, the inspecting officers should send the required support materials to the TV schools in time and supervise the utilisation of programmes.
- It has been found that majority of teacher custodians did not pay proper attention to pre- and post-telecast activities. Therefore, it is recommended that teachers must pay utmost attention to such activities that ensure effective utilisation of the medium.

8.4 Evaluation and Follow-up

- Since evaluation is treated as an integral part of effective planning, it should be done continuously from the planning stage till the programme is aired. Therefore, it is recommended that formative evaluation of ETV programmes should be done with much care by the in-house researchers who work in close collaboration with the programme producers and subject experts.
- Summative evaluation should be taken up properly to assess the overall impact of the ETV programmes on target groups. Both internal and external evaluation teams should be engaged to collect feedback from teachers and students through surveys and field studies from time to time.
- The officials of SIETs and State Governments should obtain up-to-date information/data relating to the TV schools and their utilisation status of programmes. They should find out the causes of non-utilisation of the programmes through special investigating team (SIT) and take up corrective measures accordingly.

References

Agrawal, B.C., *Television Comes to Village: An Evaluation of SITE*, Technical Report, ISRO-SAC-TR-78. Ahmedabad, Space Applications Centre, 1978.

Akutsu, Y. *et al.*, An Analysis of Factors Related to Use of School Television at the Elementary Level, *Japanese Journal of Radio-TV Evaluation*, 1978.

Aghi, M.B., *Impact of Science Education Programmes on SITE Children of Rajasthan*, Ahmedabad, Space Application Centre, 1977.

Barrington, H., The Teaching of Elementary Science by Television and Other Methods, *M.Ed. Dissertation*, University of Manchester, 1964.

Behera, S.C. and Panda, R., Educational Television Programmes for Children under INSAT: An Evaluative Study, *Journal of Indian Education*, 1988, 14(3), 29-36.

Bostick, R.N.B., The Extent of Use of ETV is Mississippi Public Schools and Factors which Encourage Limit or Prevent Usage, *Doctoral Dissertation*, University of Mississippi, 1984.

CIET, *Broad Educational Objectives of Corresponding ETV Programme Series/ Titles of INSAT Transmission*, New Delhi, NCERT, 1984-85

Chau, G.C. and Schramm, W., *Learning from Television: What the Research Says*, Stanford University Institute of Communications Research, 1967.

Childers, P. and Ross, J., The Relationship between Television and Students Achievement, *Journal of Educational Research*, 1973, 6(6) 317-19.

Choat, E., Griffin, H. and Hobart, D., Educational TV and the Curriculum for Children up to the age of seven years, *British Journal of Educational Technology*, 1986, 17(3).

Cronbach, L.J., Beyond the Two Disciplines of Scientific Psychology, *American Psychologist*, 1975, 116-27.

Dublin, R. and Hedley, R.A., *The Medium may be Related to the Message: College Instructions by TV*, Evgene, Oregon, University of Oregon Press, 1969.

Ghiassi, J., Survey of the Opinions of Social Studies Teachers in Shiraz (Iran) Regarding the Potential Use of Instructional Television in the Middle School, *Doctoral Dissertation*, The Florida State University, 1976.

Gordon, G.N., *Educational Television*, New York, The Centre for Applied Research in Education, 1960.

Greenstein, J., Effects of Television upon Elementary School Grades, *Journal of Educational Research*, 1959, 4(8), 161-71.

Greenhill, L.P., *TV in University Science Instruction*, Pennsylvania, Pennsylvania State University, 1959.

Kanade, H.M., A Study of the Impact of Instructional Television on the Behaviour of the Rural Elementary School Children, *Doctoral Dissertation Education*, M.S. University, Baroda, 1982.

Kinder, James S., *Audio-visual Materials: Television*, New York, American Book Company, 1959.

Mohanty, J. and Behera, S.C., Teacher Education Programmes Under INSAT, *EPA Quarterly Bulletin*, 1985, 8(1 and 2), 59-66.

Mohanty, P.C., A Critical Study of the Educational Television Programmes for the Primary School Children in the State of Orissa, *Doctoral Dissertation Education*, Utkal University, Bhubaneswar, 1986.

Murray, J.P., Television in Inner City Homes Viewing Behaviour in Young Boys, in Rubinstein, E.A., Comstock, G.A. and Murray, J.P. (eds.), *Television and Social Behaviour*, Vol. 14, Washington DC, US Government Printing Office, 1972.

Neurath, P., *School Television in Delhi*, New Delhi, All India Radio, 1966.

27

Impact of SITE on Attendance and Enrolment in Primary Schools

JAGANNATH MOHANTY AND P.C. MOHANTY

1. INTRODUCTION

The Satellite Instructional Television Experiment was one year project. It started functioning on August 1, 1975 and ended on July 31, 1976. By means of a satellite, it was possible for the first time to take television to the rural audience of India. Mainly six states were selected for this experiment and they were: Orissa, Andhra Pradesh, Karnataka, Bihar, Madhya Pradesh and Rajasthan. Most of the areas selected for this purpose were far away from modern means and media of communication and the people were mostly from backward classes. In Orissa, three districts, Sambalpur, Dhenkanal and Boudh-Kandhmal (Phulbani) were selected. The television sets were generally installed in the village primary school.

Three hundred fifty-four television centres were selected in Orissa, 164 in Dhenkanal, 145 in Sambalpur and 45 in Phulbani. As the TV sets were mostly installed in primary schools, the primary school teachers were selected and appointed as custodians and additional custodians of the TV sets.

The television programmes were transmitted twice a day. The morning transmission were educational in nature and the evening programmes were on agriculture, heath, hygiene, co-operation, adult education, etc. The morning programme was specifically meant for school children whereas the evening programme was for general audience. The morning programme was for 22½ minutes and it was starting from 10.22½ A.M. to 10.45 A.M. except Sundays and holidays.

The morning educational broadcasting was for the children of age-group 5 to 12 years mostly intended for primary and pre-primary section.

2. NEED OF THE STUDY

Although this SITE Project was epoch-making and world famous and a number of studies have been conducted by the Ministry of Education, Government of India, ISRO, Centre for Educational Technology, SCERT and some Universities and other agencies, no study is known to have been conducted on impact of SITE on attendance and enrolment of school children.

But it was one of the important objectives of SITE to improve enrolment and attendance as well as to reduce wastage in primary schools. That is why, the Ministry of Education and Social Welfare have suggested the E.T. Cell, Orissa to conduct a study on this and in this connection the observation of the Officer on Special Duty (Satellite Education) in the Ministry of Education and Social Welfare, New Delhi may be quoted from her letter No. F. 12—9/775.5, dt. 6.10.1977.

> "The subject is of considerable significance and the study should provide decisive information on whether there was any improvement in attendance and enrolment in schools on account of SITE, at least in Orissa."

3. OBJECTIVES

The study was undertaken with the following objectives:

(i) To ascertain the extent to which the children in primary schools were enrolled,

(ii) To find out whether the attendance increased during SITE period, and
(iii) To know whether the impact of SITE was still continuing during the post-SITE period.

4. PLANNING AND METHODOLOGY OF THE STUDY

A set of proforma was developed under the guidance of the Special Officer, SITE Education in the Ministry of Education and was tried out in a few local schools at Bhubaneswar in order to know the validity and reliability. Subsequently, the proforma was printed in three separate sheets to collect data in respect of the following:

(a) Attendance in pre-SITE period, 1974-75.
(b) Attendance in SITE period, 1975-76.
(c) Attendance in post-SITE period, 1976-77.

Then the printed proforma (Appendices—I, II and III) were distributed among all the Primary Schools under SITE in the Sambalpur cluster of Orissa through the concerned District Inspector of Schools. A letter of instruction to the Inspecting Officers was also issued with this. Although the proforma were self-explanatory, the Sub-Inspector of Schools were requested to instruct the SITE Primary School teachers to fill up the proforma carefully. They were also specifically requested to check up the last four columns of each proforma scrupulously.

These columns were as follows:

(a) Total attendance during the month,
(b) Total number of working days during the month,
(c) Average attendance for the month, and
(d) Number on roll on first working day of the month.

In course of distribution of the proforma in the field the Inspecting Officers were also oriented regarding the objectives and strategies of the study, and were given adequate suggestions for properly guiding the teachers to correctly fill up the proforma. Table 27.1 will give an idea about the distribution of proforma in the three cluster districts.

In order to elicit the responses from the Primary School teachers more freely and accurately, the proforma was made self-explanatory in nature and as brief as possible. The teacher could easily record

TABLE 27.1
Distribution of Proforma

Name of the Block	*Total No. of TV Schools*	*Total No. of Questionnaires*	
		Mailed	*Received*
1. Bargarh	6	90	90
2. Jharsuguda	24	360	360
3. Attabira	20	300	300
4. Maneswar	25	375	375
5. Jujumara	15	225	225
6. Rengali	15	225	225
7. Kuchinda	7	105	105
8. Jamankira	5	75	75
9. Lakhanpur	1	15	15
10. Dhankawda	22	330	330
11. Bhatli	1	15	15
12. Bheden	4	60	60
	145	2,175	2,175

the actual attendance of the school in the proforma. The proforma was also designed for classes I to V. The questionnaires were printed in Oriya language and wide spaces were provided to record the number of attendance. Sundays were marked in the proforma. The questionnaires were collected from the District Inspectors of Schools.

The questionnaires received from the field were checked up, the defaulters were reminded to send the questionnaires direct to the Educational Technology cell. The questionnaires which were found wrong at the time of checking were returned to the concerned schools with instruction to mail the same after due correction. Before data were processed the following abbreviations were used for facilitating the compilation work.

TAA = Total Actual Attendance.
TPA = Total Possible Attendance.
ADA = Average Daily Attendance.

Primary Data Collection

1. The class attendance charts constituted the primary data. There were three charts for each class. These were coded PQR as follows:

P = Attendance during pre-SITE year (1974-75).
Q = Attendance during SITE year (1975-76).
R = Attendance during the post-SITE year (1976-77).

2. The last four columns in the attendance charts were designed A, B, C and D corresponding to:
   A = Total actual attendance – Sum of the attendances in the month.
   B = Total number of working days in the month.
   C = The quotient A/B.
   D = Total enrolment on the first day of the month.

Secondary Data

TAA = This was the figure in column (A) of the attendance chart for each class/month.

TPA = This was the product of the total number of working days and the enrolment on the first day of the month, that was the product of the figures in columns (B) and (D) of the attendance chart.

ADA % The quotient TAA/TPA multiplied by 100. To compute the ADA % for the whole year, sum of TAA for each month was taken and was divided by the sum of TPA and then multiplied by 100.

Since it was found difficult to analyse all the questionnaires numbering 2175, it was decided to take a random sample of 20 per cent of questionnaires for analysis of the data.

5. ANALYSIS AND REPORTING

Analysis and interpretation of data collected from the schools in Sambalpur cluster were made. Month-wise data were analysed with a view to get a comparative picture of attendance during a particular month in all the three years, i.e. 1974-75, 1975-76 and 1976-77. Table 27.2 will indicate the attendance on pre, during and post-SITE period in the month of August 1974, 1975 and 1976.

It is revealed from Table 27.2 that the total percentage of attendance in all the 5 classes during pre-SITE, SITE and post-SITE periods was 82, 80 and 83 respectively. It indicates that there has been slight decrease of attendance by 1 per cent during SITE period.

TABLE 27.2

Number of Average, Daily Attendance during Pre, during and Post-SITE, year, during August of 1974, 1975 and 1976

Year	*Classes*					*Total*
	I	*II*	*III*	*IV*	*V*	
1974-75	87	68	77	92	92	82
1975-76	81	80	75	83	83	80
1976-77	83	79	87	89	81	83

But there is an increase of 3 per cent of attendance during the post-SITE period than SITE period. But there is a remarkable increase of attendance in class II during SITE period. The attendance of class II was 68 during pre-SITE whereas in SITE period it increased up to 80, the percentage being 12. In case of children reading in class III, there has been 2 per cent decrease during SITE period in comparison to pre-SITE period, but 10 per cent increase during the post-SITE period. It is, however, surprising to note that there has been 6 per cent and 9 per cent decrease respectively in class I and class IV during SITE period in comparison with pre-SITE period.

It may be inferred from the above data that during SITE, there has been decrease in attendance by 2 per cent but during post-SITE, there has been increase of attendance by 3 per cent. This may be due to the fact that SITE was launched only on the 1st August, 1975 and its impact has been felt only at the end of the year.

It is interesting to note that the attendance during SITE period has decreased by 12 per cent, 11 per cent, 9 per cent and 4 per cent, in case of classes I, II, III and V respectively in comparison with pre-SITE period but there has been an increase of 5 per cent only in case

TABLE 27.3

Average Daily Attendance during September, 1974, 1975 and 1976

Year	*Classes*					*Total*
	I	*II*	*III*	*IV*	*V*	
1974-75	94	85	92	92	96	91
1975-76	82	74	83	96	92	90
1976-77	75	82	83	77	90	88

of class IV. During post-SITE period the attendance also decreased in comparison with SITE by 7 per cent, 19 per cent, and 2 per cent, in case of class III. But on the whole the attendance decreased by 1 per cent, during SITE period in comparison with pre-SITE period and decreased 2 per cent, also during post-SITE period in comparison with SITE period.

It may be concluded that the impact of SITE is not at all felt on attendance during SITE period particularly during September.

TABLE 27.4

Average Daily Attendance during October 1974, 1975 and 1976

Year	*Classes*					*Total*
	I	*II*	*III*	*IV*	*V*	
1974-75	98	87	83	92	95	91
1975-76	80	87	81	89	95	88
1976-77	85	92	94	96	105	92

It appears from Table 27.4 that attendance in SITE period remains constant in case of class II, class V in comparison with pre-SITE but, decreased in case of classes I, III and IV by 18 per cent, 2 per cent and 3 per cent respectively. But there has been invariable increase during post-SITE period in comparison to SITE period.

It is evident that attendance increased in post-SITE period in all classes in comparison with SITE period.

It is evident from the attendance of November that in SITE period attendance decreased by 18 per cent, 6 per cent, 6 per cent, 15 per cent and 2 per cent in case of classes I, II, III, IV and V respectively in

TABLE 27.5

Average Daily Attendance during November 1974, 1975 and 1976

Year	*Classes*					*Total*
	I	*II*	*III*	*IV*	*V*	
1974-75	98	89	95	99	106	95
1975-76	80	83	89	84	104	85
1976-77	93	95	97	92	102	95

comparison with the pre-SITE period. It is very interesting to note that during post-SITE period, attendance increased more than the SITE period in all the classes except class V. However, it may be concluded that the SITE has a considerable impact during the post-SITE period on attendance in the month of November 1976.

It is evident from Table 27.6 that there has been increase of attendance during SITE in all the classes. The percentage of increase in classes, I, II, III, IV and V during SITE in comparison with pre-SITE period is 2 per cent, 6 per cent, 1 per cent, 8 per cent and 4 per cent respectively. But during post-SITE period the attendance decreased in case of classes II, IV and V by 3 per cent, 13 per cent and 11 per cent respectively in comparison to SITE period. But in case of class I, there has been 6 per cent increase and in case of class III it is constant in comparison to SITE period.

TABLE 27.6

Average Daily Attendance during December 1974, 1975 and 1976

Year	*Classes*					*Total*
	I	*II*	*III*	*IV*	*V*	
1974-75	88	87	89	96	104	91
1975-76	90	93	90	104	108	95
1976-77	96	90	90	91	97	93

Table 27.7 gives a picture of increase in attendance during SITE period in case of classes II, III and V by 1 per cent, 14 per cent and 6 per cent respectively than the pre-SITE period. But in case of class IV it is constant and a decrease of 5 per cent, in case of class I. But

TABLE 27.7

Average Daily Attendance during January 1974, 1975, and 1976

Year	*Classes*					*Total*
	I	*II*	*III*	*IV*	*V*	
1974-75	83	84	77	87	89	83
1975-76	79	85	91	87	95	90
1976-77	83	88	85	91	99	87

during post-SITE period it increased in case of classes I, II, IV and V by 4 per cent, 3 per cent, 4 per cent and 4 per cent respectively than the SITE period.

But in class III it has reduced by 6 per cent. It may be inferred that the SITE has some marginal impact on attendance during SITE period and post-SITE period.

It is evident from Table 27.8 that there has been decrease of attendance during SITE by 11 per cent, 2 per cent, and 11 per cent, in classes I, II and IV respectively whereas there has been increase by 3 per cent and 39 per cent in classes III and V respectively in comparison to pre-SITE period.

TABLE 27.8

Daily Attendance during February 1974, 1975 and 1976

Year	*Classes*					*Total*
	I	*II*	*III*	*IV*	*V*	
1974-75	89	83	85	94	51	80
1975-76	78	81	88	83	90	90
1976-77	71	82	83	88	87	80

But during the post-SITE period, the attendance has decreased by 7 per cent, 5 per cent and 3 per cent in classes I, II and V respectively. In case of class IV only 5 per cent and 1 per cent respectively is increased during post-SITE period. However, on the whole, there has been 10 per cent increase during SITE than pre-SITE and 10 per cent decrease in post-SITE than SITE period.

Table 27.9 shows an increase of attendance during SITE period by 2 per cent, 10 per cent and 2 per cent in classes I, II and V

TABLE 27.9

Average Daily Attendance during March 1974, 1975 and 1976

Year	*Classes*					*Total*
	I	*II*	*III*	*IV*	*V*	
1974-75	78	81	87	99	94	85
1975-76	80	91	85	93	96	88
1976-77	84	85	87	83	98	86

respectively, whereas there has been a decrease by 2 per cent and 6 per cent in classes III and IV respectively in comparison to pre-SITE period. But during post-SITE period, the attendance has increased by 4 per cent, 2 per cent and 2 per cent in classes I, II and V respectively than the SITE period and decreased by 6 per cent, 10 per cent in classes II and IV respectively. But on the whole, the attendance in SITE period increased by 3 per cent than pre-SITE and decreased 2 per cent in post-SITE than SITE period.

TABLE 27.10

Average Daily Attendance during April 1974, 1975 and 1976

Year	*Classes*					*Total*
	I	*II*	*III*	*IV*	*V*	
1974-75	78	80	90	94	95	81
1975-76	80	83	88	88	100	87
1976-77	71	77	85	91	84	83

It is found that the attendance during SITE period has increased in classes I, II and V by 2, 3, and 5 per cent respectively in comparison with pre-SITE period. But in case of classes III and IV, it has decreased by 2 and 6 per cent respectively. During post-SITE period, the attendance has decreased in the classes I, II, III and V by 3, 6, 2 and 6 per cent respectively in comparison with SITE period and increased by 3 in case of class IV. But the total average daily attendance increased by 6 per cent during SITE and decreased by 4 per cent during post-SITE period.

It is evident from Table 27.11 that there has been increase of attendance during SITE by 1 per cent in classes I and III, 8 per cent in case of class IV whereas in case of class II, the attendance has

TABLE 27.11

Average Daily Attendance during May 1974, 1975 and 1976

Year	*Classes*					*Total*
	I	*II*	*III*	*IV*	*V*	
1974-75	81	92	86	86	88	86
1975-76	82	88	87	94	87	87
1976-77	80	83	87	89	80	85

decreased by 4 and 1 per cent in case of class V in comparison with pre-SITE period. But during post-SITE period, attendance has decreased in all classes, i.e. I, II and IV and V except class III by 2, 5 and 7 per cent respectively in comparison with SITE period. But in case of class III, it is constant during SITE and post-SITE period. During SITE period there has been increase of attendance only 1 per cent in comparison to pre-SITE period and 2 per cent decrease during post-SITE in comparison with SITE period.

It is ascertained from Table 27.12 that attendance during SITE period has increased in all classes in comparison with pre-SITE period by 7, 10, 3, 1 and 3 per cent in classes I, II, III, IV and V respectively.

TABLE 27.12

Average Daily Attendance during June 1974, 1975 and 1976

Year	*Classes*					*Total*
	I	*II*	*III*	*IV*	*V*	
1974-75	19	83	91	88	19	86
1975-76	86	93	94	89	100	93
1976-77	98	94	96	95	91	95

During post-SITE period, the attendance increased in classes I, II, III, IV by 12 per cent, 1 per cent, 2 per cent and 6 per cent respectively in comparison with SITE period but the attendance in class V has decreased by 9 per cent. But in all the class attendance increased by 9 per cent and 2 per cent during pre-SITE period respectively.

It is revealed from Table 27.14 that there has been a considerable increase of attendance during SITE period in comparison with pre-SITE in classes I, III, IV and V 16 per cent, 10 per cent, 16 per cent and

TABLE 27.13

Average Daily Attendance during July 1974, 1975 and 1976

Year	*Classes*					*Total*
	I	*II*	*III*	*IV*	*V*	
1974-75	78	81	82	76	92	81
1975-76	94	78	92	92	95	86
1976-77	74	87	89	91	92	86

3 per cent. But during post-SITE period, the attendance has decreased by 20 per cent, 3 per cent, 1 per cent and 3 per cent in classes I, III, IV and V respectively and increased in class II by 9 per cent. However, on the whole, there has been 8 per cent increase in attendance during SITE and a decrease of 3 per cent during post-SITE period.

Table 27.14 gives a picture of total average attendance from classes I to V throughout the pre, during and post-SITE periods. The total average attendance during SITE period has increased in classes II, III, IV and V by 4 per cent, 2 per cent, 9 per cent and 12 per cent respectively and 5 per cent on the whole than the pre-SITE period. But 4 per cent has decreased in case of class I. It is also revealed that during post-SITE period the attendance has decreased by 11 per cent and 3 per cent in case of classes IV and V respectively and increased in class III by 2 per cent and remained constant in case of classes I, II in comparison to SITE period. But on the whole the attendance has decreased by 2 per cent in post-SITE period than SITE period.

TABLE 27.14

Total Average Attendance of Pre, during and Post-SITE Years

Year	*Classes*					*Total*
	I	*II*	*III*	*IV*	*V*	
1914-75	86	81	85	91	83	84
1975-76	82	85	87	100	85	89
1976-77	82	85	89	89	92	87

Enrolment

It was expected that the enrolment in different classes would increase during the SITE period in comparison with pre-SITE year and it might also increase during the post-SITE period as the television would prove as an attraction to the children in schools.

Generally the enrolment in Primary Schools is done in the months of June, July and August every year. The following three tables will indicate the position of month-wise enrolment in pre, during and post-SITE years.

It is revealed from Table 27.15 that enrolment in the month of June of the SITE year has increased by 5 per cent, 27 per cent, 14 per cent and 8 per cent in case of classes II, III, IV and V respectively and decreased in case of class I only by 21 per cent in comparison with pre-SITE year. But post-SITE period the position of enrolment is fairly satisfactory in all classes and increased by 47 per cent, 5 per cent, 26 per cent, 19 per cent and 16 per cent in case of classes I, II, III, IV and V respectively in comparison with SITE year.

TABLE 27.15

Total Avenge Enrolment on the 1st day of the June 1975, 1976 and 1977

Month	*Classes*					*Total*
	I	*II*	*III*	*IV*	*V*	
June 75	19	21	15	14	12	81
June 76	15	22	19	16	13	85
	12%	5%	27%	14%	8%	5%
June 77	22	23	24	19	15	103
	47%	5%	26%	19%	16%	21%

On the whole, the total average enrolment in the month of June increased by 5 per cent during SITE year in comparison with pre-SITE year and 21 per cent in post-SITE year in comparison with SITE year.

During the month of July 1976, the data show a considerable increase of enrolment in classes II, III and V by 17 per cent, 35 per cent and 7 per cent respectively, but in case of class I, it is almost constant but decreased by 14 per cent in case of IV in comparison with pre-SITE year. But during post-SITE year the enrolment

TABLE 27.16

Total Average Enrolment on the 1st day of July 1975, 1976 and 1977

Month	*Classes*					*Total*
	I	*II*	*III*	*IV*	*V*	
July 75	27	24	17	22	14	104
July 76	27	28	23	19	15	112
	Nil	17%	35%	–14%	7%	8%
July 77	30	27	24	23	16	120
	11%	9%	5%	19%	7%	7%

increased considerably in all classes by 11 per cent, 9 per cent, 5 per cent, 19 per cent and 7 per cent in case of classes I, II, III, IV and V respectively. On the whole, enrolment has increased by 8 per cent, in case of SITE year in comparison with pre-SITE year and 7 per cent during post-SITE year in comparison with SITE year.

TABLE 27.17

Total Average Enrolment on the 1st day of August 1975, 1976 and 1977

Month	*Classes*					*Total*
	I	*II*	*III*	*IV*	*V*	
August 75	32	22	18	19	14	105
August 76	31	26	19	20	14	110
	–3%	21%	6%	5%	Nil	5%
August 77	32	26	14	19	17	118
	–3%	Nil	25%	5%	21%	7%

Similarly, during the month of August 1975, the enrolment has increased in SITE period in classes II, III, IV by 21 per cent, 6 per cent and 5 per cent respectively, whereas it has decreased in case of class I by 3 per cent and remained constant in case of class IV. But during the post-SITE period, the enrolment has increased by 3 per cent, 25 per cent and 21 per cent in case of class II and decreased in case of class IV by 5 per cent in comparison with SITE period, has increased by 5 per cent in comparison with pre-SITE and 7 per cent in post-SITE period in comparison with SITE period.

It is evident from the above analysis that the enrolment was better in post-SITE period than SITE period. It may be due to the fact that in anticipation of TV facility to be available in the schools more students were enrolled in post-SITE period.

6. MAJOR FINDINGS

Attendance

The following findings have emerged out of the above discussion:

(1) During August, 1975 there has been a fall of 2 per cent in attendance in comparison with data during the pre-SITE period. This may be due to the fact that SITE was launched

only on the 1st August, 1975 and its impact was not felt on attendance.

On the other hand, there has been an increase of attendance by 3 per cent during the post-SITE period. This may be justified on the ground that impact of SITE has been brought upon the school attendance.

(2) It is surprising to note that there has been no impact of SITE on attendance during September of SITE and post-SITE period as there has been a fall by 1 per cent during SITE period in comparison with pre-SITE and 3 per cent during post-SITE in comparison to SITE attendance.

(3) There has been an increase of attendance by 2 per cent during the month of October, 1976 which shows that impact of SITE on attendance has been brought upon the school attendance during post-SITE period.

On the contrary, there has been a surprising fall by 3 per cent during SITE period in comparison with pre-SITE period.

(4) Data on attendance during November 1976 show that there has been increase of attendance by 10 per cent which indicates that TV has been worked as an attraction to the school children although the programmes were not on during that period.

(5) During December 1975 there has been increase of attendance by 4 per cent which shows that there has been some impact of SITE on attendance whereas there has been a fall in attendance during post-SITE in comparison with SITE.

(6) During January 1975 there has been increase of attendance by 7 per cent during SITE period, which indicates the impact of SITE on attendance and there has been decrease by 3 per cent during post-SITE period.

(7) During February 1975 average daily attendance in SITE period shows an increase by 10 per cent which may be attributed to the impact of SITE. On the contrary, there has been decrease by 10 per cent during post-SITE period.

(8) The average attendance during SITE period in the month of March has been marked with 3 per cent increase whereas during post-SITE there has been a fall in attendance in comparison with SITE period.

(9) During April 1975, there has been 6 per cent increase in the average attendance, which shows an impact of SITE during that period. On the other hand, during post-SITE period there has been 4 per cent decrease in attendance in comparison to SITE period.

(10) During SITE period in the month of May 1975 there has been increase of attendance only 1 per cent in comparison to pre-SITE period whereas there has been 2 per cent decrease in attendance during post-SITE in comparison with SITE period.

(11) During June 1975, average daily attendance increased by 9 per cent and in June 1977 by 2 per cent which shows significant impact of SITE on attendance during SITE period.

(12) During July 1975, there has been 8 per cent increase of attendance during 1976 which shows considerable impact of SITE on attendance. But during 1977, there has been as fall of attendance by 3 per cent, which indicates the absence of impact during post-SITE period.

(13) Taking the total average attendance of 1974-75, 1975-76 and 1976-77 into consideration; it is found that there has been 5 per cent increase of attendance during SITE period in comparison to pre-SITE and decreased by 2 per cent during post-SITE period in comparison to SITE year.

Thus it is evident that there has been fairly satisfactory impact of SITE on attendance. This fact is also confirmed by the decrease of attendance by 2 per cent, during post-SITE period as there was no TV during post-SITE period.

Enrolment

1. The total average enrolment in the month of June has increased by 5 per cent during SITE year in comparison with pre-SITE year and 2 per cent in post-SITE year in comparison to SITE year.
2. During July, enrolment has increased by 8 per cent, in case of SITE year in comparison with pre-SITE year and 7 per cent during post-SITE year in comparison with SITE year.

3. The total average enrolment in the month of August has increased by 5 per cent in SITE period in comparison with pre-SITE and 7 per cent in post-SITE period in comparison with SITE period.

On the whole, it is clearly evident that there has been satisfactory impact of SITE on enrolment and attendance.

Bibliography

Behera, Amarendra Prasad, *Effect of Radio Intervention on the Language and Cognitive Development at Pre-school Level*, Ph.D. Thesis, Kurukshetra University, Kurukshetra, 1997.

Behera, Kailash Chandra, *An Evaluative Study of Navodaya Vidyalayas in Haryana*, Kurukshetra University, 1998.

Behera, S.C., *Impact of Educational Television on the Competency of Elementary School Teachers*, Ph.D. Thesis, Utkal University, Bhubaneswar, 1986.

Bohidar, Jyoti Ranjan, *Problems of Tribal Education in the Context of National Policy on Education*, Ph.D. Thesis, Sambalpur University, 1995.

Maharana, S., *A Study of the Effectiveness of the Educational TV Programmes for Primary Schools*, Ph.D. Thesis, Utkal University, 1993.

Mohanty, J. and Mohanty, P.C., "Impact of SITE on Attendance and Enrolment in Primary Schools," *Studies of Educational Radio and TV Programmes in Orissa*, SCERT, Orissa, Bhubaneswar, 1984.

Mohanty, J. and Maharana, S., "Educational Television Programmes for the Age-group 9-11 Years, An Appraisal," *Journal of Indian Education*, New Delhi, NCERT, May 1987.

Mohanty, J. and Maharana, S., "ETV Programmes for the Children in the Age-grouping of 9-11 years under INSAT," *Journal of Educational Planning and Adm.*, NIEPA, New Delhi, October, 1986.

Mohanty, J. and Nayak, P.C., "An Evaluative Study of the ETV Programmes Under INSAT," *Our Education*, 1986, Calcutta University, Calcutta.

Mohanty, Jagannath, "An Investigation into the Problems and Prospects of School Community Cooperation for Democratisation and Improvement of Education," 1979.

Mohanty, Jagannath, *Early Childhood Education (ECE) for Universalisation of Elementary Education (UEE)*, NCERT, New Delhi, 1995-96.

Mohanty, Jagannath, *Impact of Democracy on Primary Education in India with Special Reference to Orissa*, Ph.D. Study, Utkal University, Bhubaneswar, 1979.

Mohanty, Jagannath, *Socio-Economic Background of the Students Studying in the High Schools of Bhubaneswar*, SCERT, Orissa, Bhubaneswar, 1987.

Mohanty, Jagannath, "Study of the Efficacy of Field Trip in the Teaching of Social Studies in Primary Schools," *The Progress of Education*, Pune, Sept., 1973.

Mohanty, Rajashree, *Science Education Programme in Secondary Schools*, Ph.D. Thesis, Utkal University, Bhubaneswar, 2002.

Panda, Manoranjan, *The Relationship between Socio-Economic Status and Achievement of Class IX Students*, Ph.D. Thesis, Utkal University, Bhubaneswar, 1999.

Patra, Subash Chandra, *A Study of the Educational Implications of Community Television Programmes*, Ph.D. Thesis, Sambalpur University, Burla, 2002.

Pattanaik, Anjali and Haritha, R., "Anthropometric Status of Child Labourers," *The Indian Journal of Nutrition and DIET*, 1995.

Pattanaik, Anjali, "Creativity: A Study of Children with Different Disabilities and Impairments," 1997.

Pattanaik, Anjali, *Nutritional Status and Its Effect on Physical Development and Educational Achievement*, Ph.D. Thesis, Utkal University, 1990.

Pradhan, Nityananda, Family-Life Values in the Tribal Communities, An Ethnographic Case Study of the Paraja," 2003.

Pradhan, Nityananda, "Research in Education of Minorities in India: Gaps and Priorities," 2004.

Pradhan, Nityananda, "Sustainable Solutions of Environmental Problems Through Community-based Education, Case Study of a Tribal Village," 2003.

Prusty, Pramod Kumar, "*A Study of the Creative Method of Teaching English on Development of Creativity Thinking of Secondary School Students,*" Ph.D. Thesis, Utkal University, 1995.

Prusty, Pramod Kumar, Effect of Creative Method of Teaching English (MTS) on Development of Creativity and School Students," 1995.

Prusty, Pramod Kumar, *Effect of Super-Learning Technique (SLT) on Development of Creative Thinking,* D.Litt. Thesis, Utkal University, Bhubaneswar, 2005.

Prusty, Pramod Kumar, "Multi-grade Learning: An Innovation in Primary Level Education."

Index